$\mathcal{P}$oetic
KNOWLEDGE

*P*oetic KNOWLEDGE

THE RECOVERY OF EDUCATION

James S. Taylor

State University of
New York Press

Published by
State University of New York Press

© 1998 State University of New York

For information, address the State University of New York Press,
State University Plaza, Albany, NY 12246

Marketing by Patrick Durocher
Production by Bernadine Dawes

Library of Congress Cataloging-in-Publication Data

Taylor, James S., 1943–
    Poetic knowledge : the recovery of education : James S. Taylor.
        p.   cm.
    Includes a bibliographical reference and index.
    ISBN 0-7914-3585-7 (hardcover   :   alk. paper). ISBN 0-7914-3586-5
(pbk.   :   alk. paper)
    1. Education—Philosophy.   2. Knowledge, Theory of.   3. Education,
Humanistic.   4. Education in literature.   5. Descartes, René, 1596–1650.
I. Title
LB14.7.T39   1998
370'.1—dc21   97-26325
                                                                          CIP

1   2   3   4   5   6   7   8   9   10

CONTENTS

ACKNOWLEDGMENTS

This book is dedicated to my parents, Jack and Mary Elizabeth Taylor, as a small return for the unpayable debt of my life and for the love and hope that was always to be found in the Missouri home of my childhood, which was so rich in the poetic way of life and which included the presence of my grandmother, Ila Gene Brossart, poet and teacher.

It is also warmly dedicated to the professors whose life and teaching inspired it: John Senior, Dennis B. Quinn, and Franklyn C. Nelick, who together taught the Pearson Integrated Humanities Program at the University of Kansas. Of these three, Professor Quinn was my main classroom teacher after Professor Senior's retirement, and it was Quinn who gave me significant advice on the philosophical aspects of wonder during the writing of the book. Dr. Senior gave freely of his time to talk over and around these ideas of poetic knowledge, hour upon hour, year after year. I never knew Dr. Nelick in the classroom, but learned all I needed to know about him one tragic morning when his sudden and rock-solid presence appeared in the intensive care unit of a Kansas hospital to give aid to me and my surviving children.

And here I dedicate this work to those family members who were lost then, Linda, Clare, Marcel, and Mary Jeanne, who began it with me but did not live on earth to see its completion and publication. Nor did Frank Nelick, or Dr. Ivan Barrientos, my first dissertation director, whose initial interest and support often sustained me after his death two years before it was finished in that form. For these: *Requiescant in pace.*

Dr. James Hilleshiem, however, who first brought me into the world of the Foundations of Education at the University of Kansas, took over as director and guided me safely through the final and narrow channels of its final form as a dissertation. His ability to give no-nonsense advice and criticism while never ceasing to encourage my work was a blessing.

Then, a special thanks to my oldest brother, David, who participated in a most significant and perhaps mysterious manner in bringing this book to the attention of David Appelbaum and the editors of State University of New York Press.

Finally, I dedicate this to Teresa, my wife, who knows what it has taken, and what it represents, to have finished this one race together.

Introduction

*T*he primary purpose of this book is to describe what is meant by a degree of knowledge, and a manner of learning appropriate to that degree, to be called, for the present study, the "poetic mode." This particular phrase appears in the writings and conversation of the teachers who taught the Pearson Integrated Humanities Program at the University of Kansas in the 1970s and 1980s. Developing an understanding of knowledge in the poetic mode is not only central in determining the approach to education in the Integrated Humanities Program, examined specifically in chapter 6, but presents the opportunity to discover the roots and history of this way of knowing.

Of course, to give a foundation for this description of the poetic mode it is necessary for me to survey and generally refer to the tradition of philosophy that informs it found primarily in the Idealist-Realist tradition of classical and medieval times. The reader should bear in mind that the present study attempts nothing philosophically new, no new epistemological or metaphysical insights into Plato or Aristotle, nor does it hammer out any new how-to agenda. Rather, this work is closer to the efforts of philosophical archeology and the attempt to resuscitate a nearly forgotten mode of knowledge.

The understanding of knowledge in the poetic mode not only requires this general philosophical survey, but also presupposes a certain culture be present that has slowly evolved into sympathetic expressions of that knowledge, in religion, art, literature, music, architecture, manners, economics, leisure, and politics. That such a culture slowly developed and even predominated for a time in the history of the West, is a fact, persisting, more or less, from a time before Socrates to the late Middle Ages. Examples from this list, typically referred to as "achievements" in Western Civilization survey courses, are really expressions of *celebration* of the higher things yearned for within the human being. The ordinary setting for a medieval village or farm, the furnishings within, the roads and bridges, are preserved in southern France as quaint sights for tourists; museums, built nearly exactly like mausoleums, now house art and artifacts never meant for such dead displays or for priceless values. They are simply the tools, clothing, tables, chairs, sculpture, and paintings that *naturally* emerged from a culture that, in spite of its relative hardships, found itself whole, integrated, and spiritually free enough to celebrate the ordinary as wonderful, as seen, for example, in the sturdy yet delicate beauty of the wood and metal tools of the kitchen and the barn from rural medieval England; or, from thirteenth-century France, the statue of the smiling Virgin holding the smiling Christ child. To show this another way: a Teflon spatula is useful, at least, for a Teflon pan; but a wooden ladle, of curved and smooth wood, is not only useful but beautiful. The first is scientific, in the modern sense, reduced to its most base utilitarian level, not to mention the strange materials wrought from laboratories; while the second tool is crafted from the poetic mode of life.

Even after the breakup of Europe after the Reformation and Renaissance, the collective memory of this cultural tradition has refused to completely die. However, one of the lessons of a survey such as this one is that one of the main prerequisites for poetic culture has been the preindustrial, prescientific West; that is, a largely agrarian-craft culture that lasted up to and even beyond the First Industrial Revolution, but which, now in its most recent evolution as Technology, has distanced more people, worldwide, at a rapid pace, from the everyday cultural experiences that manifested the acknowledgment of man's essential poetic nature. That aspect of the so-called hippie movement of the 1960s that urged a "back to nature" life, and a rediscovery of crafts—as naive and doomed as such a movement was—may well be the last spontaneous expression for the poetic idea of life for a very long time to come. Current environmental movements have become too political, bureaucratic, and "scientific" to be seriously compared with any true understanding of the more passive and simple poetic way of life.

Therefore, to present the case for the poetic mode of knowledge, I will clarify in the first chapter what is meant by "poetic" and its opposite, "scientific," and, in so doing, establish the validity of poetic knowledge. Then, in chapter 2, it will be necessary to trace the philosophical history of poetic knowledge as it was understood in ancient, medieval, and modern theories of knowledge. Following from this background, a proceeding chapter will be devoted to the main philosophical terms used to account for poetic knowledge, that is, Connatural, Intentional, and Intuitive knowledge. Next, the beginning of the great turning away from the traditional view of man and how he knows reality will be dealt with in a chapter devoted to the influence of Descartes. This period will be considered as "modern" epistemology and viewed as the decline of the recognition of the poetic mode. In spite of the Cartesian rupture in the tradition of poetic knowledge and its profound influence on how we view ourselves and the world, chapter 5 will present an experimental school in Maslacq, France, taught quite consciously in the poetic mode. Also, voices from the nineteenth and twentieth centuries who have continued to insist that man is incomplete and perhaps doomed without the poetic sense of life are recalled. Chapter 6 moves from theory to practice in examining, in particular, the Integrated Humanities Program at the University of Kansas. In fact, it was the presence of the IHP, as it came to be called, that caused me to look for and locate the exact term *poetic knowledge*. Indeed, St. Thomas Aquinas refers to "*poetica scientia*," in the First Part of the *Sentences* (prol., q. 1, a. 5, ad 3.) and again in the *Summa Theologica*, I–II, 101, 2 ad 2. These sources will be quoted in chapter 3.

Also, a book that presupposes all the philosophical background offered here, and more, is Thomas Gilby's *Poetic Experience: An Introduction to Thomist Aesthetic* (Sheed and Ward, 1934), which, while too synthesized and advanced to be called an introduction, clearly establishes the presence of poetic knowledge in the Thomist tradition. As I show in chapter 2 the acknowledgment of the poetic mode of knowledge reaches back to at least Socrates, although, as far as I can determine in this study, Aquinas is the first to use the exact term *poetic knowledge*.

Finally, a summary is offered that also poses the question, Is poetic knowledge and education possible in a society given over to the mere practical and utilitarian ends of life?

It should be said that also operating throughout this study is the second purpose for its existence: to not only explain poetic knowledge but to promote its restoration as the appropriate means of reawakening the intuitive nature of human beings who are able to know reality in a profound and intimate way that is prior to and, in a certain sense, superior to scientific knowledge. Reflections on what such a school might look like are offered in the last chapter.

Poetic knowledge is a kind of natural, everyman's metaphysics of common experience. It is a way of restoring the definition of reality to mean knowledge of the seen and unseen. With these combined purposes, it is my intention to help bridge the gap between the neglected philosophical intuition that described poetic knowledge and the approach that was followed in the IHP, often misunderstood precisely because of this loss of understanding of the poetic mode.

The need for the restoration of poetic knowledge seems particularly urgent with its prescientific cultivation of the senses, emotions, and imagination, to at least balance an education in our day now dominated in one way or another by the flat, utilitarian ends of a capitalist-socialist, technological "new world order." Of course, this all has to do with how we view the human being, and if man is seen fundamentally as a sophisticated machine possessing certain brain-driven animal appetites, then all considerations of a transcendent mode of knowledge and education are beside the point. But since the human being is only remotely analogous in some limited respects to a machine—or isn't it the other way around?—such materialist ideas of knowledge are grossly disproportionate to the most vital needs for us to know, love, and most harmoniously serve a reality whose existence is far more wonderful and mysterious than mere mathematical measurement and quantification can reveal.

1

The Validity of Poetic Knowledge

Now what I want is Facts.
—Professor Gradgrind in *Hard Times*, Charles Dickens

That there is such a thing as poetic knowledge, and consequently, that there is a mode of learning that can be called "poetic," there can be no doubt. Among the philosophers and poets of ancient, classical, and medieval times, this way of knowing was virtually a given as part of the human being's ability to know reality. Only after the Renaissance and the Cartesian revolution in philosophy does a less intuitive, less integrated view of man emerge. By the twentieth century, the idea of objective reality and man's various responses to it—has been eclipsed, for the most part, by subjectivism and a less certain, more lonely and mechanistic model of the human being and the universe.

As a result, the tradition of poetic knowledge is now all but forgotten, usually dismissed as "romantic," and otherwise misunderstood if considered at all. Therefore, it is necessary to turn to certain definitions that surround its proper understanding and return them to their original and precise meanings.

First of all, poetic knowledge is not necessarily a knowledge of poetry but rather a poetic (a sensory-emotional) experience of reality. That the ancient Greeks considered all education a matter of learning certain arts through imitation—that is, through the poetic impulse to reflect what is already there—is a point to be clarified in the next chapter. What must be at the beginning of this understanding is the phenomenon of *poetic experience*. Poetic experience indicates an encounter with reality that is nonanalytical, something that is

5

perceived as beautiful, awful (awefull), spontaneous, mysterious. It is true that poetic experience has that same surprise of metaphor found in poetry, but also found in common experience, when the mind, through the senses and emotions, *sees* in delight, or even in terror, the significance of what is really there.

This entire study rests on these admittedly difficult points. But one point that must be clear right away is that this matter of poetic knowledge is not one that belongs exclusively to the Romantics or to any realm of *feelings*, or to mystical vision. In fact, in its philosophic explanation, the basis of poetic knowledge, as we shall see, is more at home with the tradition of the Realists.

So, whatever poetic knowledge is, it is not strictly speaking a knowledge of poems, but a spontaneous act of the external and internal senses with the intellect, integrated and whole, rather than an act associated with the powers of analytic reasoning. It is, according to a tradition from Homer to Robert Frost, from Socrates to Maritain, a natural human act, synthetic and penetrating, that gets us *inside* the thing experienced. It is, we might say, knowledge from the inside out, radically different in this regard from a knowledge *about* things. In other words, it is the opposite of scientific knowledge. Concerning scientific knowledge and its predominant spirit in all aspects of modern education, by the end of the nineteenth century Charles Dickens gave us Professor Thomas Gradgrind as its great champion.

> Now, what I want is Facts. Teach these boys and girls nothing but Facts. Facts alone are wanted in life. Plant nothing else. You can only form the minds of reasoning animals upon Facts: nothing else will ever be of any service to them.[1]

From the point of view of an ancient tradition, actually from an immemorial view of the nature of the human being as knower, this position of Gradgrind's is a radically shallow idea of knowledge. Something very strange has taken place in the Western world when we keep in mind this tradition. To assist in contrasting this change it should be recalled that in the same decade of Dickens's *Hard Times*, there also appeared two of the greatest scientific and materialist statements on man, *Das Kapital* and *The Origin of Species*. How deeply Dickens understood the encroachment of the mechanistic view of man and the universe, how profoundly modern science, adrift from the metaphysical tradition of the West, had restricted the limits of knowledge to "facts," is portrayed in the opening chapter of his book. Gradgrind has called on "student number twenty," Sissy Jupe, to tell the class something of her background. She is shy, modest, and understandably quite terrified of Gradgrind. She manages to reveal that her father is a horse trainer for the local circus, an occupation far below the standards of our enlightened Gradgrind. In an attempt to expose her ignorance, he demands that Sissy tell the class what a horse is, that is, to give a brief, *factual* definition. Just as she begins an answer, he scolds her for not having any "facts" about a horse. Bitzer, a boy in the same class who has clearly excelled in the Gradgrind method of knowledge, provides the correct answer:

> Quadruped. Graminivorous. Forty teeth, namely, twenty-four grinders, four eye teeth, and twelve incisive. Sheds coat in the spring; in marshy countries, sheds hoofs too. Hoofs hard, but requiring to be shod with iron. Age known by marks in mouth.[2]

"Now girl number twenty," said Gradgrind, "you know what a horse is."[3]

The cruel irony is of course, that no one in the class *except* Sissy knows what a horse is, least of all Gradgrind and Bitzer.

This little scene at the beginning of *Hard Times* is offered under the theme of chapter 1, titled, "The One Thing Needful," that is, the kind of knowledge that derives from the *love* of a thing, a person, or place—a horse—and the loss of such knowledge, and its replacement by the superficial facts demanded by a Gradgrind, is precisely what has made these times "hard," harder than they should be. What is needed, Dickens says, the one thing, is what Sissy could have told the class about horses. That would have been her intimate knowledge of their habits and personalities, the do's and don'ts of their care and training, and her love. Her knowledge would be something closer to the essence of horses because of her simple familiarity with their wholeness as an animal, rather than Bitzer's facts most likely memorized from a textbook.

Given the burden of explaining to a modern audience influenced by an education closer to Gradgrind than to the principles of intuitive and poetic knowledge, it is fortunate that there is a remarkable advantage in having the concrete example of a college-level program in the humanities that was taught and explained in this mode.

The Pearson Integrated Humanities Program at the University

of Kansas existed for nearly fifteen years from the 1970s into the 1980s. It was a college within a university founded and taught by three professors, two from English and one from Classics, who were deeply aware of and dedicated to the philosophical tradition of knowledge and education in the poetic mode. The IHP, as it came to be called, will be considered more fully in chapter 6, but for now one of the professors from that program, John Senior, can assist in defining and distinguishing the modes of knowledge:

> The ancients distinguished four degrees of knowledge: the poetic, where truths are grasped intuitively as when you trust another's love; the rhetorical, when we are persuaded by evidence, but without conclusive proof that we might be wrong, as when we vote for a political candidate; next the dialectical mode in which we conclude to one of two opposing arguments beyond a reasonable doubt, with the kind of evidence sufficient for conviction in a laboratory testing to certify a drug for human use; and, finally, in the scientific mode—science in the ancient and not the modern sense which is dialectical and rhetorical, but science as *epistemai*—we reach to absolute certitude as when we know the whole is greater than the part, that motion presupposes agency.[4]

Unlike the various modern schools of thought on knowledge, largely skeptical, these four modes spoken of by Senior were all informed by self-evident truth, first principles founded on objective reality impossible to be "proved" by argument because they exist as givens, intuitively known by all. As Jacques Maritain observed, "the natural inclination was so strong in them (the ancients and medievals) that their proofs of God could take the form of the most conceptualized and rationalized demonstrations, and be offered as an unrolling of logical necessities, without losing the inner energy of that intuition."[5]

But it is not just the ancients or the Schoolmen of the Middle Ages or their small group of modern apologists who knew and appreciated these degrees of knowledge. The twentieth century has had its share of philosophers who have recognized at least two of these degrees. Karl Stern, from his book *The Flight from Woman*, says in the chapter titled "Scientific and Poetic Knowledge":

> Simple self-observation shows that there exist two modes of knowing. One might be called "externalization," in which the

knowable is experienced as *ob-ject*, a *Gegen-stand*, something which stands opposed to me; the other might be called "internalization," a form of knowledge by sympathy, a *"feeling with,"*—a union with the knowable.[6]

Stern, quoting Henri Bergson, helps clarify the term *intuition* for the context here, excluding the popular associations with the idea of a "hunch," but, rather, Bergson says, "By intuition is meant the kind of *intellectual sympathy* by which one places oneself within the object in order to coincide with what is unique in it and consequently inexpressible."[7]

Karl Stern continues to show throughout this chapter that modern philosophers such as Henri Bergson, Herbert Feigl, Edmund Husserl, Karl Jaspers, and Wilhelm Dithey, while at odds with much in the traditional Realist philosophy of knowledge, have all allowed for this "other way" of knowing that Stern and Senior have called "poetic" and which modern education, for the most part, has rejected.

How this tension and misunderstanding between the modes of knowledge have actually played out in our day can be partially illustrated by a brief look at the greatly debated areas of how children learn to read and, accordingly, how best to teach them to read. For example, modern scientific theories of learning have given us the battle over look-say, phonics, basal readers, with all manner of audio-visual machines, graphics, and "high-tech" aides and methods. Frank Smith, from his book *Insult to Intelligence*, offers what may seem an oldfashioned and simplistic alternative:

> One of the leaders in research on how children learn to read, Margaret (Meek) Spencer of London University, says that it is authors who teach children to read. Not just any authors, but the authors of the stories that children love to read, that children often know by heart before they begin to read the story. This prior knowledge or strong expectation of how the story will develop is the key to learning to read, says Professor Spencer.[8]

This is simply an example of poetic learning, in the sense that the child is left alone, undistracted by methods and systems, so that the senses and emotions come naturally into play when being read to, where wonder and delight gradually lead the child's imagination and memory toward the imitative act of reading. Smith continues to say that the same approach can be used for the child learning to write, that is, by first simply listening to stories. Poetic experience and knowledge is essentially passive, and listening is above all the gateway, along with looking, to the poetic mode.

The problem, according to Smith, with what he calls the "drill and kill" method of language arts programs is not that they fail to give skills to decode words and write correct sentences but that they destroy the delight of learning in the process; and, as it is an axiom that learning requires, especially in the child, a high interest level, the scientific system of reading and writing threatens to defeat the very goals promoted by such systems.

> Teacher researchers Donald Graves and Virginia Stuart exam-
> ined how children were taught to read and write all over the
> United States. . . . Like many observers, Graves and Stuart
> conclude that kindergarten and first-grade children love to
> write, but "it doesn't take too many years of filling in the
> blanks, copying words and diagraming sentences before chil-
> dren decide writing is no fun at all."[9]

Given that the scientific idea of education is a mechanical model that manifests itself in some form of the "drill and kill" system, and given, in contrast, that the human being is not a machine and has not, for centuries, responded to learning by such methods, the conflict produced by the imposition of the scientific idea of learning will also have its negative effect on the emotional life of the learner. "We don't just learn about something," Smith says, "we simultaneously learn how we feel as we learn."[10] It is in this way that we hear more and more that young students have come to "hate" math or English, or, slightly worse, that it is all "boring."

It is the firm position of this study that some essential perception about the human being, about the world, and how we learn about our world, has been dumped from the modern educational experience. That which has been abandoned is the poetic mode of knowledge, even though its existence and importance has been referred to and assumed to be in place for centuries. It is the history of this largely forgotten tradition of knowledge that now must be examined.

2

The Philosophical Foundations
of Poetic Knowledge

This, to my way of thinking, is something
very much like perfection.

—The Odyssey

ontrary to a popular notion of Book III in *The Republic*, Plato
did not dislike poetry or literary works, nor did he exclude them
from his great model of justice in the soul and the educational means
to achieve it. For example, in Book II we see that Socrates is very
keen that the way to begin educating for mind and character is by
beginning with stories, ". . . true stories and fiction. Our education
must use both, and start with fiction. . . . And we will tell children
stories before we start them on physical training."[1] This last remark
is probably offered as a distinction from Spartan education of the
time. But this much-misunderstood censorship of Plato's was a limited one; namely, a theological concern that led him to a position
from which to expunge from the poets, especially the works of
Homer, those passages that would appear to children as blasphe-
mous, irreverent, immoral, or sacrilegious. He was anxious over the
passages that would portray God as responsible for all of men's mis-
ery, or show the gods as no more than wretched demons sent to de-
ceive men. As Julius A. Elias says:

> Thus the attack on poetry takes in his [Plato's] concerns as a
> religious reformer. . . . It is surely the moral focus that is central
> in Plato's thought and we should be reversing the natural order
> of his programme if we took the attack on poetry narrowly con-
> ceived as the point of departure . . . The passages most fre-
> quently cited to document the attack on the arts are those

11

dealing with the misrepresentation of the gods as spiteful, venal, and immoral.[2]

In other words, this was a narrow and restricted censorship, and, really, a rather commonsense position that would be understood and, to some degree, practiced by modern orthodox religions, as well as by those less orthodox who believe that what children are exposed to should be regulated.

Socrates could not have proposed *The Republic* without poetry and the poetic sense of life and education. Again Elias comments: "Plato's writings contain and imply an acknowledgment of the indispensability of poetry . . . his writings contain examples of good poetry—the myths."[3] Furthermore: "Plato was aware, surely from his own experience, of how mysterious the process is that prompts the juxtaposition of images. . . . His work is full of imagery of all kinds: similes, metaphors, analogies, isomorphisms."[4] Plato's poetry, the famous myth of the cave, for example, arises "where the logic of discourse is incapable of definitive demonstration, we fall back of necessity on poetry to persuade."[5]

Therefore, while it is true that Socrates offers in *The Republic* the earliest systematic theory of education in the West, it must also be recalled that that theory came *after* the first great educator in Greek antiquity, Homer. "As Plato said, Homer was, in the full sense of the word, the educator of Greece. . . . He was this from the very beginning, as Xenophanes of Colophon insisted as far back as the sixth century."[6]

Werner Jaeger, in his three volume study of Classical Greek literature and philosophy, *Paideia: The Ideals of Greek Culture*, reminds the modern reader that Homer, "[like all the great Greek poets] is something much more than a figure in the parade of literary history. He is the first and the greatest creator and shaper of Greek life and Greek character."[7]

We have to frequently remind ourselves in our utilitarian age that poetry, and all art, for the Platonic-Aristotelian tradition, was considered a means of real and valuable knowledge, a knowledge of the permanent things. "Art has a limitless power of converting the human soul—a power which the Greeks called *psychagogia*. For art possesses the two essentials of educational influence—universal significance and immediate appeal. By uniting these two methods of influencing the mind, it surpasses both philosophical thought and actual life."[8] Here, in this last statement, Jaeger touches on the educational value of what is treated here as poetic experience, poetic knowledge that "surpasses" discursive methods of inquiry, testing of hypothesis, and so on; and, instead, tends to take us inside the objects of knowledge through the immediate powers of the senses and emotions. For example, this would be the difference, for the beginner, between studying music—theory, harmony, rhythm—and actually *doing* music, by singing and dancing, to become, in a sense, music itself. It is the difference between Bitzer's and Sissy Jupe's knowledge of horses. This position of poetic knowledge has no quarrel with the realm of the expert—the opera star or the physician—but it does hold that there is a proper order of knowledge, as outlined by John Senior in chapter 1, beginning with the poetic; without the observance of this order, one can "produce" pianists who can perfectly play the notes of the great composers, without playing the *music*, and doctors who treat diseases, but not the whole person who is ill.

Still, this is not likely to stir the modern reader much without recalling that in addition to the immediate, proximate, and remote ends of Greek education, and the final end of *paideia*, and *psychagogia* (leading the soul) under Platonic education, there was a transcendent vision of reality. Notice, as certainly Socrates did, how Homer has Odysseus penetrate the ordinary, sensory details of a banquet to reveal the poetic, transcendent significance:

> I myself feel that there is nothing more delightful than when the festive mood reigns in a whole people's hearts and the banqueters listen to a minstrel from their seats in the hall, while the tables before them are laden with bread and meat, and a steward carries round the wine he has drawn from the bowl and fills their cups. This, to my way of thinking, is something very much like perfection.[9]

This visionary movement from the particular concrete objects of beauty, this penetrating gaze into the transcendent nature of things, is essentially a poetic act, yet, distinct (not separate), as was stated in the beginning, from the crafted thing called verse. And it is this kind of experience, these moments of being led by the ordinary objects of delight and wonder into "something very much like perfection," that occurs everywhere in Homer.

Notable, too, and equally illustrative of what would have been Socrates' education for the caretakers of civilization, is the stark contrast with the banquet to the confrontation between Odysseus and the Cyclops. Odysseus explains these monsters in terms his listeners at the banquet will understand immediately.

> The Cyclops have no assemblies for the making of laws, nor any settled customs, but live in hollow caverns in the mountain heights, where each man is a lawgiver to his children and his wives, and nobody gives a jot for his neighbors.[10]

The first description at the banquet hall of Lord Alcinous is not merely an image of manners and civility, although it is clear by implication that without this poetic sensibility toward things, life deteriorates into brutality and chaos; what is also revealed is the upward movement of the senses and emotions with the intellect that sees the invisible meaning of things. What can be located as well, in contrast with the brutality of the Cyclops, is that the vision of "perfection" at the feast takes place, as all poetic knowledge does, in a setting of *leisure* of some kind. It is quite appropriate to learn that in Greek, the word for leisure is *skole* and, in Latin, *scola*, which, as can easily be seen, becomes *school* in English. Josef Pieper, the German Thomistic philosopher, explains that " '*school*' does not, properly speaking mean school, but leisure. The original conception of leisure, as it arose in the civilized world of Greece, has, however, become unrecognizable in the world of planned diligence and 'total labor'."[11] Here is precisely another way of stating the distinction between the poetic mode—requiring a condition of leisure—and the scientific; that is, the world of effort, work, the labor of proof, and, in the "drill and kill" methods mentioned earlier. Pieper seems to be describing exactly the experience of Odysseus at the banquet: "The power to know leisure is the power to overstep the boundaries of the workaday world and reach out to superhuman, life-giving existential forces that refresh and renew us before we turn back to our daily work."[12] This notion of leisure—its poetic nature, its way of knowledge in the *paideia* of Plato—is far, far removed from contemporary ideas of leisure that usually result in, rather than renewal, exhaustion, if not a certain degree of dissipation from over stimulating the senses in the great quest to escape from stress and, with great effort, to have "fun." To be placed at a 45° angle in a reclining chair, drink in one hand, remote control in the other, in front of the television, is not leisure but something closer to sloth of mind and body.

The more *The Republic* is considered under the poetic mode of knowledge, the more it is seen that poetry, either as art or as the spirit of teaching through music and gymnastic, is Plato's chosen mode of education for the crucial first stages of training for the guardians. Thus, a tradition of learning that began with Homeric epics as models of imitation in virtue and delight are now taken up for serious reflection and discourse under the genius of the West's first great philosopher. All of the educational experiences detailed in *The Republic* for the child—songs, poetry, music, gymnastic—are meant to awaken and refine a *sympathetic* knowledge of the reality of the True, Good, and Beautiful, by placing the child *inside* the experience of those transcendentals as they are contained in these arts and sensory experiences. Of course, this way of education for the beginner is based on the child's natural disposition to learn by imitation; that is, not only to attempt to duplicate what they hear and see but to become the thing that is imitated, as the child becomes the galloping horse, by snorting and whinnying; the snake or alligator by sliding across the floor; the pirate; the cowboy; and so on. Jean Piaget's modern research methods in psychology simply confirm what was always known about the child in this regard:

> The child, like the uncultured adult, appears exclusively concerned with things. He is indifferent to the life of thought and the originality of individual points of view escapes him. His earliest interests, his first games, his drawings are all concerned solely with the imitation of what is.[13]

How deeply poetic experience can achieve this first and quite profound, though obscure, knowledge of things, is seen by Socrates' minute sifting of the particular passages of poetry, music, and movements of physical exercise to be taught, so that only a balanced and refined character emerges to take up much later the rigor of those higher modes of knowledge contained in geometry, logic, and, finally, dialectic. But the first experiences in the poetic mode will never be forgotten, nor rejected, as if one had outgrown them and found them silly. That is the modern mechanical view of growth, moving from one compartment of knowledge to the next, lopping off the one behind as now inferior. The educational tradition of

Socrates is organic and living, more like the image of the growth rings in a tree, rather than the consumable and disposable stages of growth so prevalent in modern education. As Socrates explains:

> We shall thus prevent our guardians being brought up among representations [music, sculpture, poetry, architecture] of what is evil, and so day by day and little by little, by grazing widely as it were in an unhealthy pasture, insensibly doing themselves a cumulative psychological damage that is very serious. We must look for artists and craftsmen capable of perceiving the real nature of what is beautiful, and then our young men, living as it were in a healthy climate, will benefit because all the works of art they see and hear influence them for good, like the breezes from some healthy country, insensibly leading them from earliest childhood into close sympathy and conformity with beauty and reason. . . . [T]his stage of education is crucial. For rhythm and harmony penetrate deeply into the mind and take a most powerful hold on it.[14]

The "rhythm and harmony" is not meant to be restricted to music, but under the Greek notions of proportion and integration, would be applied to all prerational modes of knowledge. However, it is true that it is the actual music that gets deeply inside the psychosomatic dimensions of the human being, and this is precisely why Socrates is careful with it, because of its effect on *character*, the formation of which is, after all, the end of all his concerns.

> We'll consult Damon [the musician] and ask him what combinations [of rhythm and harmony] are suitable to express meanness, insolence, madness, and other evil characteristics, and which rhythms we must keep to express their opposites.[15]

And 2,000 years later, Shakespeare gives his "music" to this musical wisdom:

> The man that hath no music in himself,
> Nor is not mov'd with concord of sweet sounds,
> Is fit for treasons, stratagems, and spoils.
> The motions of his spirit are dull as night
> And his affections dark as Erebus.
> Let no such man be trusted. Mark the music.

Ever so briefly, in passing, I should mention that against the charge that Socrates represents an exclusive Western idea of education in this matter of poetry and music, stands his virtual contemporary, Confucius, who reminds his pupils: "Be stimulated by the *Odes*, take your stand on the rites, and be perfected by music."[16] It is noteworthy indeed that this Eastern master teacher reserves music and its powers as the means for perfection of character.

And, when Socrates thinks of physical training (gymnastic) as a crucial discipline, it is not just complementary to literary and musical knowledge, but is in its own way integrated with its powers upon the senses and emotions into a larger view of musical (poetic) education.

> And so we may venture to assert that anyone who can produce this perfect blend of the physical and intellectual sides of education and apply them to the training of character, is producing music and harmony of more importance than any mere musician tuning strings.[17]

And, how sublime is the need of such an education?

> But to love rightly is to love what is orderly and beautiful in an educated and disciplined way . . . for the object of education is to teach us to love what is beautiful.[18]

Viewed from the perspective of sensory and emotional education as the beginning of the poetic mode of knowledge in *The Republic*, Socrates' entire discussion that follows on Forms, the allegory of the Cave, the myth of Er, and the immortality of the soul, no matter how lofty, incomplete, or misunderstood, the whole of Plato's so-called Idealism rests on a carefully cultivated, vibrant, sensory-emotional contact with a very real and knowable objective reality. But in a post-Cartesian, rationalist world, the fact that Plato insisted that this knowable universe is ultimately spiritual in nature, and that "Genuine knowledge was immaterial, intellectual, and eternal as were the perfect forms upon which it was based,"[19] are positions simply no longer fashionable or "correct," rather than theories that have been disproved.

Projecting the great philosophical argument in the world of *The Republic* into the twentieth century, it would appear the modern sophists have won the day, that, as Thrasymachus said long ago—"I say that justice or right is simply what is in the interest of the stronger party"[20]—has dominated in nearly all areas of culture. The Sophists, then and now, justify an education driven by the power brokers of the marketplace, and, therefore, it is an education bereft of all traditional principles.

In spite of this lopsided current struggle, the past does not change, and it was Homer and Socrates who first gave clear images and reasoned speculations, respectively, concerning poetic knowledge, where, as John Senior said, "truths are grasped intuitively." However, it remained for Aristotle, the great pupil of Plato, to explain *how* such necessary, prephilosophical knowledge was possible without appealing, as did his master, to a separate world of ideas creating, it is said, a radical dualism. In this famous disagreement, the full details of which are beyond my present focus, Aristotle said it is in the nature of the mind to simply abstract (draw out from) the essences from objects, that there is no need to construct another "world" for these forms and essences. "It must be held to be impossible that the substance, and that of which it is the substance, should exist apart; how, therefore, can the Ideas, being the substance of things, exist apart?"[21] Realist psychology and epistemology, under Aristotle's insights, contained primarily in his *Metaphysics* and *De Anima*, assert that all existing things contain an invisible life—forms and essences—that must be perceived by the mind in order that there be knowledge. The essence of bread, for example, is grasped intuitively by the mind regardless of the sensory "accidentals" of color, shape, and so on, and in this way the universal idea of bread, or bread-ness, is achieved. Realist philosophy says that the invisible life, the form, is *in* the thing, not elsewhere. It is simply in the nature of the mind, the soul, to correspond with this invisible reality. Aristotle says in *De Anima* that "the soul is in a way all existing things; for existing things are either sensible or thinkable, and knowledge is in a way that is knowable, and sensation is in a way that is sensible."[22] This statement of the soul becoming "in a way all things" is a point of greatest importance when St. Thomas Aquinas's commentary is examined on this category of knowledge in the next chapter and is, of course, a central contribution to understanding the poetic way of knowledge.

What Aristotle offers, then, is a moderate dualism that joins physical and metaphysical reality in an objective order of existence that the human being is naturally equipped to perceive and "become," first through the senses and then through the ability of the mind to abstract essences and form concepts.

As interesting and important as this famous distinction is between Idealism and Realism, more significant for the history of poetic knowledge are the observations of Aristotle that carry forward the treatment of Homer and Plato, especially in those areas where they are dealing with the foundations of truth—which is, as I have shown, the province of poetic knowledge.

Thus, it is in the *Politics* of Aristotle, his rewriting, as it were, of *The Republic*, that a great continuity is found between these two geniuses of philosophy concerning the education of youth. Aristotle's survey of the educational climate of his day could have been written this year.

> As things are, there is disagreement about the subjects. For mankind are by no means agreed about the things to be taught, whether we look to virtue or the best life. Neither is it clear whether education is more concerned with intellectual or with moral virtue. The existing practice is perplexing; no one knows on what principle we should proceed, should the useful in life, or should virtue, or should higher knowledge, be the aim of our training.[23]

However, Aristotle wastes no time in announcing that there is no confusion in his mind about the first stages of education.

> To young children should be imparted only such kinds of knowledge as will be useful to them without vulgarizing them. And any occupation, art, or science, which makes the body or soul or mind of the freeman less fit for the practice and exercise of virtue, is vulgar; wherefore, we call those arts vulgar which tend to deform the body, and likewise all paid employments, for they absorb and degrade the mind.[24]

Here, then, is the end of education for Aristotle, "the practice and exercise of virtue," which corresponds with Socrates' desire for the guardians to produce "good character," with both philosophers depending on the same kind of means of education to take the student's whole being into experiences of virtue, at least, in some sympathetic, vicarious way, which, as has been explained, is the heart of poetic knowledge. As with Plato, so with Aristotle, these still remain as fundamental for education: music, gymnastic, and poetry.

> The customary branches of education are in number four; they are, (1) reading and writing, (2) gymnastic experience, (3) music, to which is sometimes added, (4) drawing. . . . Concerning music, in our own day most men cultivate it for the sake of pleasure, but originally it was included in education because nature herself, as has been often said, requires that we should be able, not only to work well, but to use leisure well; for, as I must repeat once again, the first principle of all action is leisure.[25]

Concerning this startling last sentence, it can simply be restated that, beginning with the ancient Greeks and extending, no matter how meagerly, even into the twentieth century, the idea that real education requires a certain contemplative spirit (leisure) has persisted. It is in leisure (skole) that we prepare for an active life of virtue, and, in the experience of music, a species of leisure, we gain our first touch through the sensory-emotional (poetic) mode, of our final purpose, which is to experience happiness, a resting from activity, a return to where we began, to a state of repose: leisure. For the purpose here, it can be said with Aristotle in mind that the poetic precedes the scientific, the passive precedes the active, and, in the order of importance based on what must come first, these beginning conditions for virtue are greater. To know music, the sublime expression of leisure in this ancient tradition, was to grasp, remotely, that is, poetically and obscurely, something of the end of all action. As Aristotle says: "Both [action and leisure] are required, but leisure is better than occupations and is its end."[26]

While Aristotle speaks of gymnastic, reading and writing, he always returns to music, and it is music as the foundation of virtuous education with which he mostly deals. Why is it so important?

> May it [music] not have also some influence over the character and the soul? It must have such an influence if characters are affected by it. And that they are so affected is proved in many ways, and not the least by the power which the songs of Olympus exercise; for beyond question they inspire enthusiasm, and enthusiasm is an emotion of the ethical part of the soul.[27]

Always remembering that music is being considered here as one of the most powerful means of poetic experience and knowledge, notice that Aristotle displays the same intense concern as Plato, not just for music in the formation of youth, but for a certain kind of music.

> Since then music is a pleasure, and virtue consists in rejoicing and loving aright, there is clearly nothing which we are so much concerned to acquire and to cultivate as the power of forming right judgments, and of taking delight in good dispositions and noble actions. Rhythm and melody supply imitations of anger and gentleness, and also of courage, temperance, and of all the qualities contrary to these, and the other qualities of character.[28]

Notice also how the acknowledgment of imitation as the primary means of education gains another dimension. Not only does the child imitate what is presented to his imagination, but the fundamentals of music, rhythm, and melody imitate the virtues of just anger, gentleness, courage, and temperance that, under the physical power of music acting directly on the senses, takes these admittedly difficult and complex concepts and reverberates them throughout the body and mind as a kind of real *experience* of the concept. There existed in the time of Plato and Aristotle a kind of "rock and roll" music associated with the wild celebrations of the cult of Dionysus with its emphasis on percussion instruments that attracted large numbers of youth. So, when Aristotle speaks in the tradition of Socrates of the qualities of music contrary to the virtues, to grasp his meaning we have only to recall the obvious effects, worldwide in our day, of rock music and musicians on manners and style of life on millions of children. Braving a generalization in the spirit of Socrates, I would say such music perfectly promotes the contraries of the virtues: violence, brazen vulgarity, and intemperance.

The words of Socrates noted earlier—"the object of education is to teach us to love what is beautiful"—are, of course, informing Aristotle's entire position here. The beauty of "right judgments," the "delight in good dispositions and noble actions," the "pleasure" of virtue itself, all form a portrait of ancient education that has unfairly been narrowed and isolated by modern audiences as solely rational. Yet, all character excellence and virtue are here prepared with the most thoughtful of sensory and emotional experiences, which represents a clear expression of knowledge in the poetic mode. Aristotle concludes this point on music, thus:

> Enough has been said to show that music has a power of forming the character, and should therefore be introduced into the education of the young. . . . There seems to be in us a sort of affinity to musical modes and rhythms, which makes some philosophers say that the soul is a tuning, others, that it possesses tuning.[29]

In case it has been forgotten, recall that both Plato and Aristotle referred to poetry and to music as parts of a particular art, the form of song, so that in their considerations for virtuous or character education, they are inquiring into the appropriateness of words as much as particular rhythms, scales, and melodies. Be that as it may, the point continues to be that all these fundamental considerations for education take place with an understanding that a direct appeal to the sensory-emotional life of the human being are held to be necessary and essential *knowledge*. The place of sensory-emotional experience that gives knowledge is prerequisite in this tradition leading to rational discourse, as if to say in this "musical" way of experiencing reality there is a judgment of the senses that begins to "tune" us to our world, naturally. Thus, the famous passage of Aristotle:

> All men by nature desire to know. An indication of this is the delight we take in our senses . . . we do not regard any of the senses as Wisdom; yet surely these give the most authoritative knowledge of particulars. But they do not tell us [the] "why" of anything—e.g. why fire is hot; they only say that it is hot.[30]

The answer to why fire is hot introduces another branch of knowledge, that is, the experimental and scientific, a mode of knowledge given to the expert who isolates certain aspects of the phenomena of fire. But there is nothing to suggest here that, while that kind of knowledge is more exact as to causes and elements of fire, it is, therefore, a "better" kind of knowledge, for it is also a narrow and disintegrated kind of knowledge, compared with the more whole and existential reality of the *experience* of fire taken in at once by the various senses. Even Faraday's famous lecture *The Chemical History of a*

Candle rests upon him and his class closely observing a burning candle prior to experiments. Only after the shape and colors of the flame have been carefully noticed does he move forward to various demonstrations, but it is obvious that all that follows is informed and held up by the initial gaze at the flame. As I explained that poetic knowledge moves far beyond the knowledge of verse, so too it can be said that the term *gymnastic* can be understood in its broader and poetic sense to include how Faraday began his lecture; that is, as a "naked wrestling" with reality, unencumbered by microscopes, textbooks, or tests.

To summarize: an education with the foregoing in mind, an education for beginners, would be poetic, which means, to draw heavily on direct and vicarious experience that engages and awakens the senses; for example, gymnastic, poetry, music. And, with Aristotle, we would distinguish that mode of knowledge that is in its own right higher than poetic knowledge, which he calls wisdom. "Wisdom is knowledge about certain principles and causes."[31] Wisdom, or metaphysics, is the study of things in their causes, a very rigorous, mature, complex discipline for the carefully trained philosopher. (Later, I will examine how wisdom, knowledge about certain principles and causes, can be arrived at without the discipline of formal metaphysics when connatural knowledge is presented.) But whereas, the "delight we take in our senses" is the first knowledge of the thing itself, as it is, undisturbed, unanalyzed by the beginner and average man, "That we take pleasure in the sheer exercise of our sensory faculties is a sign that we do have a desire for knowledge,"[32] comments Jonathan Lear in his work on Aristotle and knowledge. How so? "One does not know the content of a desire unless one knows what ultimately satisfies it. By its satisfaction [pleasure] we learn what the desire is desire for. That is why Aristotle speaks of the delight we take in our senses."[33]

The point is that both Plato and Aristotle recognized that the senses, of their own nature, make a proportionate selection of what is pleasant, what is the "mean"—not unlike the tale of Goldilocks who finally selected the bowl of porridge that was not too hot, not too cold, but "just right." This "just right" is poetic knowledge, the judgment of the senses, without which all higher learning tends to become dehumanized and increasingly destructive. Jonathan Lear traces Aristotle's following of the role of the senses and knowledge.

> Man starts life with the ability to discriminate among sensory
> phenomena, an ability he shares with other animals. . . .
> Through repeated encounters with items in the world, our sen-
> sory discriminations develop into memory and then into what
> Aristotle calls "experience." Experience Aristotle characterizes
> as "the whole universal that has come to rest in the soul." The
> world that provides a path along which man's curiosity can
> run. Because the universal is embedded in particulars, a per-
> son's first explorations among particulars will naturally lead
> him toward a grasp of the embodied universal.[34]

Complementary to the discussion of the senses and knowledge
is David Summers, who, in his book *The Judgment of Sense* says that,
"Aristotle occupies an essential place in the history we are tracing
because he defined the structure of sense and therefore the nature of
the judgment of sense. . . . [He] agreed with Plato in associating its
[the senses] discriminations with the beginning of knowledge."[35]
Furthermore, Summers is helpful in defining Aristotle's "pleasure"
(delight) as the experience of the senses that is "a kind of proportion
between any faculty and its object. Although the highest of such pro-
portions is that between the intellect and its object, there are also
pleasures of sense."[36] Summers speaks of this pleasure as a corre-
spondence between the senses and the object, natural or artificial, as
a kind of "perfection," known immediately to the senses. Aristotle
concludes this point clearly near the beginning of the *Metaphysics*
when he recognizes that there is a poetic impulse to know in all men,
an experience he calls "wonder," that initiates all learning.

> It is owing to their wonder that men both now begin and at first
> began to philosophize; they wondered originally at the obvious
> difficulties, then advanced little by little and stated difficulties
> about greater matters. . . . A man who is puzzled and wonders
> thinks himself ignorant (whence even the lover of myth [po-
> etry] is in a sense a lover of Wisdom, for the myth is composed
> of wonders). . . . For all men begin, as we said, by wondering
> that things are as they are.[37]

Because wonder is so much a part of poetic experience in that
it is rooted in the sensory-emotional response of man to "things as
they are," it is well to clarify this term before proceeding. First of all,
wonder is an emotion of fear, a fear produced by the consciousness

of ignorance, which, because it is man's natural desire (good) to know, such ignorance is perceived as a kind of abrupt intrusion on the normal state of things, that is, as a kind of evil. Something is seen, heard, felt, and we do not know what it is, or why it is now present to us. There can be mild or extreme degrees of fear, wonder, at these times. But notice—unlike modern perversions of this natural impulse, such as the extraordinary and fantastic sounds, sights, and sensations artificially produced for a designed effect in films and video games—the traditional idea of wonder expressed by Aristotle operates within the *ordinary*, simply "things as they are." Dennis B. Quinn, one of the three professors of the Integrated Humanities Program, has written in his study of wonder that:

> Wonder, always considered a passion, was classified by Aquinas and many before him as a species of fear. This is bound to strike the modern reader as out of tune with his experience of the emotions of both fear and wonder. . . . Fear, we must remember, is one of the emergency emotions: it arises when we perceive some evil that seems to be insuperable. . . . There are, of course, many kinds of fear . . . [and] it is helpful to distinguish wonder from some passions in its immediate family. When we do so, we see that wonder is the most rational form of fear.[38]

It is important to stress, Quinn points out, that "It is frequently forgotten that wonder arises not from ignorance but from consciousness of ignorance."[39] Quinn also clarifies what could appear to be now (and later when the emotions, especially those of pleasure, are treated more fully in connection with poetic knowledge) a confusion or contradiction in this explanation.

> Wonder intensifies . . . pleasure . . . because wonder increases desire and therefore the joy of discovery. It seems at first that the pleasurable character of wonder is at odds with its being a form of fear, which is usually unpleasant. It is true that wonder arises from something that is unpleasant, consciousness of ignorance, and that until one knows, one remains in this condition. But the only way that one can profitably flee from ignorance is by desiring and attempting to know, and these are pleasant activities. A man imprisoned will find his condition unpleasant, but he will take delight in planning his escape.[40]

It is in this flight from ignorance that *philosophical* knowledge can begin, but it is crucial to keep in mind that wonder *qua* wonder is what it is precisely because it is not yet "philosophy" in any kind of structured system of thought. Although wonder may lead to knowledge (as Quinn says, it is the most rational of the emotions of fear), because it is an emotion (fear) charged with the recognition of ignorance giving birth to the desire to know, the knowledge that does take place at this level of experience is what we call poetic, that is, prerational knowledge. Cornelis Verhoeven, in his book *The Philosophy of Wonder* prefers to view the Platonic idea of philosophy, distinct from structured systems of thought, as a "radicalization of wonder in all directions."[41] With Plato immediately in mind, there seems to be nothing in Verhoeven's explanation that is not also informing what was quoted above from Aristotle. For Verhoeven, to *begin* to philosophize, as Aristotle says, is not to somehow pass beyond wonder. In fact, "The whole history of philosophy lies in a broad circle about the loose space of wonder, even when this wonder is regarded as a starting point."[42] This thought is exactly consistent with what was said earlier of Socrates' careful cultivation of the musical and gymnastic modes so that at the height of this formation, one has never lost the experience of wonder; passing through the contemplative nature of all subjects, geometry, arithmetic, and to dialectic, rising from the Cave of shadows, one is prepared to gaze into the Sun, and see the transcendent light of all things. Therefore, as Verhoeven explains this fundamental understanding of wonder, it must be clear that he is referring to *beginning philosophy,* as best seen in the dialogues of Socrates, which is indeed a different matter than the later system of philosophy, written by others, called "Platonism."

> Philosophy is not knowledge; as a form of desire (love) it is more a pathos, a state, than an actual knowing. Plato gives this pathos a name: wonder. . . . An introduction to philosophy is an introduction to the wonder that makes philosophy move. . . . It [wonder] is not founded on knowledge nor has it knowledge as its goal. Rather is it an obstinate ignorance, as in Socrates the art of avoiding institutionalized and certain knowledge. Knowledge leads to science, not to philosophy. Science has a firm grasp of reality which it uses as a tool. In this operation, as endorsed by the data of reality, science is verifiable. It can be expanded by hypotheses and experiments. But philosophy is not

a science; it is not a means of transmitting knowledge. It is what
it is before it can be termed knowledge.[43]

These are, quite likely, unfamiliar and perhaps difficult uses of
the terms *knowledge, philosophy,* and *science,* and perhaps I should add
that the "knowledge" I speak of as poetic, is certainly not the knowledge referred to by Verhoeven that takes place in the deliberate acts
of philosophy. However, if there is to be a correct understanding of
poetic knowledge and its nature, these close distinctions held by the
long philosophical tradition of the West must be observed. When
modern education with its neglect of wonder and the poetic mode
are examined later, it will be good to recall what has been said here
since there will be occasion to quote again from Verhoeven and his
commentary on general education and philosophical wonder.

But for now, offered as a kind of "breather" from these important but somewhat difficult clarifications, and before following the
ancient Greek tradition of knowledge into the Middle Ages, it is re
freshing to remember that we really have not gone so far after all
from the banquet hall and Odysseus' vision of perfection, his wonder at the commonplace details of the feast, as if seen for the first
time in their significance, "the universal embedded in particulars."

It is a repeated observation in the history of philosophy to say that
St. Augustine represents a bridge from the ancient and classical
worlds to the Christian and medieval era; it is repeated because it is
true. And as I examine Augustine on this matter of poetic knowledge, it should not be far from our memory that this famous convert
was immersed in the letters of the Greco-Roman world, the works of
Plato, Virgil, Cicero, and was himself a teacher of literature. Because St. Augustine recognized in Plato the higher, spiritual nature
of man; because of his refutations of the heresies of his day, which
laid the foundation for a Christian theology; by giving to the world
one of the great classics of the spiritual life, *The Confessions;* by writing
the broadest theological interpretation of history ever attempted,
The City of God—by these works alone, from pagan humanist to
Christian saint, Augustine is indeed this tremendous link with a past

that makes it possible to consider that past as a continuous tradition, and, therefore, still informing our thoughts today on these subjects of knowledge, learning, and education. As John Henry Cardinal Newman said, St. Augustine is the teacher who "has formed the intellect of Christian Europe."[44]

But it so happens that Cardinal Newman has also written of another voice and force of the poetic mode of Christian culture, nearly a contemporary of Augustine's but not nearly as well known or likely to be considered in a discussion of the modes of knowledge; that is, St. Benedict, the father of Western monasticism. With the presence of St. Benedict, we do not find treatises or discussions on knowledge. In fact, to have had such an influence at all on Western thought does not seem to have been intended; and yet the life and example, especially of the early monastic foundations, based on the letter and the spirit of *The Rule of St. Benedict,* were living testaments of the poetic mode of life reaching to the heights of spiritual perfection.

Precisely because of the enormous and various influences of the Augustinian and Benedictine presence in the West and because of the immediate focus of the topic at hand, I will offer only a survey of the more specific contributions to the tradition of poetic knowledge.

St. Augustine understood very well that we are first drawn to a contemplation of reality by a sense of wonder, pleasurable in some way, when we are motivated to know through our senses within the general appetite of love. Knowledge of a thing, for Augustine, requires possession of it, and he said we are not in possession of a thing until we love it. It is also clear that Augustine includes in the term *love* all the associations of sensory delight and desire given to this initial act of knowing identified by Plato and Aristotle. Augustine, of course, would be quick to counsel that the end of knowledge of things is not sensory pleasure; our end would be to possess a vision of beauty and perfection above the object of the senses that would lead us to the contemplation of God. Even here, the Christian belief in the body's eventual joining with soul in the Beatific Vision includes as part of the joys of heaven, pleasures proper to the body's external and internal senses. However, because of the great need to rescue such terms as *love* and *pleasure* from devalued modern connotations, a general understanding of Augustine's idea of the senses and knowledge must be outlined. In *On Music* he says:

> When the soul experiences physical sensations, it is not being affected by the body, but rather it is acting with more deliberate attention than usual because of what the body is experiencing. The body's actions [i.e., the senses] . . . do not escape the notice of the soul. This is precisely what is meant by sense perception. The function of sensation, which is in us even when we are sensing nothing, is one of the body's instruments, which the soul employs with restraint so that it may be better prepared to give conscious attention to physical conditions.[45]

Notice that it is the mind, the soul, the intelligence that experiences *sensations*, while the "body's actions" are the realm of the *senses*. Sensation, therefore, is a kind of knowledge, a perception that results from the action of the senses.

All knowledge, then, begins in the senses, but Augustine would not call all knowledge poetic, or, let us say, aesthetic, simply because it passes through the senses— although it will be said later that there is something poetic, broadly speaking, in this spontaneous, intuitive connection between the senses and the mind. "Unless a thing is enjoyed for its own sake," comments Emmanuel Chapman in his study *Augustine's Philosophy of Beauty*, "and for no other reason, it cannot enter into the aesthetic experience."[46] This understanding of the senses in delight of an object leading to an immediate though obscure knowledge of a thing, rests with the mind not the senses; but it is the act of *sensation* distinguishing what is useful in the object from what is delightful. Augustine says elsewhere: " 'To use' is to put something at the disposal of the will, whereas, 'to enjoy' is to use a thing with satisfaction, which is no longer a matter of hope but of actual reality."[47]

In other words, the reason there is no need to hope for a thing is because, through delight in the contemplation of the object for itself, love has obtained possession, and where there is possession of the object of desire, there is no need for hope, which, as a result produces the experience of "satisfaction." For example, to *en-joy*, to enter into joy, is to gaze at the full ripeness of the round, red apple on a wooden kitchen table on a bright fall afternoon, to marvel at its perfect beauty in being what it is. To use such an apple to make a pie is a very good thing to do, certainly in anticipation of filling one's hunger with its goodness, but it is not the same thing as the first experience. Though there is an admixture of the two, the first encounter of the apple that takes place in leisure satisfies the desire for an immaterial possession of its essential beauty; the second satisfies the *feeling* of a particular physical hunger. In the way that Augustine is describing, on the sensory-emotional level, poetic knowledge can be said to soar above the descriptive knowledge of the metaphysical and give instead the *experience*, no matter how remote and obscure, of the thing itself.

Chapman, alertly, but with a certain complexity, attempts to explain this difficult point raised by Augustine.

> In every act of sensation, which is of the mind through the senses, there is the compresence of intellect. Without the compresence of mind a verse could not be heard, nor for that matter even a word or syllable of it. . . . It could not be heard unless at the end of the sensation of hearing the memory retained its beginning as well as all the intermediate stages. . . . Aesthetic pleasure is saturated with intelligibility and by that very fact is much more in conformity with the nature of man. Man is primarily an intelligence using a body. . . . The simple expression [of Augustine's] *delightful contemplation* contains the two essential characteristics of the aesthetic experience: not any delight but delight in contemplating an object, not any contemplation but contemplation with delight. Delightful contemplation, that is to say, the concurrence of joy and a vision, *intuitive knowledge* with delight, is required to experience an object aesthetically.[48]

And, keeping in mind that for the purposes here I use the term *poetic* to be considered and included with the term *aesthetic*, Chapman approaches something of a final statement about Augustine's thought on sensation and knowledge: "The object of the aesthetic experience is essentially the object of intelligence, because what contemplates in the full meaning of the word is the mind."[49]

So, when St. Augustine says, "There is no enjoyment where there is no love,"[50] he means that to enjoy a thing is to gain a real knowledge of it. Enjoyment is spontaneous, surprising, unplanned, and immediately captivating to the senses and emotions as well as to the mind; in other words, poetic. Augustine explains:

> Because love is a movement [of the soul] and every movement is always toward something, when we ask what ought to be loved, we are therefore asking what it is that we ought to be

moving toward. . . . It is the thing in regard to which possession and knowing are one and the same.[51]

He continues to make clear that there exists important distinctions in what objects are to be loved, as a moral man, and a Christian, would. But, over and over again, he returns to the principle that extends the history of thought on poetic knowledge.

> To possess any subject of study is to know it . . . [and] however good a thing is, if it is not loved, it cannot be perfectly possessed, that is, known. For who can know how good a thing is if he does not enjoy it?[52]

Certainly we need to recall that Realist and Christian philosophy would say that love is ultimately in the will, but what is also being recalled to mind from this tradition is that the objects of love are first placed there by the senses, sensation, and the emotion of love. An important point of the ancient, classical, medieval tradition on man as knower was the consistent view that it was the *whole* person who experienced the world—not just the eyes or just the mind, but the composite being, body and soul, man.

Unlike the scientific mode of learning that proposes *methods* and *systems* for acquiring knowledge, the tradition that has been thus far reviewed reveals rather a *way* of knowledge, like a path or winding road, with interesting detours off the road, more than the superhighway of modern education. It is a way more akin to the natural human response to discovery of the world. It is a way of leisure and reflection of what is there, the way things are, and when one is considering the kinds of knowledge, it is seen that there is a natural order after all that corresponds to the learner and his universe, beginning with what is known, immediate and accessible, and proceeding to the unknown.

Andrew Louth has devoted a book to examining the gulf between science and poetry, and concludes concerning the ancient and medieval tradition:

> We can see in the writings of the twelfth century—on both sides of the growing divide—a separation between mind and heart that had not been the case with the [Church] Fathers. With Augustine . . . knowledge and love are held together: there is a coherence of love and knowledge—we cannot love

what we do not know, nor do we progress in knowledge if we do not love.[53]

And, George Howie, a modern translator of and commentator on Augustine's educational works, adds in his introduction on this particular mode of knowledge:

> Whatever a man may desire to possess, desire itself is the most conspicuous and undeniable fact of learning. . . . In Augustine's telling metaphor, love is like the weight in physical objects, which propels them to their natural resting places.[54]

It was in St. Augustine's *De Magistro* [The Teacher], "one of the most influential of his earlier writings,"[55] that he explores the curious fact that "words have no power to make us know physical realities unless we have previously had some experience of these objects through the senses."[56] But even the presence of sensible objects in the memory require something more than words to bring to life the knowledge they hold.

Now, in the Christian tradition, what has been presented as the legacy of Plato's and Aristotle's recognition of the senses and their link to the intellect becomes with Augustine a doctrine of inner illumination, where "One is your teacher, Christ."[57]

> As physical light is necessary that we may perceive corporeal realities, so the divine wisdom must "illumine" the human mind, verifying St. John's description of Christ as *the true light that enlightens every man that cometh into the world.*[58]

God Himself sits at the center of the soul, the mind, he says, as the interior teacher, the light within that loves and knows. It is God who illuminates the storehouse of sense impressions in the memory. This would explain those moments, spontaneous, and unaided by methods or prior training, where the reality of things is seen in metaphysical wonder, as if seeing, not as God sees, but as a being enlightened by God. This is, under Christian psychology, the explanation of the experience of poetic knowledge. Augustine expresses both the validity of sense knowledge and the doctrine of illumination. One explains the other.

> He [the student] learns not by means of spoken words, but by means of the realities themselves and his senses. . . . Hence, I

do not teach even such a one, although I speak what is true.
For he is taught not by my words, but by the Realities themselves made manifest to him by God revealing them to his
inner self.[59]

And, now, what of the other great Western Father, St. Benedict? How did he advance the case for poetic knowledge? As mentioned earlier, it was a *way* of life, not a treatise, that Cardinal
Newman called "poetic."

> To St. Benedict, then, who may fairly be taken to represent the
> various families of monks before his time and those which
> sprang from him (for they are all pretty much of one school), to
> this great Saint let me assign, for his discriminating badge, the
> element of Poetry.[60]

To grasp the importance of the inclusion of this broader category of
"Poetry" in the history of poetic knowledge, and why Newman la-
bels the Benedictine era as poetic, requires an understanding of the
enormous influence of the words of St. Benedict contained in his
Rule.

> Dom Paul Delatte, second Abbot of Solesmes, in the best mod-
> ern commentary on the *Rule* says of it that like the Ten Com-
> mandments of the Law it is *justificate in semetipsa* [justified in
> itself]. It needs no style or intellectual or spiritual brilliance be-
> cause it has transformed the history of Western Civilization.[61]

That *Rule* simply but profoundly called for the pure and uncompli-
cated devotion of men who had fled from the world to follow an arduous and unglamorous routine so as to free their hearts and minds
from the cares of the world for God alone. It was the spirit of the
Rule that gave, eventually, to a world dark and dead, the rounded silence of the Romanesque cloister, where the weary eye may rest on
the sight of graceful, simple architecture, where the play of light and
shadow tends to quiet the mind, and where the ear transports the
heart and mind upward along the prayers of the freest of all music,
Gregorian chant. Newman explains this spirit and the reason he
calls it "poetic," instead of, say, "rational."

> The monks were too good Catholics to deny that reason was a
> divine gift, and had too much common sense to think to do

without it. What they denied themselves was the various and manifold exercises of the reason; and on this account, because such exercises were excitements. When the reason is cultivated, it at once begins to combine, to centralize, to look forward, to look back, to view things as a whole, whether for speculation or for action; it practices synthesis and analysis, it discovers and invents. To these exercises of the intellect is opposed simplicity, which is the state of mind which does not combine, does not deal with premises and conclusions, does not recognize means and their end, but lets each work, each place, each occurrence stand by itself, which acts toward each as it comes before it, without a thought of anything else. This simplicity is the temper of children, and it is the temper of monks.[62]

And, I would add, this is the temper of poetic experience and knowledge.

In other words, the Benedictine Age, unlike past times treated here, was not a time of theoretical conversation on the character-forming value of music and gymnastic, or the components of aesthetic experience, or the distinction between sense and sensation, and long before the subtle clarifications of Aquinas's definitions of intentional and connatural knowledge—although, the Benedictine experience contained all of this knowledge in its radical simplicity of life. Rather, this was a movement of adventurous men who had "dropped out" from what they saw as a corrupt world and began to live with the sense knowledge of their hands, with their hearts and minds in immediate confrontation with nature, as the beginning, and, in the theological sense, the end, of their salvation.

> Their object was rest and peace; their state was retirement; their occupation was some work that was simple, as opposed to intellectual. . . . They had eschewed the busy mart, the craft of gain, the money-changer's bench, and the merchant's cargo. . . . All they desired, was the sweet soothing presence of earth, sky, and sea, the hospitable cave, the bright running stream, the easy gifts which mother earth, *justissima tellus* yields on very little persuasion.[63]

And what was the spirit of *The Rule of St. Benedict* that moved these men to reside in caves, to fell thick forests, to clear and till the rocky fields? It was a call, a poetic voice that spoke to their senses of something wondrous in the created world, that asked them to watch and listen closely for the lessons there in a state of "wise passiveness" that Wordsworth would call for again centuries later. That voice is heard in the first words of the *Rule*: "Hearken, O my son, to the precepts of thy Master, and incline the ear of thy heart: willingly receive and faithfully fulfil the admonition of thy loving Father."[64] John Senior comments, concerning the spirit of the *Rule*, that "it is only to the patient, silent, receptive listener that the meaning of the poem, or the mystery of the number, star, chemical, plant—whatever subject the science sits at the feet of—is revealed."[65] In other words, to listen—to "Hearken"—and "to incline the ear of thy heart" is not only the first disposition for learning anything, it is also a poetic disposition. It is just as Aristotle said, that the state of leisure, passive receptivity—essentially, a poetic disposition—is prior to activity.

Again, we must remind ourselves that the age of St. Benedict was no lark or quaint period of history but was the single, most transforming cultural force in the rebuilding of Western Europe, informing in one way or another all those aspects of what is called "civilization" to such a degree that virtually every person of Christian medieval society, from popes and pirates to peasants, viewed the world as a vibrant arena of visible and invisible reality. Newman continues:

> Therefore have I called the monastic state the most poetical of religious discipline. It was a return to that primitive age of the world, of which poets have so often sung, the simple life.... It was a bringing back of those real, not fabulous, scenes of innocence and miracle, when Adam delved, or Abel kept sheep, or Noe planted the vine.[66]

In chapter 1, I defined and distinguished the terms *poetic* and *scientific*, particularly as they apply to modes of knowledge, education, and the difference between being and doing. Here, with Newman's commentary on the poetic mode in Benedictine life, I am greatly assisted in advancing the understanding of the essential difference in these two ways of viewing the world. The length of the following quote from Newman reflects the importance of this point, central to this entire study.

> Poetry, then, I conceive, whatever be its metaphysical essence, or however various may be its kinds, whether it more properly

belongs to action or to suffering, nay, whether it is more at home with society or with nature, whether its spirit is seen to best advantage in Homer or in Virgil, at any rate, is always the antagonist to *science*. As science makes progress in any subject matter, poetry recedes from it. The two cannot stand together; they belong respectively to two modes of viewing things, which are contradictory of each other. Reason investigates, analyzes, numbers, weighs, measures, ascertains, locates, the objects of contemplation, and thus gains a scientific knowledge of them. Science results in a system, which is a complex unity; poetry delights in the indefinite and various as contrasted with unity, and in the simple as contrasted with systems. The aim of science is to get a hold of things, to grasp them, to handle them, to comprehend them; that is (to use a familiar term), to master them. . . . [Poetry] demands, as its primary condition, that we should not put ourselves above the objects in which it resides, but at their feet. . . . Poetry does not address the reason, but the imagination and affections; it leads to admiration, enthusiasm, devotion, love.[67]

Are we so far from Socrates, who taught that philosophy was just what the word means, a love of wisdom, and that the end of education is to teach us to learn to love what is beautiful; or from St. Augustine, who said that to know a thing we must come to love it? No, we are in the same tradition with St. Benedict where poetic experience leads to love, that is, to real knowledge.

To make sure these thoughts and images from Newman are not confused with a false idea of the poetic, that is, the popular "romantic" perception of things poetic, he advises:

They [the Benedictines] were not dreamy sentimentalists, to fall in love with melancholy winds and purling rills, and waterfalls and nodding groves; but their poetry was the poetry of hard work and hard fare, unselfish hearts and charitable hands.[68]

Indeed, the poetic response to reality, for it to be real, finds an awful beauty in the "hard work and hard fare" of life—the sorrows of great losses, the disasters of nature, the betrayal of friends—all are first "celebrated" by our senses, imagination, and affections, long before we apply reason to what has happened, or why.

In keeping with this clarification that the poetic mode is not a deranged "flight of fancy" in need of being advanced to a higher mode of knowledge to justify itself, John Senior explains in speaking of the *Rule* that the entire Benedictine response to the universe and to God was in the poetic mode.

> The theory, not in the sense of hypothesis but of intellectual insight, of this way of [Benedictine] spirituality is based upon the fact that there are two Revelations, the one is the Book of Nature where visible things of this world signify the invisible things of the next, and the other of the Book of scripture where the invisible things of the next are made visible in the life and death of Christ.[69]

To learn to "read" by first learning to *listen* to the voice in the book of nature, which includes our own human nature, was the first task of the monk, as a prerequisite for taking up later the book of Scripture, which often contains both "voices" as in Psalm 18. The clear connection is still with us here, echoing what St. Augustine said, that one cannot really read and know the words—the signs of things—without first a knowledge of the things themselves, which we must come to love. The pre-Christian audience of the Homeric and Virgilian epics and the unlettered peasants of the Christian, premodern world could never have grasped, as they did, the spiritual dimensions of the poets in the first case and the supernatural teaching of the apostles and disciples in the second, had they not already read deeply first in the book of nature.

It would be nearly five hundred years before the formation of the Dominican order and their more systemized learning, and even the culmination of this knowledge in the works of one man in the thirteenth century who had been nurtured by the "rest and peace" of the Benedictine age. The slow and quiet growth of monasteries and the monastic influence throughout Europe, in discipline, manners, spirituality, morals, crafts, music, agriculture, and architecture, become "the cradle of scholastic theology"[70] from which emerged a boy, raised since he was five years old with the Benedictines in Italy, as the man considered to be the greatest Catholic theologian, St. Thomas Aquinas.

Umberto Eco is best known in America for his popular and somewhat fantastic novel, *The Name of the Rose*. However, it is his scholarly work—namely, *The Aesthetics of Thomas Aquinas*—that is of importance in continuing to follow the history of poetic knowledge.

Before directly examining Aquinas's contribution to understanding knowledge in this mode, Eco calls to mind that, in general, "the medievals were disposed to conceive of beauty as a purely intelligible reality, as moral harmony or metaphysical *splendor*,"[71] which sounds very much like the goal of learning set forth by Socrates. It was from Socrates, to Aristotle, to Augustine, that we learned there must be present something of the beautiful embedded as a universal in the particular object that gives rise to wonder and delight for there to be poetic experience. Education and learning, was more to guide the student to these objects so that the innate powers of knowledge, through the senses, would be awakened. This manner of knowledge permeated a whole civilization of Eastern and Western Christianity. Eco continues:

> An abundance of medieval literature demonstrates an awareness of sensible beauty, the beauty of natural objects and of art. . . . Medieval thinkers were quick to point out that sensible beauty could not be discarded simply because a higher value was ascribed (on the theoretical level at least) to spiritual beauty.[72]

Of course, there was also a constant teaching extending from the Church Fathers to the medieval scholar-saints against the distractions of beauty and the overattachment to sensible pleasures insofar as they could become impediments to the soul's union with God. However:

> It is one thing to maintain that aesthetic pleasure is out of place; it is quite another to have no aesthetic sensibility in the first place. . . . Even when the mystics were rejecting the pleasures of sensible beauty, they were elevating their aesthetic sensibilities to another level. They rejected the beauty of outward things only when those were contrasted with inner beauty.[73]

There was a deep understanding, albeit usually unspoken, in all of this of the intuitive mind, the judgment of sense, of poetic knowledge: "The soul recognized in material objects a harmony identical with that of its own structure, and this recognition was the genesis of aesthetic pleasure."[74] This "recognition" is the connection between sense and intellect that precedes scientific knowledge, especially the "science" spoken of by Newman. Perhaps the most difficult point to grasp is that there was nothing unusual about this aesthetic sense of things in medieval life, nothing remarkable or merely theoretical. "There was . . . an everyday sensibility [in the middle ages] of beauty grounded upon ordinary taste, and not just theory."[75] In every village where the narrow streets followed some spontaneous impulse of the builders in relation to the different sizes of the shops and houses, rather than conforming to an imposed grid planned by a city engineer; along the rising and falling rural roads that yielded to the contours of the countryside, roads marked with shrines and inns set in distances a man could walk following the sun from morning to evening, rural roads that became a natural part of the landscape connecting monasteries and towns; the rustic chapels, the great cathedrals in the cities; the sound of bells measuring the boundaries of each parish— all of medieval life could be said to have "taught" in the poetic mode, for "there was a direct connection linking the earth with heaven, and this must be taken into account when one considers their aesthetic perceptions."[76]

Therefore, as I present the last source from the Middle Ages, St. Thomas Aquinas, this poetic perception must be taken into account, in addition to what Eco says, that "If art could simultaneously instruct and delight . . ., this was because the medieval sensibility, like medieval culture as a whole, was an 'integrated' sensibility."[77] In other words, unlike modern society—which is more scientifically arranged and focused on the part, the bit, and the "byte," the exception, and the bizarre isolated example not necessarily connected with anything—medieval man, like ancient Western man, considered the universe a whole and living reality, significant and mysterious. In fact, mention of the "integrated sensibility" is exactly what Jaeger noticed when he spoke of the Greek's *psychagogia* of art, where the two essential elements of learning are contained: universal significance and immediate appeal, or delight.

It was, then, into a society, a culture, built on centuries of slow

Benedictine influence so eloquently described by Newman, that Aquinas was born in the thirteenth century. It is Aquinas who gives the final formal distinctions to this mode called "poetic," and since the popular image of this philosopher and theologian is often that of a cool and aloof thinker, a kind of mathematician of argument, demonstration and proof, there are some most interesting facts about him, in balance, to discover.

Standing underneath all the precise, rational architecture of the *Summa Theologica* is a very calm sense of serene purpose, wherein if one listens closely can be heard a voice peacefully assured of itself with no trace of arrogance, able to soar because it knows so well of that sensibility "linking the earth with heaven." Why? Certainly to be considered is the fact that Thomas was placed with the Benedictines of Monte Cassino at an early age. This would have been largely a musical education in all the respects spoken of by Socrates. Music was all the monks taught young boys, the Latin and chant of the *schola cantorum*, a school of song drawn from Psalms and history of the Old Testament: "There were numerous stories of Aquinas's cultivation in music . . . [his] quotations from the musical treatises of Boethius and Augustine, and various passages which reveal an undeniable mastery of the subject."[78] The more celebrated, formal learning of the *trivium* and *quadrivium* came much later, in Naples; but even here there was still music ever present in his course of studies. The insights and advice of Socrates that called for a proportioned experience of rhythm and melody as part of the earliest education was fulfilled in Aquinas. Further evidence that Aquinas was a man immersed in the poetic mode is seen when it is recalled that toward the end of his life he considered all his philosophy and theology as mere straw (compared to the possession of God Himself) and returned to the writing of some of the finest examples of Latin poetry and hymns, still treasured today by the Church. In addition, he composed in his maturity an entire Mass and Office dedicated to the Blessed Sacrament, still included in the liturgical books of the Latin Rite. "When Aquinas writes about beauty and artistic form he was not dealing with mere abstractions, cut off from experience. He was referring, implicitly, to a world which he knew well."[79]

> Aquinas was always conscious of the possibility of a pleasure which was pure and disinterested. He identified it with the pleasure produced by the apprehension of beauty in objects.

> Disinterested pleasure means pleasure which is its own end,
> which is not connected with the satisfaction of animal needs or
> with utility. An embryonic form of such pleasure already exists
> in play. What is play? It is an activity whose end is its own ful-
> fillment, and which causes a psychic relief necessary for our bi-
> ological rhythms. "The activities of play," writes Aquinas, "are
> not aimed at some extrinsic end, but aim rather at the well-
> being of the player."[80]

How different this is from some popular studies and attitudes on
play that declare its value as being the means to some other end,
usually to advance some "skill" in the curriculum, and resulting in
the glut, ala "Sesame Street," of so-called educational toys. But
under Thomas's idea, this would no longer be play but more like
activities approaching play's opposite—work—where Aristotle's
principle of "leisure preceding action" is reversed. Furthermore,
Aquinas's definition of play is squarely in the poetic mode of knowledge, remembering all that has been said before of its taking place in
leisure, for "disinterested contemplation is similar to play, because it
is an end in itself. It [contemplation of the object] also resembles
play in that it is not a response to some compulsion rooted in the ex-
igencies of life, but is rather a higher activity appropriate to a spiritual creature."[81]

In what has been explained so far, from Socrates to Augustine,
concerning poetic knowledge and, namely, that to know a thing we
must in some way possess it, it has also been far from clear how this
"works," even though the role of the senses and emotions has been
described. That all the powers of the knower—senses, emotions,
will, and intellect—are integrated is the main view within this tradition, and this opens up a more detailed description of how poetic
knowledge operates. It is Aristotle, and St. Thomas's commentaries
on the Greek philosopher's several works in this area, that reveal this
integration of the powers of knowledge.

Because my purpose here is to discover what Thomas said and
not to debate his findings, some explication of these topics found in
the *Summa Theologica* is needed to prepare a context for a clearer understanding of this integration. It is only because there exists unique
and precise distinctions from Aristotle and Aquinas that it becomes
appropriate to use the language of reason to explain that which is
prior to reason.

The modern Dominican scholar, Robert Edward Brennan, was a prolific writer, especially on Thomistic psychology, which covers exactly the insights needed to illuminate the intuitive, or poetic, mode of knowledge. All that will follow now is based upon St. Thomas's commentary, with Brennan's guidance, on Aristotle's *De Anima* and the refinement of the idea that man is not more of a body or more a soul but is a whole being made up of a mixture of matter and spirit; that is, a composite being. In restraining the theory that the soul is a separate and imprisoned force within the body, as some of the neo-Platonists came to believe, Aquinas lays the foundations, and offers explanations for, the sensory-intellectual harmonious relationships of our being, where "body and soul are regarded as incomplete in themselves, so that it requires the joining of both to make a complete substance."[82] St. Thomas says that "whereby a thing primarily acts in its form,"[83] so that, in this sense, the soul is the *form* of the body, the most intimate of relationships, "so intimate, indeed, that he could not be a man unless his body and soul were united to produce one substance."[84] In the Socratic-Aristotelian-Thomistic tradition, this is the glory of man.

> If we do not see that man is made out of matter and form
> [soul], we have no final point of reference for what he does . . .
> we have no clue to the inner meanings of his operations. . . .
> For what he does must be the result of what he is, and what he
> is, is a person whole and entire . . . it is not the eye that sees or
> the ear that hears or the mind that thinks. It is *man* who does
> these things with the aid of his eyes and ears and mind.[85]

With this intimate union in mind, St. Thomas prepares us to see how knowledge in the poetic mode takes place. One of the previous and main reasons for using the term *poetic* was that it is a sensory experience and, at the same time, a passionate one, where we are *moved*. And, as has been said all along, this constitutes a kind of knowledge. St. Thomas explains: "For we see that the senses are for the sake of the intellect, and not the other way about. The sense, moreover, is a certain deficient participation of the intellect."[86] This point that the senses *participate* in some way, no matter how obscurely, in the intellect, is of supreme importance in accepting the presence of poetic knowledge. And a better understanding of this is based on Thomas's borrowing of Aristotle's distinction between the senses; that is, the exterior and interior senses, especially the latter. The senses, taken together, exterior and interior, constitute the "sense knowledge of man," says Henri Renard, another modern commentator on St. Thomas. Even more germane is Renard's observation that "the subject of sense knowledge has a definite capacity to become intentionally another being."[87] But for now the focus will be on the description of the interior senses, and in treating this specific area, Part I, Question 78, Article 4, of the *Summa Theologica* will be followed.

The inner senses, or powers of the soul, in traditional philosophy, are four in number: the common sense, imagination, memory, and the estimative sense. (Interesting to the previous digression into aesthetics, Aristotle grouped these four, using slightly different terms, under the category of man's "aesthetic" powers.) While these are material in nature, they "have a greater freedom from the pressures and confinements of matter than the outer senses. . . . They do not come in direct contact with the sensible qualities of bodies but must depend on the outer senses for their knowledge of these things. . . . They are lodged, so to speak, midway between his outer senses on one side, and his intellect on the other."[88]

Taken in order, the common sense, unlike the popular idea of the term, is rather, as St. Thomas says, "the common root and principle of the exterior senses."[89] (See figure 2.1 for a general outline of the Order of Poetic Knowledge, which should prove to be a helpful graphic to the explanations that follow.) It is the power of the common sense to distinguish one sensation from another—sight, touch, smell, and so on—as it "links up several sorts of sensations so that we get a unit-experience of things. Such an experience is called a percept, and the act by which it is achieved is a perception."[90] Perhaps it is easier to think of the common sense as "a common receptacle for the products of the outer sense," with "all the outer senses . . . rooted in the common sense. From it they derive their power of consciousness."[91] Without the common sense, the impact of reality on the ears would simply be sounds; on the eyes, colors, light and dark, and so on; whereas, the common sense forming whole-making percepts of these, they are now experienced as definite patterns, which in turn will be formed into images of things—music or trees. All of these powers, in their function of grasping reality, do so effortlessly. And

Figure 2.1

Order of Poetic Knowledge		
SENSES	**Exterior**	**Sight—Hearing—Smell—Touch—Taste**
	Interior	Common: *Synthesizes all exterior senses*
		Imaginative: *Pictures material things absent*
		Memorative: *Recalls past images as experiences*
		Estimative: *Judges inwardness (good or evil) of things*
EMOTIONS	**Irascible**	Fear—Reverential (piety and wonder)
		Anger—Courage—Sadness
		Hope (awaits attainable objects of desire)
	Concupiscible (Pleasure)	Love—Desire—Joy (possesion of the good, true, beautiful)
WILL	**Deliberative**	Chooses from particulars
	Loving	Spontaneously follows the good
INTELLECT	**Intuition**	Degrees of Knowledge:
	Conception	Poetic
		Rhetoric
	Reason	Dialectic
	Cognition	Science

Designed by James S. Taylor

here, in the lower levels of cognition, the principle of common sense is *integration* and *synthesis* in conjunction with all the other senses.

Next, the role of the imagination receiving the sense impressions from the common sense is, as St. Thomas says, a power or an ability to picture material things in their absence. "Like the percept [of common sense], the image has a value for the mind which is both synthetic and whole-making."[92]

> Like the common sense . . . it is rooted in the sensitive part of our nature. As Aristotle would say, it is a mixed power, working through the composite forces of body and soul.[93]

Even though the imagination remains a sense faculty, confined by time and space, St. Thomas says that it is these material images that help to build up our immaterial ideas. The special significance and excellence of imagination "lies in the fact that it can form images of things that we are not here and now looking at or hearing or smelling or tasting or touching and so forth. All it needs to bring forth its fruits is that we shall have had some previous experience of these matters."[94] Therefore, for a blue sky to be imagined one would have had to have actually seen the color blue; to imagine a cold, blue sky, one must have felt real cold as well, since the range of the imagination (from the Latin *imitari*, to imitate) is not restricted to things seen, but heard, smelled, tasted, and felt. Since poetic knowledge is that knowledge grounded in reality, things as they are, the cultivation of this power of *imitari* is enormously important in giving the stuff upon which ideas are formed in the intellect, especially in an increasingly insulated society that spends more time inside cut off from the world—inside houses, cars, airplanes, and buildings. Recall too, that Socratic education presupposed the child's innate ability to imitate, and given this broader understanding of imagination and its Latin origin, much more than the sounds of poetry and music, more than the movements of gymnastic were being followed, but an *image* of them and of their experience is set in the interior of the human being.

Both the memory, the next of the interior senses, and the imagination form images of things that have made an impression on the senses, but, as Aquinas distinguishes, the memory is a power of recalling past experiences and as identifying them as past. Memory is the power of "reliving of the past, in the form of images."[95]

> The thing to notice in the recollective power is that memory is being guided by reason *in a purely natural way*. That is to say, there is no forcing or pushing of the memorial power toward something it does not want. It tends, *of its own accord*, to link together various items of experience that are alike. Reason merely takes advantage of this tendency.[96]

This natural tendency of the interior sense of memory to "link together various items of experience that are alike" is an exact description of the poetical power of the human being that, prior to any acts of rational analysis, begins noticing and storing the image-laden connection of things.

Aristotle remarks in a passage, noticed by Aquinas, at the end of the *Posterior Analytics*, that demonstration is impossible without first a rich and varied sense perception, leading to experience of reality that, in turn, enlivens the memory. It is the memory that prepares us to think, to understand, based on sense-perception experiences, which, as presented here, are the immediate powers of poetic knowledge, the intuitive instruments of grasping reality; and intuition, Aristotle says, is excelled in its accuracy of thought only by a scientific—discursive—knowledge.[97]

It is not unusual to experience what seems to be a blurred distinction between imagination and memory, and indeed they are at first glance very close because they both depend upon images. But to illustrate their very real difference, if one is asked to picture a glass of wine, that is imagination; if one is asked to recall the last time wine was drunk at a feast, that is memory. Imagination is the stuff of all stories; memory is the story itself, and likewise in all the areas of education in the poetic mode, there is the *story* of science, history, mathematics. But it all begins in the lively cultivation of the senses, especially imagination in confrontation with reality and the arts; it all unfolds as a kind of story from the memory—the discovery of penicillin, the discovery of America, the discovery of *pi*—illustrating again why the ancient Greeks held the knowledge of Homer's epic poetry to be the prerequisite for all further education.

Turning to the fourth and final interior sense, the estimative power seems to be the master of them all. Both Aristotle and St. Thomas notice and agree on the close correlation between instinct and estimative power in men and in animals, although they function differently in human beings. There is, however, a movement in both animals and man from knowledge to emotion to action, which is at the root of estimative behavior. The crucial difference is, of course, that animals cannot think and they continue to respond to their instinct in the same way, following patterns of action, as did their ancestors. Whereas, man, able to think, to reflect, and to choose more or less freely, may improve his instinct, estimative responses, or may even decide not to respond to some situation that touches the estimative power.

The estimative power, then, is part of every instinct and the root of estimative behavior is the power of estimation. What does it do? It is the ability of the animal—including the human being—to know, without any previous information, what is good and what is bad for itself. Estimation has also been defined as "the apprehension of the inwardness of a thing together with its external appearance."[98] Possession of the estimative sense in a high degree is what won Odysseus the epithets of "clever," "cunning," "wily," and "resourceful." The estimative sense is the sensitive reflex that lays the foundation for the virtue of prudence. Any number of Aesop's fables or Uncle Remus stories portray quite clearly the standard example of the estimative sense, or, often, the tragic ignoring of it; for example, in Aesop, when the lamb sees the wolf and fails to run away, or from the classic fairy tales, when Little Red Riding Hood is foolish enough to give the wolf all the information concerning her presence and destination. In the first case, it is not exactly the sight of the wolf that should poetically alert the lamb to danger, "but rather the hostility of the wolf apprehended at the time that it is seen."[99] David Summers, quoted here, and earlier, from *The Judgment of Sense*, offers the following review of the estimative sense, the one sense above the others so important for the poetic response to experience; that is, the ability to know (judge) without the labor of discourse.

> Estimation was firmly lodged among the internal senses and the qualities grasped by estimation were called "intentions," a term Avicenna used for what could only be apprehended by internal sense. . . . It became part of the basic language of medieval and Renaissance psychology and philosophy [as] *Estimatio*, [which] might be defined as the activity of the first faculty by means of which the spiritual or inward could be intuited in particular things. . . . *Estimatio* according to Gundisallinus, "may be said to transcend the order of abstraction" because it

apprehends intentions, which are not material, even if they
exist in matter.[100]

The fact that this interior sense, the estimative power, has the ability
to "transcend the order of abstraction" is precisely one of the main
points made regarding poetic knowledge, and why it needs to be
taken seriously once again as a way of knowing, distinct from but in
no way inferior to scientific knowledge.

Furthermore, man has a rational nature and he can, for example, train his instincts—he can even achieve virtue by guiding or
restraining his instincts. This means that man's estimative sense,
like the memory and imagination, is tied very closely with his reason.
It is

> a power subject to the intellect and used by the latter to do
> what St. Thomas describes as "a kind of thinking." To be sure,
> estimative power does not really think or penetrate to the inner
> nature of things, but it does put things together . . . in terms of
> images. . . . Aquinas regards it as the highest of all our senses,
> and its knowledge as the most perfect that is possible to a power
> which is mixed with matter. So he calls it a "cognitive sense"—
> as though it were able to reflect on things and come to conclu-
> sions.[101]

There is much to note here. First, there is the poetic operation
of the estimative sense in that it does "a kind of thinking"—the object that is the wolf that is also intuited as hostile—by putting *images*
together, just as poets do, rather than reasoning things out. Also,
there is the restraint from a popular romanticism, or even a false
mysticism, when it is recognized that the estimative sense, as with
the rest of these powers, is not confused in its normal function with
the special power of the intellect. And, then, the estimative sense is
regarded as the highest cognitive sense by St. Thomas because it can
determine what is *good* for the whole human being, not simply that
something is *there*.

It is necessary to point out again that the background for poetic
knowledge is developed from the Realist tradition of philosophy,
particularly the Platonic-Aristotelian-Thomist tradition that eventually refined the exaggerated dualism of Plato*nism* and harmonized
the view of man as a composite being of body and soul in intimate
union. In fact, it is only with the Realist view that we are able to

understand the idea that the outer and inner senses, which are material powers, have an integrated participation in the intellect, the supreme immaterial power. It is thus that Aquinas can refer to the estimative power as a "cognitive sense." But even with this clarification, this taming of Plato's so-called other world of ideas, our debt is still clearly owed to this great pupil of Socrates who first demonstrated the importance of an education that begins with the senses and the discovery and cultivation of harmony and beauty in the soul by way of the sense's natural affinity for the harmonious, proportionate, and the beautiful in nature and the arts.

With the Realist tradition of psychology as guide, it is possible to now move from the exterior-interior senses to the *appetites*, and, always with the understanding within this tradition that man is directed, by nature, toward the good. In keeping with the overall direction here to demonstrate the presence of the poetic mode of knowing, it is to the point to recall, with modern Thomists, that this natural movement in man toward the good "exists . . . as a blind drive which functions independently of his knowledge . . . nor is it dependent on reason for its existence."[102] Remember that the estimative sense determines whether a thing is good or bad, and, in turn, this "cognitive sense," as is the case for all types of cognition, has a corresponding appetite. (Appetite: from the Latin *petere*, to seek for; or *appetere*, to strive after, to long for.) Two of these appetites or, to use their more modern names, "emotions," come into play when an object is sensed: the concupiscible (pleasure) or the irascible appetites. The first, the pleasure appetite, is apparently more closely related to poetic experience, insofar as it is associated with aesthetic experience; however, as I explained earlier, considered as wonder, it actually belongs to the irascible emotions as a species of fear, that is, as the consciousness of ignorance in the face of some reality as explained by Quinn and Verhoeven. When it is understood, as Quinn explains, that "St. Thomas says the irascible passions defend the concupiscible,"[103] then the emotion aroused by wonder, fear, or fear of not knowing (i.e., consciousness of ignorance) is seen in this light as the impulse to preserve the good that is found in rest (joy), the concupiscible-pleasure emotion of knowledge—in this case, poetic knowledge. And, finally, poetic knowledge means possession of the object in some way and is therefore in its end, pleasurable. When Wordsworth writes "My heart leaps up when I behold / A rainbow in the sky," there has been no movement toward scientific knowl-

edge of what has been seen; rather, this is the precise moment suspended between wonder (fear) and possession (joy), for to be-*hold* is
to possess, to hold with the cognitive sense of the sensory-emotional
response of near simultaneous, fear-joy: the sensation of one's heart
leaping up in the chest. At this moment, *something* of the rainbow's
reality is truly known, but rational explanation alone is insufficient,
in fact, impossible, for this is the gaze of contemplation, of love. It is
the difference between being unexpectedly moved by an unknown
attractive face—desiring to know the person better—and the desperate premeditation of computer dating. It is the difference between *thinking* about the mystery of a rainbow, and *being in* the
mystery of its presence. In another poem, Wordsworth describes the
movement from the aftershock of wonder to joy:

> Almost suspended, we are laid asleep
> In body, and become a living soul:
> While with an eye made quiet by the power
> Of harmony, and the deep power of joy,
> We see into the life of things.

From the point of view of Realist psychology, it can be detected that
Wordsworth is disrupting the body-soul harmony: "we are laid
asleep / In body," as if the soul alone is now free to experience the
vision; whereas the tradition that informs Scholastic philosophy re-
peats over and over again that it is man, whole and entire, the composite being that sees "into the life of things." In any case, it is
indeed when we are "suspended" by the presence of some event,
when the laws of time and gravity seem to have paused, when we
possess the gaze "into the life of things," that there is poetic knowledge—mysterious, obscure, the antagonist to science, as Newman
said—yet nonetheless undeniable knowledge.

So, with this very fine distinction between the fear that is part
of wonder and the joy, the pleasure derived from where it leads us,
it is possible to continue with a focus on the concupiscible-pleasure
emotions and poetic knowledge. The irascible appetites—fear,
courage, hope, and anger—are all to serve the pleasure appetite to
achieve the goal of some good, some point of rest. If the good seems
unobtainable, then hate or despair is experienced. Certainly there is
something poetic about these emotions that arise at the perception
of goods that now appear arduous, hard to get at. Because great

poets such as Sophocles were able to give *form* to such difficult experiences in attaining the good, Aristotle recognized, in viewing such tragedies, a *catharsis*, that is, a purgation of the fear or the sadness that the viewer had taken from the conflict of the play and a return to emotional satisfaction. For example, though Antigone dies, her struggle toward the good, to honor the gods before man, is actually accomplished in the end: she does in fact bury her brother, and Creon, chastised by the gods, ends in wisdom. Classical music can reveal the same movement through the emotions of wonder and joy: the startling beginning of Beethoven's famous Fifth Symphony is the music of sudden alarm. Emotionally speaking, we don't know what is happening or what is about to happen, and that is a kind of knowledge; poetically, it is the knowledge of a mystery of the sounds of surprise and alarm, but for no apparent reason. Then, the smoother, quieter, flowing strains of the same theme appear. We recognize the theme from the beginning, but now it is presented in such a way that the fear gives way to pleasure. Our fear has been purged, we have been strengthened, as it were, and prepared, sustained by joy, for the recurring loud announcements of the beginning. Never do we rise to rational, scientific knowledge in such experiences, but it is a knowledge nonetheless, for the poem, the tragedy, the music, has moved our cognitive sensory-emotional powers inside, to a view from *within* wonder and joy. Such poetic experience and knowledge is beyond the most careful and precise descriptions of such emotions, for we have in this way experienced the things themselves.

Modern psychology continues to recognize that it is the pleasure appetite and not the irascible emotions that must finally prevail in a mentally healthy person. Here, it is extremely important to broaden the idea of pleasure. Dr. Conrad Baars, a modern Thomist psychiatrist, explains:

> Our claim that the pleasure appetite of man is more spiritual and intuitive—as compared with the more "rational" and mechanistic character of the utility appetite—can be understood only in the realization that we are not restricting sense pleasure to the meaning which is often given it: namely, to indicate simply and solely the gratification of the sense of touch and taste. In man the intellectual prevades and elevates the entire sensory life, including the pleasure appetite.[104]

Therefore, poetic experience—knowledge, education—comes about, ultimately, as it escapes, so to speak, from the irascible emotions— namely, of fear—and rests in pleasure.

At no time, however, is it being suggested that reason resides anywhere other than in the intellect; what is being said, with the entire Realist tradition, is that the exterior and interior senses are penetrated by the light of the intellect and have a cognitive value. Furthermore, in this same tradition a distinction is recognized in the intellect itself; not only does it possess the ability to abstract essences from material objects to form concepts—essentially a spiritual act— but there is a function of the intellect that can be stimulated to elaborate on these concepts and abstract ideas, analyzing them, and so on. This is called the reasoning or discursive intellect. Baars notices in this regard another function.

> The other element of man's intellectual power is the *intuitive intellect*, by which man collects and reads (*intelligere* comes from "intus" and "legere," which means: reading in or at a deeper level) the deeper meaning of reality, which cannot be represented by ideas or pictured by images. . . . In this connection, it should be noted that we can speak of "the connatural knowledge of the heart" whenever the pleasure emotions—in their intimate relationship with the intuitive intellect—are elevated and transformed into psychic motors that completely support man's contemplative intellect and loving will.[105]

Brennan, following Aristotle and Aquinas, as does Baars, regarding these two aspects of the intellect, is perhaps more precise than Baars in some points that are more relevant to revealing poetic knowledge at work. Whether it be the *nous poietikos* and *nous pathetikos* of Aristotle's distinctions of a creative (actually, close to our poetic) intellect in the first place, and a receptive (that is, sympathetic) intellect in the second; or, if it be what Aquinas calls *intellectus agens* and the *intellectus passivus*, both describing how we abstract forms through images of things to arrive at ideas—in both cases, we see that the body-soul reaction to objects *out there* is to spontaneously, effortlessly seize upon their material and immaterial reality, at a glance, it might be said.

This whole operation is poetic, first, because it is sensory, this sensing-abstracting function of sense-intellect; and, also because the movement is spontaneous and metaphoric: the subject-object, juxtaposed like metaphor, produces the third thing, the immaterial idea of the thing, and possession (love-knowledge) of the universal concept. This is, after all, the stuff of poetry, this joining of things, this way of *seeing* that assembles, connects, and integrates reality. Those who seem to gaze and reflect, poets and those with keen poetic senses, only appear to be alone, for it is impossible to experience an emotion alone, that is, without some object. *Feelings*, so often confused with emotions, strictly speaking lack the "out there-ness" of the appetites. Baars explains this interesting distinction.

> Though one can say that all emotions are feelings, the reverse is not true. Not all feelings are emotions . . . for example, those of pain, hunger, thirst, cold, warmth, fatigue, tension, relaxation, sleepiness, and dizziness. These feelings originate in our body and cause us to be aware of certain changes . . . we eat in response to the feeling of hunger, we take a rest when we feel tired . . . we turn on the heat when we feel cold. An emotion, on the other hand, is primarily a psychic reaction to stimuli from the world around us.[106]

So poetic knowledge is emotional and moves to deeper realities beyond mere feelings, but always through the concrete things of the world. Poetic knowledge operates through images, as does the cognitive sense process where the intellect gazes and penetrates with light our memory's storehouse of images.

This innate ability of the intellect to "read within," spontaneously—this power of the intuitive intellect, moved by the emotions, especially of love—is, at bottom, the realm of poetic knowledge. Baars continues to say that in addition to the intellect, which provides spiritual knowledge, there is a power that causes man to long for the immaterial goods known by the intellect. This spiritual appetite is as different from the sensory appetite as the intellect is from the sensory cognitive power. He says that this spiritual appetite sees beyond the concrete sense goods and embraces the immaterial universal good; "this spiritual power is called the will,"[107] or, as he named it, "the loving will."

And what poetic treatment can be applied to the will in the manner in which has been accomplished with the other aspects of the cognitive process? To begin with, the philosophical tradition that I have followed maintains that the proper object of the will is the good; that is, something that is desirable. When the senses, all of them working together, *see*, supplying not only the image to the intellect for abstraction of the form, but when what is seen is desirable—

having a kind of beauty—according to St. Thomas Aquinas, "*id quod visum placet*," that which, being seen, pleases,[108] then the concupiscible (pleasure) emotion of love moves the intellect and gives to the will, first, before any deliberation, simply a love, a desire of the object. And, as has been said, nothing can be desired except it first be known, so that knowing a thing is the first condition of loving it. While it is true that this first knowledge is poetic in that it resembles a state of rational rest, and, because, on the other hand, the acts of the will are associated with volition, two movements of the will must be distinguished, one more closely aligned with intuitive knowledge and poetic experience than the other. Baars looks at this distinction: "Just as there is an intuitive and a reasoning movement in man's knowing power, so there is also a double element in the will: the loving will and executive will."[109] Brennan contributes to this understanding, adding that "the acts of the will . . . fall into two general groups: *natural* movements of the will, which are impulses toward the good; and *deliberate* movements which are impulses toward particular goods.[110]

Brennan explains that, in regard to the first acts, the word *natural*, or nature, is from the Latin *nasci*, that is, to be born. "Hence, the natural movements of the will are those that it is born to exhibit. . . . It is born to be moved by goodness as such, or universal good."[111]

> In the first case, will acts as *will*; that is to say, as a power which is led, by the deepest instincts of its nature, toward goodness in general or toward the good which is its highest perfection. In the second case, will acts as *free will*, that is to say, as a power which can take or leave the particular goods that are presented [by the intellect] to it.[112]

Then, Brennan makes a parallel distinction that reveals exactly the poetic aspect that resides at every turn in knowledge:

> The difference between will and free will, as St. Thomas tells us, is the same as the difference between understanding and reason. Thus, understanding [intuitive] deals with first principles; whereas, reason deals with conclusions [scientific knowledge].[113]

Therefore, it is understanding, and natural will, that effortlessly see and love the universal good, which is also to say, the *ends* of things, whole and intuitively. The reason and deliberative will, on the other hand, where the activity of choices reside, is the realm of particulars and *means*. Conrad Baars describes this distinction in less formal but nonetheless direct terms:

> The basic activity of the will is love. Love is the passion of the intellect. The *loving will* is a blind power which follows the enlightenment of the intellect. Just as the activity of the intellect comes to its perfection in a judgment about what really and objectively is, so the will comes to its perfection in accepting and approving what is insofar as it is. [The will] . . . approves the known being as valuable in itself. . . . Therefore, the loving will is characterized by the activity of passivity. The core of love is: let it be, because it is good as is. Love [as it is in the will] is respect and adoration of the loved being. Love allows the being to be, and it enjoys its being.[114]

How different this "loving will" is from the popular image of the will in general as the realm of high energy, exertion, and the powerhouse of "getting things done." This other understanding of the will, so crucial in forming an appreciation of the permeating presence of poetic knowledge, rests in *being* rather than *doing*, which is to indicate a kind of metaphysical tendency within these interior powers. Notice also how this traditional aspect of the will conforms to the gaze of poetic experience—"adoration," and enjoyment, where, as Baars says, "The loving will follows the wondering intellect which is open to the mystery of being."[115] Since Baars has used the expression "wondering intellect," it is important to remember that this is exactly what has already been said in regard to the intellect being awakened by wonder. It is also important to restate that this is all an integrated experience, not occurring in mechanical steps or linked together as a chain, and to remember that this knowledge begins in the senses, touching the sensory appetites, first fear, then resolving to the pleasure appetites—love, desire, joy—and that "it is the nature of man's sensory appetite to function in accordance with the will. Thomas Aquinas expressed this forcefully with the words: 'It is the nature of the sensitive appetite to follow reason.' "[116] That this aspect of the will is clearly in the poetic mode and not the rational is stated by Aquinas elsewhere. It is not the reason that draws us to things—not the mind—but the appetites, namely, of love, that is, desire, which possesses a cognitive sense of goodness, or badness.

> Now the soul is drawn to a thing by the appetitive power rather
> than by the apprehensive power, because the soul has, through
> its appetitive power, an order to things as they are in them-
> selves. . . . On the other hand, the apprehensive power is not
> drawn to a thing in itself, but knows it according to an intention
> of the thing.[117]

This should also assist in distinguishing between the poetic *aspect* of acts such as intentional knowledge (to be treated next) and the more fully realized poetic experience where all the knowing powers are functioning prerationally with reality. It is, then, love, the loving will, that draws us to things more than discursive systems of thought. And, though the distinction between intellect and senses is strictly observed, under the view of poetic knowledge, they are never sepa-rate. Further, this love is not the subject of mere *feelings*, as Baars distinguished earlier. However, Baars also pointed out that "all emo-tions are feelings." It was only the reverse that was not true. There-fore, when speaking of the loving will, and remembering that St. Augustine explained that the senses treated alone are one thing but the act of *sensation* is an integrated act involving the whole person, this aspect of the will is not some act of the soul that is detached from feeling. The emotion of love carries with it an appropriate feeling or sensation. John Senior says, when applying these principles to ed-ucation:

> The final cause of schools is feeling in the knowledge of things
> the throb and thrill of them. . . . Sensation is a very large gift
> of nature without which nothing in emotion, intellect or will
> can breathe. If you don't feel Cupid's arrow at the sight of pass-
> ing beauty you can't forever see God's beauty face to face.
> Beatitude insofar as it is known and expressed in this life is
> sensational—witness the Song of Songs.[118]

Of course, modern empirical psychology does not admit the existence of these distinctions, or even the particular powers of the senses, emotions, will, and intellect. But empirical psychology is con-fined by its commitment to measure material phenomena, and, as Baars remarks, "If empirical psychology rejects the immaterial pow-ers, it oversteps its own boundaries, because this is not a question for purely empirical investigation."[119] In addition, under the terms of traditional Realist psychology, modern empirical psychology arrives at its conclusions against the immaterial powers, ironically, by immaterial inference.

I can now summarize regarding the two ways in which the term *poetic* has been applied to the subject of knowledge. First, there is an aspect in every act of intellection, in all its parts, that is effortless, spontaneous, requiring no stimulation other than the presence of the object of apprehension itself, where the mind arrives at material and immaterial knowledge of a thing by way of the senses, and the universal quality is abstracted—a *natural* transcendental gazing into the forms of things. This is a virtually unconscious act where the will *sees* with the intellect the universal good in all reality, in being *qua* being. This is the foundation of poetic knowledge because it is all prior to the work of the deliberative will and any rational testing and probing into the existence of the object.

Then, secondly, there are simply particular experiences beginning in wonder and moving to the concupiscible (pleasure) appetite (touching on the subject of aesthetics), where there is the harmonious integration of the exterior and interior senses, emotions, will, and intellect, knowing the good and beautiful in some thing, knowing this simply in repose, love, and adoration, where these things are regarded as "something very much like perfection." Things of nature and the things of man's craft, insofar as the latter conform to a proportion that is found in nature, provide poetic experience and knowledge, without which (according to the principle first stated by Socrates) all following modes of knowledge are empty and lacking the first remote knowledge of their ends.

This survey has arrived at a kind of threshold that has given a foundation for employing two key terms in identifying this first mode of knowledge, terms shared by Aristotle and Aquinas: *connatural knowledge* and knowledge by *intentionality*. Furthermore, there are a handful of modern philosophers who have contributed abundantly to the understanding of these terms in the light of poetic knowledge—Jacques Maritain and Josef Pieper in particular. In fact, their insights are so profound and relevant to this study that the next chapter must begin by preparing the way for their important commentaries.

3

Connatural, Intentional, and Intuitive Knowledge

> There are more things in heaven and earth, Horatio,
> than are dreamt of in your philosophy.
>
> —*Hamlet*

From the philosophy of Aristotle and Aquinas emerged a "metaphysics of cognition"[1] in which intuition means the nondiscursive act of the intellect that grasps first principles without the aid of proof by demonstration. For example, when it is said that a thing cannot be and not be at the same time and in the same way, the mind *sees* this as self-evident, intuitively. There is something poetic in this aspect of cognition, in that it is a spontaneous, spiritual act that recognizes immaterial reality in the immediate object. For, there must be some *thing* for there to be, or not to be: the stone, or at least the idea of the stone. And although this book is devoted to the poetic mode of knowledge, gymnastic was always considered as an integrated and complimentary mode with the poetic spoken of by Plato and Aristotle. For a simple understanding for our times, and for the purposes here, we can think of the gymnastic mode first of all as direct experience with reality, for example a life lived more out of doors; the difference, say, between a child walking to school in all kinds of weather and being driven in a climate-controlled automobile or bus. The direct confrontation with the most simple realities of nature, the gymnastic, participates in the poetic mode. But the gymnastic can also be seen in more refined circumstances: the difference, for example, between listening to a Strauss waltz and actually dancing, in full evening dress, to a live orchestra playing the Blue Danube. In other words, in spite of distinct treatments of the acts of the intellect and the modes of knowledge here, they are in reality

59

never separate, but more like the notes of the musical scale, similar to the image used by Socrates in *The Republic* quoted earlier, notes of knowing that can be sounded distinctly but have no meaning outside their relation to the others. To sound the gymnastic note strikes the sympathetic reverberation of the poetic, up to the highest notes of metaphysics. To recall and widen the legitmacy of the metaphor of the soul and music, it is no mere quaint or naive tradition that begins with at least Pythagoras (sixth century B.C.) to the school of Plato and the subsequent Neo-Platonists, and many others, that understood there was such a thing as the music of the spheres as *real* music that also informed the harmony of the soul as part of the same musical nature.

In any case, a stunning example of the harmony of the modes of knowledge, leaping as it were from the gymnastic to the realm of experimental physics, awaits us in chapter 5.

These sensory-based intuitions (exterior and interior senses) create images upon which the memory reflects, for "no other kind of thought except intuition is more accurate than scientific knowledge," says Aristotle, and, as a result, "intuition will be the originative source of scientific knowledge."[2] I will clarify this definition of intuition in this and following chapters.

To prepare for that point, it is necessary to return to *De Anima* where Aristotle stated, and Aquinas keenly noticed, the great principle of Realist epistemology: " The soul is in a way all existing things; for existing things are either sensible or thinkable, and knowledge is in a way what is knowable, and sensation is in a way what is sensible."[3] He continues:

> Within the soul the faculties of knowledge and sensation are *potentially* these objects, the one that is knowable, the other what is sensible. They must either be the things themselves or their forms. The former alternative is of course impossible; it is not the stone which is present in the soul but its form.[4]

St. Thomas found the occasion in this passage to affirm the spiritual character of knowledge:

> Hence, as we have said above, forms according as they are the more immaterial, approach more nearly to a kind of infinity. Therefore it is clear that the immateriality of a thing is the reason why it is cognitive, and the mode of knowledge is according

to the mode of immateriality . . . sense is cognitive because it can receive species without matter, and the intellect is still further cognitive because it is more "separated from matter and unmixed," as said in the *Soul* [*De Anima*].[5]

Again and again, in this long tradition, from Socrates to Aquinas, the spiritual nature of the knower able to know his world, is repeated. It is this spiritual character of first knowledge that is called poetic, while continuing to recall that this first knowledge of being (that things are as they are) is not only intuitive but is never surpassed in its initial importance. Poetic knowledge is never outgrown. As Vincent Smith observed, "In the opinion of Aquinas, metaphysics, though superior in dignity to other branches in philosophy, uses truths which these lesser lights have searched out."[6] Furthermore, Smith echoes what was said earlier by Verhoeven, that true philosophy is a reaction of wonder to what is, and the intellectual movement beyond this point, while advancing in its descriptive understanding of reality, also moves away from the spontaneous philosophy of nature to a philosophical science of nature:

Genuine philosophy discerns two notions of being. The first is the view of the ordinary man who, even though not formally a metaphysician, has a spontaneous conviction that being is. . . . the other notion of being is that of the metaphysician. This is a refined, reflex, scientific notion of being, explicitly recognized as being and rigorously defended as to its reality and its principles. . . . [But] the philosophical science of nature builds on the ordinary man's notion of being.[7]

What happens in this "spontaneous conviction" of being? A modern Thomist commentator, Henri Renard, says: "Aristotle says that the soul somehow can become all things, meaning that the soul can know all things, because it is what it is."[8] What both Aristotle and Aquinas say, generally, is this:

In order to know, one must somehow *become* another; for to know is to be another. It is a sort of participation in the "to be" of another, not inasmuch as this other, the object, is an individual existing distinct and separate from the knowing subject, but inasmuch as the subject by knowing becomes *in the intentional order* and lives the idea, the reality, which is the object.[9]

Before going further, a pause is in order to allow these terms to stand more clearly in relation to one another: *intuition* is the spontaneous awareness of reality, that something is *there*, outside the mind but that the mind cannot help but know. It is included in the poetic mode because of its dependency on the sensory life of the soul and the effortless, spiritual nature of awareness at this level. The *intentional* order of knowledge is prelogical knowledge in the poetic mode because it knows reality by *inclination* toward the object in a sympathetic manner, like seeking like, still based in the senses, though higher than intuition, but still far from rational or analytical activity.

Therefore, since the mind as the immaterial power of knowledge must, in order to know, be able to receive something likewise immaterial from the objects of reality, it follows that there be a *form* of the thing, its immaterial substance, obviously not its physical presence, that is impressed into the mind in the manner of Aristotle's famous analogy of the impression left by the seal pressed into wax. This reception of the intentional form of the object is a most basic and intuitive cognitive impulse, the first reflex to experience knowledge as union, possession, with the essence (the form) of the thing to be known. And this is the poetic tendency of the cognitive life, this getting within the immaterial reality of the objects of knowledge prior to rational thought. So deep and involuntary is this impulse, that among the various definitions of a human being, one is certainly that we are poetic beings, for it is always the end of poetry to bring us sympathetically inside the experience of reality, always in search of union, fulfilling our innate desire to know. Aquinas adds that "the knowing being is naturally adapted to have also the form of some other thing."[10] We are naturally proportionate to knowing in this way, a *necessitas naturalis* of knowing. And, this "to have" that Thomas speaks of is similar to, if not the same as, the love (possession) spoken of by St. Augustine in his definition of knowledge. The becoming of the other carries this possession in the mode of passive love, which is never dominating or critical, being prior to any acts of analysis, and, as Baars says, is a power that "allows the being to be, and it enjoys its being."[11]

As was shown earlier, it is the art of poetry to take one into the imaginative experience of things; however, not just the craft of verse does this, but the vision, the movement of poetic knowledge as well. This "metaphysics of cognition" recognizes that the most basic, involuntary processes of knowing have an analogy to poetry in the sense that to know simply that a thing is, that is, to have a knowledge of being, involves this getting inside the object and possessing it spiritually. It is always union that poetry seeks, and it is union that the mind seeks to achieve in order for there to be knowledge at all. Renard pursues this carefully:

> What does this "to be another" or "to become another" really mean . . . what is this process of knowing in which the knower becomes the known? The answer is not far to seek. Knowledge is *union*, an immaterial or *intentional* union, between the knowing subject and the known object.[12]

St. Thomas Aquinas puts it this way: "The noblest way of possessing a thing is to possess it in an immaterial manner, that is by possessing its form without its matter; and this is the definition of knowledge."[13]

The "intentional union," this intentional knowledge, are the terms used to distinguish that part of man that "becomes" the thing. Clearly, it is not the man in the order of nature that achieves union with objects, but rather the *tendency toward* (*in* + *tendere*, to stretch forth) the mind as it receives the immaterial representations of objects, that is to say, their forms. This knowledge of objects comes about intuitively, unassisted by rational discourse, and, as in a twinkling of an eye, proceeds from one act of the exterior senses, to the interior senses, leading to the appetites, intellect, and will. But each aspect of these powers is operating naturally: the appetite of natural desire; the passive intellect that receives; and, the nonvolitional will that inclines effortlessly to being.

By definition, poetic experience is free from analysis. Likewise, intentional knowledge "becomes" another, free of the rational checkpoints of scientific knowlege, by entering into an *interior* knowledge of reality, possessing the object in "the order of immaterial representation."[14] It is partly because this process is immaterial, that is, spiritual, that it is called poetic, effortless and pure, as it participates in the thing known. For example, it is in this way that one is able to know the color and shape of a tree without, obviously, receiving the tree itself. Modern theories of knowledge, dominated by the mechanistic model of man, attribute these powers to the brain, but as remarkable and mysterious as the brain is, it is still a material organ of the body, and, therefore, it must be the mind, the soul, that uses the powers of the brain to achieve this immaterial union.

While it is true that scientific knowledge is more precise from the viewpoint of truth achieved through dialectic, and, by comparison, poetic knowledge is obscure and even defective as St. Thomas says;[15] nonetheless, all first knowledge, knowledge of being and the universe, to the highest act of abstraction, rests on this fundamental intuition that leads to the intimate knowledge in the intentional order that things are, and that we are at home with them for we have taken their substance into the parlor of our souls. St. Thomas continues elsewhere (Sum. Theol., I–II, 101, 2 ad 2.) to say that poetic knowledge and theology—because neither are directly proportioned to the reason—make use of the "modus symbolicus," that is, the symbolic or poetic mode, to communicate their truths. It is this level of poetic knowledge and not science that comes first to our assistance in knowing our world, and the other world. Poetry discovers, science proves.

Given the accumulated experience of knowledge in the intentional order, the knower comes to possess what St. Thomas described as *connatural* knowledge, the way of knowing that is placed deeply within the poetic mode. For the purposes here, it can be said that connatural knowledge is a step beyond the intentional order and even closer to the poetic.

To be connatural with a thing is to participate in some way with its *nature*, as distinct from its intentional form, to share a likeness of nature. St. Thomas used the term to designate one of two ways in which we form a rightness of judgment. The first way is by reason, following the steps of discourse and dialectic. But the second way of judging correctly is "on account of a certain connaturality with the matter about which one has to judge in a given instance."[16] For example, in terms of moral virtue, one can arrive through the steps of reason as in a syllogism to the *principles* of right judgment. But there is prudence required to *act* with right judgment when dealing with particular circumstances. It so happens that there are those who, lacking the rigor of rational discipline, act in accordance with prudence displaying a recititude of the will in a given circumstance. How so? Because they have become, through habit, through familiarity, not rational discourse, *connatural* with the circumstances that tend to turn out a certain way, over and over again. About such people—such as a Julius Caesar or a skilled but illiterate craftsman—one notices not simply an alert mind but an overall alertness of keen senses. And this is precisely what the poets are always saying: look,

look at this, and look at that. It is the habit of noticing what is happening here and now and reflecting with the natural powers upon that experience that cultivates the connatural degree of knowedge.

This is why St. Thomas says that given a familiarity with a thing, a *habit* of its being, the rigors of reason are bypassed and one "judges rightly . . . by a kind of connaturality."[17] Aquinas also offers a related term that assists greatly in understanding this mode: *sympathy*. Knowledge by connaturality is a sympathetic knowledge, a term more in the spirit of what takes place in poetic knowledge, and is in keeping with what Karl Stern described, when quoting Bergson's definition of intuition, as "intellectual sympathy."[18]

With this background, it is now possible to turn to the modern philosopher who has written specifically and profoundly on poetic knowledge, Jacques Maritain.

> In this knowledge through union or inclination, connaturality or congeniality, the intellect is at play not alone, but together with affective inclinations and the dispositions of the will, and is guided and directed by them. It is not rational knowledge, knowledge through conceptual, logical and discursive exercise of Reason. But it is really and genuinely knowledge, though obscure and perhaps incapable of giving an account of itself, or of being translated into words.[19]

Although Maritain usually speaks of connaturality with a view to understanding the poet as the possessor of a particular kind of knowledge leading to the act of poetry, here, for my purposes, the treatment is intended to broaden the application of the principles of poetic knowledge to extend to all unpremeditated intellectual acts of knowing. Therefore, it is necessary to observe that Maritain, in his extension of the Thomistic definition of connaturality, places the origins of poetic knowledge in the preconscious life of the intellect, but with no contradiction to the traditional dynamics of intuition established by the Realist-Scholastic school. In fact, in all that has been presented on this topic, from Socrates, Aristotle, Augustine, Aquinas, and their modern commentators, Brennan, Baars, and Renard, there is a remarkable continuity, culminating with Maritain. Maritain says:

> We are confronted with an intuition of emotive origin, and we enter the nocturnal empire of a primeval activity of the intel-

lect, which far beyond concepts and logic, exercises itself in vital connection with imagination and emotion. We have quit logical reason, and even conceptual reason, yet we have to do more than ever with intuitive reason—functioning in a nonrational way.[20]

This "intuitive reason" has been met earlier, where the first principles of being and causality are grasped spontaneously and seen as self-evident. Also, adds a sympathetic commentator, "in this depth—but remember that it is a depth of the intellect, not a subrational, Freudian abyss—is the activity of the intellect whose operation precedes the conscious world of concepts and syllogism; and also in this depth is the perceptive power of poetry."[21]

And, now, Maritain joins Socrates and Plato twenty-five hundred years earlier, as he takes up his reflections on the muse of knowledge.

> *Music*, thus, in Plato's vocabulary, does not mean only music, but every artistic genius which depends on the inspiration of the Muse . . . [but] I think that what we have to do is to make the Platonic Muse descend into the soul of man, where she is no longer Muse but creative intuition, and Platonic inspiration descend into the intellect united with imagination, where inspiration from above the soul becomes inspiration from above conceptual reason, that is, poetic experience.[22]

Because this term *poetic experience*—defined earlier as distinct from the craft of poetry and used here by Maritain in exactly the way intended in that ongoing definition—may seem to be a misplaced departure from the terms of a trained Realist and Thomist, Ralph McInerny clarifies:

> It must be kept in mind that the act of judging is always an act of intellect; it is not that something other than the intellect makes the judgment when connaturality is spoken of, but rather that the rectitude of the intellect's judgment is due to something outside the intellect itself.[23]

As discussed in the previous chapter, the primary powers that are "something outside the intellect itself" are the appetites. Poetic knowledge, like poetry, is, in a certain sense, "an emotional thing," but, as was described, is also integrated with the rest of the cognitive powers. When it is recalled that the Idealist-Realist tradition considers the appetites (emotions) part of the cognitive (interior) senses, this ability of the judgment of sense is not so puzzling. This point gives rise to the distinction that was central to Maritain's interest, that, as McInerny observes:

> Intellectual knowledge is abstractive, immaterial, universal. Appetite, on the other hand, tends towards things as they are in themselves. We love things for what they are and in themselves; not as we know them but as they are. We could thereby say that the mode of appetite is more existential than that of intellect.[24]

Still, a reminder is necessary, that while making these difficult distinctions among the cognitive powers, it is the intellect, that region of the mind that sees and judges *per modum inclinationis* (by inclination), rather than the intellect *per modum cognitionis*. This is the realm of Maritain's focus, where with Aristotle, he says, there is "the dreamer of what is true . . . [where] the moving principle seems to become stronger when the reasoning is relaxed."[25] And how well this squares with common experience and conventional wisdom can be recalled in the numerous stories throughout history and in our daily lives where the answer to some problem that has puzzled us is revealed exactly when we cease to address it directly. Often these moments occur at a time of recreation, or in semiconsciousness, or while performing some routine act such as bathing, as in the case of Euripides.

Where poetic knowledge was neglected, repudiated, then virtually forgotten by modern philosophy, Maritain reclaims this area of the preconsciousness where there is "the recognition of the existence of a spiritual unconscious," one which "Plato and the ancient wise men were well aware."[26] However, Maritain is quick to distance this recognition from the Freudian notion of the unconscious, a connection, he also concludes, is "a sign of the dullness of our times."[27]

Instead, this spiritual preconscious is where poetic intuition and intellect are seen as the same race and blood, where one calls naturally to the other. This is also what Maritain calls the "musical unconscious"—none of this to be confused with any number of trendy "mystical experiences" popularized in the 1960s. Rather, as has been said from the beginning about this realm of first knowledge: "It is enough to think of the ordinary and everyday functioning of intelligence . . . and of the way in which ideas arise in our minds."[28] Not only do the operations of the cognitive senses have a poetic aspect to them, in that they give knowledge spontaneously via the external and internal senses, but what is described here as the "ordinary and everyday functioning of intelligence" also reveals the habit of poetic intelligence as a way of seeing the world, seeing the significance in the superficial, what most would dismiss, ignore, or never notice. Indeed, "the way in which ideas arise in our minds," while not poetry, is poetic. This means the instant the senses deliver an image of physical reality to our minds, we have knowledge that something is there, that there is an existence beyond ourselves and at the same time part of ourselves. Then, the estimative sense attempts to determine if the thing is good or bad for us—a tree, a snake, a man. At this point, knowledge is accomplished without the aid of the rational act; rather, it is the *intellectus* that has penetrated the powers of the senses. Of course, at this level of knowledge we could be mistaken about the goodness or badness of the thing known. But with intuitive-poetic knowledge, whether the particular knower be a bright poet or a small child, the scholar or a learning disabled person, the powers of the soul have composed a "musical" thing, sounding a note from the external senses and resonating throughout the interior faculties, a poetical act that effortlessly assembles impressions and images and spontaneously gives a spiritual knowledge of being, a kind of song of reality.

On the other hand, there is the habit of poetry practiced by poets and those who see by the light of poetic experience, whose gaze catches the "ordinary" and sees that the surface presence, rather than to be repudiated as mere matter that veils its airy form, is quite significant just as it is. Here, where the ordinary becomes illuminated, is when the habit of poetry sees something marvelous *in* the thing itself, especially in its relation to another real thing where the art of juxtapostion and metaphor produce a third thing. This is *not* mystical experience, at least, not the pseudo-mystical experience that fired the more enthusiastic of the Romantic poets such as Coleridge and Blake to regard the actual as something to get beyond, to distort if not destroy, dismiss as mere means to mystical vision. Blake's famous, "To see the World in a grain of sand . . . to hold Eternity in the palm of your hand" and Coleridge's *Kubla Khan* are perfect examples of the tendency to associate poetic experience with a radical neo-Platonism where all that really exists are Forms: and, with Coleridge, where poetic truth is hallucination, drug induced, or the druglike effect of a distorted reality. Poetic knowledge does not describe essences; that is the world of advanced philosophy. Poetic knowledge is the wonder of the thing itself—not the essences of trees but the stately presence of the hawthorn in summer is the stuff of poetic experience.

How different pseudo-mystical poetry is from either Shakespeare or Robert Frost, whose poetry always works with, not past, the thing itself. This is a poetry that already knows the deep significance of things as they are, so that all that is needed is to arrange them alongside, in vibrant sympathy, the wide range of human responses to life.

> That time of year thou mayst in me behold
> When yellow leaves, or none, or few, do hang
> Upon boughs which shake against the cold,
> Bare ruined choirs where late the sweet birds sang.

This is a world of real leaves, boughs that bend and shake, real cold, and real birds, that, as contingent beings, carry in their song the sadness of their transient presence as well as the transcendent reality of their origin from Ultimate Being. Suddenly, in the illumination of poetic light, these real objects become analogous to our deepest thoughts and emotions of the passing of time and the coming of old age.

And this power of knowledge must be the constant point of poetic experience and knowledge: it always deals with the really real. All discussion of the acts of abstraction having a poetic aspect due to our being's natural desire for union, should never be thought of apart from the thing itself as when pushed to an extreme doctrine—for example, in some Eastern philosophies that teach that the physical world is illusion and nothingness real. It is important to remember that abstraction, the mind's yearning for union of like seeking like between spiritual substances, is still below the order of poetic knowledge, which is not the mind knowing but the body-soul knowledge immersed in the life of the object before it. To borrow from drama: it is not the setting, not the plot, not the time or characters, but as Shakespeare said, the *play's* the thing. *Wholeness* and *inte-*

gration are the words that come to mind in attempting to describe our knowing power's relation to the world. Thomas Gilby says regarding St. Thomas and the tradition he represents:

> The mind, for him [Aquinas], is physical, that is, it is part of nature, for by *physical* a Thomist does not mean *bodily* chiefly. It is the highest form of life . . . a noble energy by which the subject . . . goes out and mingles in the life of others without ceasing to be itself. It is the power of possessing them, not of caging them in concepts.[29]

In this inclusive view of nature, Gilby says, "thought and things are both made of the same stuff; knowledge is a real action and nature is its principle."[30]

It is the same with Frost, noticing with reverential wonder the hummingbird in one's own backyard:

> And make us happy in the darting bird
> That suddenly above the bees is heard,
> The meteor that thrusts in with needle-bill,
> And off a blossom in mid air stands still.

Poetry, and poetic knowledge, discovers the invisible principles in real things without destroying the thing itself, which is, by the way, exactly how intentional knowledge operates and thus its poetic character. Abstraction, concepts, analysis, by themselves, isolate us from the real. Certainly, this mode of knowledge has a mysterious dimension to it, because, unlike science, which cannot enter into these depths, it is quite at home in these intuitive connections with reality that become connatural. But real mystical experience is the result of a grace from God usually given in mystical contemplation to souls in a high degree of faith and charity. Furthermore, mystical experience is concerned with interior silence and an ineffable union with God, whereas, poetic experience soon becomes animated with the connections of created things. Although, it must be said, honoring the above distinctions, the best of poetry, like the best of music, touches on this interior silence; silence being the basis of all sound and music.

What I would summarize here is that from the most imperceptible connections of the "spiritual preconscious" that rests within the reflexes of the first knowledge of being in the senses, to the more cultivated habit of poetic sensibility and vision, we are, throughout, poetic beings even as we live and move among the most ordinary and everyday experiences. Also, I would repeat that the beginning of poetry, philosophy, and science is wonder. Wonder is the principle, the *arché* and therefore as soon as philosophical inquiry begins, science begins, and results in an advance away from wonder. Yet, this poetic spirit never ceases to operate throughout real philosophy. For example, when Aristotle stated that the first principle of all activity is leisure, even after examining the rightness of this idea, we are still struck with the trace of wonder surrounding its absolute clarity, as perhaps was the case with the statement just made that the basis or first principle of music is silence. In fact, both are so simple we are dazzled by the light. And likewise, when Henri Fabre gazed for hours at wasps and bees, unaided by microscopes or any other laboratory paraphanalia, it was then he noted all the remarkable patterns of instinct; when Pasteur proved that it was the presence of bacteria that spoiled food, not spontaneous generation by the most obvious demonstration; when Faraday carried out his chemistry experiment with a plain lighted candle; they, too, like the poets and philosophers, were trailing clouds of wonder, to change a line from Wordsworth, up to the highest scientific regions of their work.

It is this "ordinary" and "everyday functioning" of the mind with reality that is poetic, that is knowledge, and informs all that can be learned, that most people in the present day have ceased to believe in. But, Maritain believes, and deeply. Reworking Aquinas's distinction of the two powers of the intellect, Maritain designates the function that has been called poetic with the *intellectus agens*, and speaks of it as the "Illuminating Intellect," where it "is in no way limited to the process of abstraction and formation of ideas; the Illuminating Intellect is rather the *activator* of intelligence in all its operations."[31] With the insight and precision of Aquinas to lead the way in this area of creative intuition, Maritain is able to follow his muse:

> We possess in ourselves the Illuminating Intellect, a spiritual sun ceaselessly radiating, which activates everything in intelligence, and whose light causes all our ideas to arise in us. . . . they [the distinctions of Aristotle and Aquinas on the powers of the Intellect] enable us to see how the notion of a spiritual unconscious or preconscious is philosophically grounded. I have

suggested calling it, also, musical unconscious, for, being one with the root activity of reason, it contains from the start a germ of melody.[32]

This "germ of melody" is the work of connaturality where knowledge is grasped, not by the intellect's other power of abstraction, but by "poetic intuition . . . directed toward concrete existence as connatural to the soul pierced by a given emotion."[33]

To help prevent confusion here, I should say that in light of the difference between the power of abstraction of the intellect to know essences and connatural knowledge of a thing as a concrete object, both of course are acts of the same intellect, and both produce an intimate union with the object—the first in concept, the other in a kind of vicarious experience, by way of inclination, sympathy, and congeniality (terms all used by Aquinas, and others, to describe this mode).

The charge of subjectivism can be anticipated here, as if to say that this matter of poetic intuition is simply a private affair, too personal to establish itself as universally valid. And, interestingly, Maritain does announce that this is an area of the mind that is "free from the laws of objective reality," at least, "as to be known and acknowledged by science and discursive reason."[34] But the popular notion of subjectivism must be separated from the appropriate term subjectivity. The first submits to no reality outside of self; whereas, Andrew Louth, author of Discerning The Mystery, returns the latter term to its broad and integrated meaning, more in the direction that Maritain intends. This point is so crucial to answering misunderstandings about subjectivism and poetic knowledge in general, a lengthy quote is necessary.

Science is concerned with objective truth . . . independent of whoever observes it . . . experiments must be repeatable by other experimenters. Objective truth, in this sense, seeks to be detached from the subjectivity of the observer. In contrast to such objective truth, subjective truth is a truth which cannot be detached from the observer and his situation. . . . Put like that, it seems at first sight obvious that objective truth is real, and subjective truth falls short of such ultimacy. But further reflection suggests that so to suppose is to over-simplify. When Kierkegaard claimed that all truth lay in subjectivity, he meant that truth which could be expressed objectively (so that it was the same for everyone) was mere information that concerned everyone and no one. Real truth, truth that a man would lay down his life for, was essentially subjective: a truth passionately apprehended by the subject. To say, then, that truth is subjective is to say that its significance lies *in the subject's engagement with it*; it does not mean that it is not objective in any sense: indeed if it were simply a collection of subjective impressions, there would be no engagement, and consequently no questions of truth at all.[35]

In other words, truth that is subjective is truth that one has made one's own—the observer is now engaged in the thing through connatural knowledge, and one has, through sympathy, *participated* in the reality (albeit obscurely) of the experience, so that knowledge ceases to be mere information and becomes existential and recalled as real. Poetic experience leading to poetic knowledge is concerned "with bringing men into *engagement* with what is true. What is important is engagement with reality, not simply the discerning of reality."[36]

Speaking of the poem and the poet in this context of intuition and knowledge, Maritain responds to the problem of subjectivity with the same distinctions as does Louth.

> Poetic knowledge proceeds from the intellect in its most genuine and essential capacity as intellect, though through feeling, feeling, feeling. At this point I would wish to insist that it is in no way a merely emotional or a sentimentalist theory . . . I am suggesting. First, I am speaking of a certain kind of knowledge, and emotion does not know: the intellect knows, in this kind of knowledge as in any other. Second, the emotion of which I am speaking is in no way that "brute or merely subjective emotion." . . . It is an emotion as *form*, which, being one with the creative intuition . . . is *intentional*, as our idea is, or carries within itself infinitely more than itself.[37]

This function of the emotion "as form" is critical to review and understand, and it is necessary to return to the more traditional term, *appetite*, and how, in Realist psychology it is the appetites that *move* us toward the perceived good. A commentator on Maritain, Ralph McInerny, quoted earlier, remarks on this particular point: "Since appetite . . . moves toward things as they are in themselves,

as they exist, appetite assimilates one to what is desired; one becomes like what one loves, becomes connatural with it."[38]

The point to be stressed and reinvoked here is that regardless
of the particular focus Maritain has on the poet and the poem as the
expression of poetic intuition, and with all the review concerning the
metaphysical aspect of the reflexes of the senses with the intellect toward grasping immaterial reality, a view consistently expressed from
Socrates, to Aquinas, and beyond, it is still the poetic nature that resides in every human being in the act of first knowledge that remains
remarkable. It is with this poetic nature in mind that Socrates laid
down his fundamental ideas on education, discoveries of the cognitive dimension of our sensory and emotional powers, especially in
the gymastic and poetic modes, that have been observed in one way
or another for over two thousand years. Even though both St. Augustine and St. Thomas wrote treatises on education, both titled *De
Magistro* (and there are indeed numerous articles on teaching and education throughout the Middle Ages and the Renaissance), still,
there is no specific and detailed treatment of the poetic mode of
knowledge, no self-conscious attention given it, simply because (pre-
sumably from some point before Homer) the credibility of intuitive
knowledge was a kind of given in the power of the knower. The deliberate treatment of poetic knowledge by Maritain and others
becomes necessary only after the seventeenth century and the ascendancy of science as the preeminent method of learning.

For Maritain, the poet and the poem are the obvious examples
of poetic intuition and knowledge, but he also accounts for a broader
understanding of this first knowledge, which succinctly gathers together the longer descriptions already presented into three kinds of
knowledge in this regard: (1) knowledge by intellectual connaturality
where a concept is formed intuitively, as in philosophical and scientific modes of knowledge; (2) a nonconceptual knowledge by connaturality, as in contemplation where divine realities are experienced
yet are inexpressible by the union of love; (3) knowledge of creative
intuition, when "reality comes to be buried in subjectivity . . . [and]
is attained in its concrete and existential consonance with the subject
as subject. This is poetic knowledge . . . by affective connaturality."[39]

It is from this knowledge, "by affective connaturality," Maritain says, that the poem emerges as the fulfillment of the desire to express the experience. At first, Maritain seems to be saying that the

only way poetic experience can be expressed is in some work of the creative intellect; namely, the poem, although he includes painting as well. In any case, there is nothing in Maritain to deny the extension of real poetic experience and knowledge, as was presented at the beginning, to include Odysseus and his illumination of a particular moment, moved by the force of sensory beauty, his mind enlightened by the presence of concrete objects; and, as Louth remarked, *engaged* in the reality of the feast, where the "poem" of the mind becomes a kind of vision of "something very much like perfection." Indeed, this is poetic knowledge, "when reality comes to be buried in the subjectivity" of the knower, a state of comprehension very far beyond Gradgrind's world of "facts." Why? Because Odysseus (and ourselves too, insofar as we learn to *look* with him) is carried *inside* the objects of desire, intentionally, and in sympathy with their being, and achieves a spiritual union.

Then, as it turns out, Maritain does acknowledge the broader distribution of poetic experience. He says, "There is no poem without poetic experience. . . . [But] there can be poetic experience with no poem. (Although there is no poetic experience without the secret germ of a poem, however tiny it be.)"[40]

Socrates' idea of natural philosophy was the love of wisdom, or as Aristotle recasts this, all men desire to know, and both say this knowing begins in wonder. Because wonder is poetic experience, it can be said here, in the wide sense, that all men are poets. Every time we know anything, we possess "the secret germ of a poem." When the secret germ becomes the fruit, there is knowledge, and there is the possibility of the poet and his poem upon which philosophy grows but never outgrows. This movement of knowledge is what is behind the whole idea of Socrates' painstaking considerations for "musical" education, so that in the end we learn to love what is beautiful and in this way know also the true and the good.

That we truly do possess these poetic moments of intuitive knowledge is acknowledged by another modern Thomist philosopher, Josef Pieper, who, reminiscent of Verhoeven, refers to these experiences as a kind of shock:

> The act of philosophizing, genuine poetry, any aesthetic en-
> counter, in fact, as well as prayer, springs from some shock.
> And when such a shock is experienced, man senses the non-
> finality of this world of daily care; he transcends it, takes a step
> beyond it.[41]

This step beyond the world of daily care is the step of poetic knowledge where the *nunc fluens,* the flowing of successive "nows" of time, is
transcended and we touch, or we are touched by, even if ever so
briefly and obscurely, the *nunc stans,* where the time of this world
does more than stand still, it is no more, and in its place stands the
eternal now. While it is true that religious mystical experience, especially those documented cases in Christian mysticism, represent the
height of this transcendence, for the study at hand it should be kept
in mind that common and everyday examples hold within them this
aspect of losing time: the time lost in childhood play; the time that
seems to vanish when lovers are together, alone; the hours that have
simply slipped away during a meal where there was wine and lively
conversation. And here is a very important distinction, set forth by
Maritain, between emotional knowledge of poetic experience and
mystical experience, too often blurred by sentimentalism:

> This seizure of an intelligible reality immediately sensible to the
> heart, without resorting to the concept as formal means, cre-
> ates, on an entirely different plane and by an entirely different
> psychological process, a distant analogy between aesthetic
> emotion and the mystical graces. . . . In reality, mystical con-
> templation takes place by virtue of the connaturality of love;
> here, on the contrary, love and affective connaturality with re-
> gard to the beautiful thing are a *consequence* or a *proper effect* of the
> perception of aesthetic emotion.[42]

In other words, poetic experience, or aesthetic emotion, has the
power to take us spiritually into the object of wonder, true; but what
we see there, what we experience is still the result of our natural
powers. Mystical experience, on the other hand, though it too is a
connatural knowledge, that of love, depends upon the illumination
of mystical graces from outside, beyond, our natural powers. Maritain notes in this observation that, in his opinion, Thomas Gilby
does not always stress this difference enough.[43]

Be that as it may, we are dealing with a degree of transcendent knowledge with poetic experience, and it is also Pieper who understands precisely that an education by the Muses as called for by Socrates is one of leisure, as defined earlier, with its etymological links to education. And, to better understand this notion of leisure and education, it is necessary to grasp what has risen up against it. Pieper prepares for this contrast by covering what should be by now some familiar ground:

> *Ratio* is the power of discursive, logical thought, of searching and of examination, of abstraction, of definition and drawing conclusions. *Intellectus*, on the other hand, is the name for the understanding insofar as it is the capacity of *simplex intuitus*, of that simple vision to which truth offers itself like a landscape to the eye.[44]

But, since modern philosophies have emerged that no longer regard knowing the truth as natural, or even possible, where what was recognized as self-evident is replaced with a system of doubt, under such conditions, Pieper says, learning is now perceived exclusively as *work*, rather than an act of leisure. In other words, the modern idea of learning is dominated by the *ratio*, and the *simplex intuitus* acts of the mind are dismissed as irrelevant under a scientific idea of knowledge. There are no "givens" nor can "inspiration" be taken seriously as valid knowledge—all is mental work and the student, more and more, becomes the intellectual laborer. Leisure and poetic knowledge suffocate under the weight of this new scientific philosophy where the way is opened for the school and all its operations to function quite comfortably with imagery analogous to a factory where products are produced for a marketplace.

In contrast to the modern perception of the knower as laborer, is the poetic nature of the human being. And the poetic mode at this level easily merges with a philosophy not yet ruled by methods of academic procedures, as can be seen in the setting for the meeting between Socrates and Phaedrus as they begin their talk. Socrates describes the location they have chosen for their conversation on beauty:

> Here is this lofty and spreading plane-tree, and the agnus castus high and clustering, in the fullest blossom and the greatest

fragrance; and the stream which flows beneath the plane-tree is deliciously cold to the feet. Judging from the ornaments and images, this must be a spot sacred to Achelous and the Nymphs. How delightful is the breeze:—so very sweet; and there is a sound in the air shrill and summerlike which makes answer to the chorus of the cicadae. But the greatest charm of all is the grass, like a pillow gently sloping to the head. My dear Phaedrus, you have been an admirable guide.[45]

For a man who claimed to hardly ever leave the city of Athens, Socrates is actually quite familair with the countryside, not only knowing the correct names of things—the agnus castus—but is over-whelmed with the fragrances, the bath of cold water on his hot and dusty feet, the gentle breeze, the song of the birds, the feel of the grass. If ever there was a poetic setting for a philosophical conversation on beauty, this is it. And, I should note, a sacred one as well. For, seeing the ornaments and devotional images that apparently decorate the trees, Socrates realizes that they have come upon a place where Achelous, the longest river in Greece that coursed through beauteous ravines and countryside, useless for commerce, is worshipped. He knows that this place will be inhabited by the Nymphs, probably the Acheloids named after the river, lovely female spirits who represent the divine powers of mountains, waters, and woods, among other places.

And Pieper is in the tradition of the life described here, that carries the "secret germ of a poem" in every act of all the knowing powers, whose only "work" is to stand and wait before an intimately knowable reality. In spite of the misplaced "work ethic" of the modern world, there is no intrinsic value to difficulty as such, especially when it comes to knowledge. It is enough, say the poets, Maritain and Pieper, to simply grasp "existing things and in unveiling reality."[46] And, as Aquinas said in this regard: "Not everything that is more difficult is necessarily more meritorious; it must be more difficult in such a way that it is at the same time good in a yet higher way."[47] Certainly, no one can seriously imagine someone working hard and being proud of the difficulty encountered in falling in love; or of the great effort needed to listen to beautiful music; or of an honorable endurance required to watch an evening's setting sun. When difficulty becomes meritorious is when one will give one's life for the beloved, or will go to great sacrifice to conserve a life that includes beautiful music and the sight of setting suns; but that is only because one has first *loved* (known) these things in leisure, experienced the rest, the union, and as a consequence, always yearns to return to them.

Again, I must pause at this point to obviate any misunderstanding in the distinctions between these modes of knowledge. It is only a rigorous modern science, cut off from metaphysics, that is really at war with poetic knowledge. The *scientia* of the ancients and medieval thinkers is distinct from poetic knowledge, but never separate. Josef Pieper explains perhaps better than any modern philosopher the history and integration of these modes, especially what had been considered the natural relation between philosophy and poetry:

> Plato, as everyone knows, virtually identified philosophy with Eros. And in regard to the similarity of philosophy and poetry, there is the little-known and curious saying of Aquinas which occurs in his commentary on the *Metaphysics* of Aristotle: The philosopher, he there says, is related to the poet in that both are concerned with *mirandum*, with wonder, with marveling and with that which makes us marvel. That saying . . . acquires added significance because, as thinkers, Aristotle and Aquinas are both cool-headed, sensible men, altogether averse from any kind of romantic blurring of the orders [of knowledge]. Thus, poetry and philosophy are more closely related to one another than any of the sciences to philosophy; both, equally, are aimed, as one might say, at wonder (and wonder does not occur in the workaday world)—and this by virtue of the power of transcending the everyday world, a power common to poetry and philosophy.[48]

So, with the loss of poetic knowledge from serious consideration in modern theories of knowledge, it follows also that the proper notions of leisure and education are lost along with the proper conditions in a society for *mirandum*; for "wonder [from which all knowledge begins] does not occur in the workaday world," either from the modern idea of work (living to work, instead of working to live) or in modern education that has turned even play into a kind of work in that it is usually conducted as a means to learning something else rather than treated as an end in itself.

Of course, there is real effort required at some point in learning, and often great effort is required to learn something well. But this is a situation that arises *after* the experience of wonder—if it arises at all—and the exertion for this kind of learning is usually in the student on the way to becoming a specialist or expert. And, even in the case of the specialist, the true scientist for example, there would always be the memory of the original *love* of the thing about which he first wondered. Consider again Pasteur, Fabre, and Faraday in this light. They all retained the initial vision of the beginner, the amateur, the one who loves.

For Aquinas and the tradition he represents, the effort to know beyond the state of wonder is actually still to be considered as a means to clear the way for our natural powers "to follow our natural bent in the right way"[49] of knowledge. It is in such a context that we better understand Aristotle's intriguing remark that "the principle of all action is leisure";[50] that is, the end of all endeavor is to return to a state of rest. Furthermore, there is still not a better image of poetic experience and knowledge than Homer's portrait of Odysseus, overcome by the vision of perfection in the sensory and emotional delights at Alcinous's banquet. As a matter of fact, Pieper sees, too, that "The feast is the origin of leisure. . . . To hold a celebration means to affirm the basic meaningfulness of the universe and a sense of oneness with it, of inclusion within it."[51] It is the life of poetry and the poetic sense of things to feast, that is, to celebrate the reality that can only be found in leisure. It is the natural, preconscious mind that celebrates the illumination of things, as a song stirs the heart, the rhythms move the body to dance; or, too, the soul's deep inward gaze in stone-cold grief, for it must be said that the terrifying look into one's own emptiness and inability to surmount, alone, certain ultimate obstacles to happiness, and the gaze into what appears to be an abyss when all that was once believed to be held together by our determining will crumbles in an instant into chaos. This also takes place in a kind of leisure and the shock of wonder, that is, a state of suspension from the routine of the workaday world. Here is where the mind is suddenly wrenched from the sleep of illusion and self-deception, and the senses and mind are schooled in the ancient knowledge that Sophocles gives to Creon, learning in sorrow to be wise.

All this is so because of the nature of our *whole* being where the mind comes into play under the stimulation of leisure and unveiled reality, where our "effortless awareness"[52] participates in, and has the capacity for, apprehending "the spiritual in the same manner that our eye apprehends light or our ear sound."[53] It is this spiritual aspect of reality that is "seen" by the *intellectus* that allows us to sense "the nonfinality," that is, the eternal. Our *simplex intuitus* leads us to the inner knowledge of the perfection of pleasure or to the perfection of grief, as in the awful beauty of the deaths of Romeo and Juliet. This is the meaning of leisure—not just a cessation of labor, but the means by which the poetic powers celebrate the mysterious reality of things as they are, in joy or sorrow; yes, even that strange pleasure experienced in sorrow. We experience in leisure "the basic meaningfulness of the universe and a sense of oneness with it," for there is a sadness in reality—the *lacrymae rerum*, Virgil's "tears of things"—as experience sooner or later makes clear. To have seen in the poetic mode is to have touched a joyful rest, and to depart from that joy is a sad affair indeed. The parting from those we love ultimately by death, the loss of youth, the end of day, the passage of a season, all are real and sad. Normally, the irascible passion of hope sustains us with an anticipation of the rest and joy that sooner or later will return. So, prior to the poem or the work of art, as the trophy won from the confrontation with poetic experience, is poetic knowledge that is shared by all, the recognition and restoration of which is absolutely prerequisite for the restoration of humane education.

Before I examine in the next chapter the ideas of one man that led to the greatest departure from the foundations for poetic knowledge, a summary of connaturality and the backgrounds of poetic knowledge are in order so that the contrast may better be observed.

Four degrees of knowledge were distinguished: poetical, rhetorical, dialectical, and metaphysical, which were discovered in antiquity and held as valid through the Middle Ages and up to the Renaissance. While St. Thomas Aquinas held that *poetica scientia* was the least reliable mode when it came to logic,[54] he still considered it quite real as a means of getting at the truth of things, and, as a matter of fact, the foundation for all discursive reasoning.

Furthermore, while discursive reasoning attains to metaphysical truth by carefully moving from one thing known to another, these same truths can be *approximated* by the mode of poetic knowledge. It is in this mode that St. Thomas designates knowledge by *connaturality*. It is simply an intuitive way, refined by habit, of knowing immaterial reality and transcendent truth.

In an interview with John Senior, one of three professors of the
Integrated Humanities Program, in January 1994, he said, concerning intuition:

> For example, our most immediate brush with metaphysical
> knowledge is that of *being* where we intuitively know that some-
> thing *is* due to our experience of being. This certitude contin-
> ues as it is seen that other things share in this being—trees,
> dogs, cats—and that the cat and ourselves are alike in that both
> participate in being, both are living things.[55]

In contrast to this traditional view, Vincent Smith points out
that "Modern thought . . . does not tend to admit that man's first intellectual attainment is the general idea of being. Hegel [among
many other modern philosophers] held that thinking starts with the
individual. . . . this is true also in the case of . . . all others who, following the empiriological method, deny abstraction and set out to
reconstruct the world from atomistic units, the true backdrop of all
empiricism in philosophy."[56]

To have, however, this intuitive first knowledge of things is to
have a *sympathy* with them, with being, and in this sense poetic
knowledge is higher than metaphysics because its knowledge is one
of *participation within* the thing itself, rather than a mere description of
the metaphysical properties and principles of existence. Recalling
what was said of *intentional* knowledge in this regard, it is the soul that
becomes the thing known (in the intentional order), possessing this
immaterial, spiritual knowledge—a poetic rather than an actual
knowledge arrived at by discourse and reasoning.

The opposite of poetic knowledge was called scientific, that is,
knowledge used to know externals; for example, the stars—their
light is caused by burning gases, or reflection, they are so many light
years from earth, and so on. But the act of the interior senses, the
imagination, drawing on the memory and estimative sense, extends
connatural knowledge to know things from within; that, for example, the stars are immediately pleasant and mysterious, and it is
never very long when looking at them before one drifts into a vast-
ness beyond everyday experience, and we participate in some way in
their life, which accounts for the sensation of awe that descends
upon us in their silent, distant presence. Senior added in the same
interview:

Poetic knowledge can be seen in play, when a child imitates, for example, the movements and sounds of a horse in such a way that he *becomes* the horse through his imagination. The child approaches more nearly the essence of the horse than by the study of either the scientific properties of the horse, or by the study of the principles of its being. From a scientific point of view, this knowledge of the horse is not very precise; but from the poetic position it is a knowledge more real than the scientific due to its vicarious experience of the object.[57]

The point all along has been that the science of metaphysics, though higher in rational perfection, still remains *outside* the object of knowledge; it is still external knowledge. To know in the poetic mode is not only accessible and natural to all, it is, in this sense, more real. In fact, scientific knowledge in general dwells on the measurement of sensory details and not on the life of the senses with nature. While it is true that metaphysics ascends to the knowledge of essences, it remains an external knowledge that describes but does not participate or experience objects as does the sympathetic nature of poetic knowledge. Poetic intuition, connaturality, possesses a vicarious knowledge prior to the scientific, and in this way becomes more present as something real than the acquisition of metaphysical causes and principles. From this it can easily be concluded that a modern science that has rejected the poetic sense of life also rejects universal and spontaneous human responses to an objective reality that perceives the world as good (beautiful) and true. But if there is only dull, one-dimensional matter "out there," then it is not surprising that modern science, in spite of all its good intentions, also gives the world the weapons, machines, and toys to destroy itself.

Drawing upon his contemplative approach to Latin, Senior illustrated poetic knowledge in the following way:

Romance languages, and Latin in particular, contain interesting and revealing distinctions for the understanding of poetic knowledge in the terms for knowledge: *scio* and *cognosco*. The "sc" in both words has the idea of movement, but the former (scio) has the notion of a kind of superficial movement parallel to the thing known, as when it is said, "I know Robert." However, the latter (cognosco) carries with it something much deeper, actually, a knowledge *to be born into* the thing known— na*sc*ent—an intuitive birth with the thing known, to become the thing itself, in sympathy, as to say, "I *know* Robert," and, in this way meaning, "I *am* Robert."[58]

St. Thomas Aquinas said poetry occupies the lowest order of knowledge because it is less distinct and tends to be obscure compared to scientific knowledge. Poetry carries no explicit knowledge of causes or first principles, only of their effects. It relies on the cognitive aspect of the senses and emotions. But poetry does give vicarious experience of causes, getting the knower inside the thing to be known by intuition, by being connatural (sympathetic) with the object. For example, Newton *explains* gravity and its laws; poetic experience and knowledge *knows and can recreate the imaginative experience* of gravity.

With Jacques Maritain, "creative intuition," that is, poetic knowledge, takes us into the experience of metaphysical being. Our senses, for example, clearly tell us that life is variously sad, happy, good, bad, and so on; but poetic experience goes beyond the senses and dwells within the cause—the art of poetry does this exactly—and in so doing, creates, as it were, the cause itself. Maritain's "creative intuition" was extended to define poetic experience broadly, as experience known to all, not just the poet in the act of creating.

Still, this connatural knowledge in all its aspects is vague and obscure and does not satisfy the precision called for by science. However, it is the poet, and anyone who reflects with poetic experience, that can give *form* to experience, so that the thing, the experience, can be repeated in the memory and imagination, and in so doing, gain a kind of *being*, a creation. The poetic view calls forth the subjectivity of the knower to become *engaged* with the object of knowledge. It is in this way that the habit of poetry, the habit of the poetic view of things, takes raw experiences and forms them into essences. This must be the case, since experience by itself cannot be repeated, it is simply lost. But the poetic impulse to imitate that leads to form the poem, even the germ of the poem in the preconscious intellect, that causes one to reflect on experience, gives to experience repeatability and thereby becomes real knowledge. When this habit of poetic knowledge is discovered in the life of the teacher, all subjects are seen in a new light. The teacher becomes as it were the poet of history, science, arithmetic, as well as rescuing languages and literature from the deadening treatment of scientific analysis.

A final example: this edge that poetic knowledge possesses can be seen in theology, in miracles, which are to bolster faith, to move the will toward God. But these are still *extrinsic* examples of faith. On the other hand, poetic knowledge of miracles would be when the miracle is in some way *actually communicated*, at least, for a moment, to us, and at that point is an expression *beyond* faith, for then we momentarily move into *possession* of what up to this time has been believed by faith.

In ordinary experience, not of miracles, poetry and the poetic sense of things presents nature, and ourselves, in such a way that essences are revealed as timeless, always being born in an endless moment of creation, in the act of poetic creation so we may *see* the thing as it is. Willa Cather, the American writer, understood this way of seeing, the knowledge, the movement of the inner senses, when desire moves, "From being a shapeless longing, it becomes a beautiful image; a dumb rapture becomes a melody that can be remembered and repeated; and the experience of a moment, which might have been a lost ecstasy, is made an actual possession and can be bequeathed to another."[59]

In concluding this chapter and summary, it must be said that something indeed happened to the tradition that carefully divided and recognized the degrees of knowledge; some radical departure in the philosophy of man took place after the Reformation and the Renaissance—a new philosophy that can be said to have ended the predominant view of ancient-medieval psychological anthropology and ushered in what is designated the *modern* view of man. This new view, for all the ideas of liberation and fulfillment associated with it from the Renaissance down to the present day, is actually a much narrower, more confined, and restricted perception of man and his powers to know his world than all that preceded it.

4

Descartes and the Cartesian Legacy

The eye—it cannot choose but see;
We cannot bid the ear be still;
Our bodies feel, wher'er they be,
Against or with our will.
—*William Wordsworth*

The Western philosophical tradition before the Reformation and Renaissance had slowly developed as characteristically uncritical. This is not to say it was unquestioning and did not contain disputes. After all, there had been the bitter war between Socrates and the Sophists. Plato's Idealism was strongly opposed by Aristotle's Realism, and St. Augustine's Platonism was given sharp precision by Aquinas. St. Thomas himself speaks directly of a certain kind of philosophic doubt, *dubia*, appropriate to metaphysics, although he gave it "no existence as a discipline distinct from metaphysics."[1]

The questioning spirit before the breakup of medieval Europe was dominated by a belief that there are certain givens that can be embraced by the inquirer into truth that do not require an elaborate system of proof. As a matter of fact, there are what may be called "primordial certitudes" that simply cannot be proved. There are, "self-evident aspects of reality which lie open to our senses and intellect—aspects of reality so clear and evident that they do not need demonstration. It would be contradictory, in fact, to try and prove them, since they are implied in all proof."[2]

As the position has been throughout, we know reality first through the "fundamental intuition of the senses and the intellect—of the intellect *in* the sense, so to speak. Before we know *what* a thing is, we know *that* it is; and we know this not necessarily by conscious reflection but implicitly, as taken for granted in all our concepts and judgments."[3] This is why it is foolish to deny that things exist, for such a denial must contain the affirmation that such things indeed are present.

Therefore, in this ancient tradition of philosophy, the knower's mind was not the first object of knowledge, but rather corporeal objects that indubitably exist; that is, the universe with all its observable reality was intuitively accessible. The mind, this older tradition held, was uniquely equipped to grasp reality and to move upwards to contemplation of existence and being. Man, then, was not removed from his world, alone with his mind as his only certitude, but existed with his mind in a world of knowable reality. But this view was soon to be seriously challenged.

René Descartes was born March 31, 1596, in Touraine, France. He attended a Jesuit college at La Fleche where he studied logic, philosophy, and mathematics. There seems to be nothing to suggest he was unhappy with his education there, and he regarded the Jesuit Fathers with great respect. However, in time he came to the conclusion that much of his traditional learning was not based on a solid foundation. Remarkably, much of this conclusion was based on a strange dream of his. Sometime after 1612, he decided that mathematics was the only branch of knowledge that offered certitude, because of its clarity. In 1637, he published the *Discourse on Methods of Rightly Conducting the Reason and Seeking for Truth in the Sciences*, or as it has come to be known, *The Discourse on Method*. It was a major decision for Descartes to rely solely on his own reason and not on the tradition and authority of the philosophical legacy embraced by the Roman Catholic Church, which included those parts of ancient Idealist and Realist insights that admitted the validty of different modes of knowledge. He also believed that once this one method was discovered it would lead the inquirer to new truths. This being the case, a break with the past, he felt, was necessary, along with a new method to demonstrate truth in an exclusively rationalistic and systematic way. Frederick Copleston, the eminent historian of philosophy, observes:

> It is undeniable that in one sense at least Descartes consciously and deliberately broke with the past. First of all he was determined to start again from the beginning, as it were, without trusting to the authority of any previous philosophy. . . . Descartes was resolved to rely on his own reason, not on authority.[4]

Taking up this position led him to establish a method that would avoid what he considered the vague notions of the Scholastics and leave place only for certain knowledge. He would accept only clear and distinct ideas as valid. Interestingly, the etymology of *method* reveals exactly what has become known as the Cartesian influence in education. In this sense, *method* is an approach that is "between" or intersects "the way," as in the way home—in other words, the use of *method* attempts a kind of short cut, a point observed in some detail at the beginning of the next chapter.

It is important to keep in view the distinction that while the Realist tradition used certain set procedures to arrive at truth, Descartes proposed a universal method for *all* sciences. In fact, Descartes believed that all sciences are ultimately one and therefore what was needed was one universal scientific method to arrive at certain knowledge. Ironically, his argument was not so much with the Scholasticism of the past but with skepticism, a tendency he noticed in current education, the result of the influence of Montaigne. Again, there seems to be no question that Descartes believed his method of doubt was designed to lead one to certain truth. However, the introduction of his method, from the beginning, presents difficulties even in clarifying what were once accepted, defined terms. For example, in dealing with ancient and medieval philosophy there was a certain amount of difficulty encountered due to the fact we are not used to making such sharp distinctions and so closely considering the operations of the cognitive powers. But with Descartes, this difficulty moves toward confusion because some terms now familiar from the older tradition are being used in different ways. Descartes reduces our mental functions to only two, and names them deduction (reason) and intuition; but this is *not* the intuition described so far in this study. Intuition, in Descartes' usage, instead of arising from the engagement of the outer and inner senses with reality, penetrated by the light of the intellect, is now focused as a function exclusively with the mind. Copleston explains that by intuition Descartes means "a purely intellectual activity, an intellectual seeing or vision which is so clear and distinct that it leaves no room for doubt."[5] Consider, now, that it was traditional Realist philosophy that said precisely that knowledge by intuition, while clear enough to see self-evident truths, was also rather obscure in comparison with the mode of logic and metaphysical reasoning. But, as it turns out, "Descartes does what he can to reduce deduction to intuition,"[6] since he requires each step of the deductive process, each truth seen, to be clear and distinct before proceeding.

Basically, Descartes has isolated one mode of knowledge, of the four described earlier—that of mathematical certainty, or dialectic—and imposed it on all the others. Further, he has changed the traditional meaning of the term *intuition* and then insisted that all knowledge, to be valid, carry with it the clarity and precision of a solved problem. This last aspect introduces the pernicious notion that knowledge itself is a "problem," which, in turn, gives rise to the error Josef Pieper spoke of, quoted earlier, that all knowledge is obtained by work, and thus, the emergence of the intellectual laborer.

With Descartes, the learner must now begin with exactly what was not the beginning before: a self-conscious systematic method and an assumption of doubt about previous givens. These replace the spontaneous knowledge of being and a reality that was in no need of demonstration and proof.

In Part Two of the *Discourse*, Descartes sets down four rules to be observed in his method:

> The first rule was never to accept anything as true unless I recognized it to be certainly and evidently such: that is, carefully to avoid all precipitation and prejudgment, and to include nothing in my conclusions unless it presented itself clearly and distinctly to my mind that there was no reason for occasion to doubt it.
>
> The second was to divide each of the difficulties which I encountered into as many parts as possible, and as might be required for an easier solution.
>
> The third was to think in an orderly fashion when concerned with the search for truth, beginning with the things which were the simplest and easiest to understand, and gradually, and by degrees reaching toward more complex knowledge, even treating, as though ordered, materials which were not necessarily so.
>
> The last was, both in the process of searching and in reviewing when in difficulty, always to make enumerations so complete, and reviews so general, that I would be certain that nothing was omitted.[7]

All of this is quite familiar to modern readers. It is, after all, exactly the procedure followed by, for example, laboratory science, as well it should be, if one is testing for a cure to some disease. But

Descartes applies this method to all knowledge. Taking the first two precepts, it is seen that not only will methodic doubt and a method of analysis (taking apart) operate as the two main components of knowledge, but underpinning the entire method is Descartes' conviction that the rigor and effort of mathematics is the *only* certain means for discovering and demonstrating truth. Descartes clearly says:

> Considering that among all those who have previously sought truth in the sciences, mathematicians alone have been able to find some demonstrations, some certain and evident reasons, I had no doubt that I should begin where they did.[8]

With just a little reflection, keeping in mind the tradition from which Descartes broke, it becomes evident that we know, and know that things are true, in more than one way. There is, for example, intuition where we know directly and immediately certain universal truths, referred to in traditional philosophy as self-evident truths of first principles, truths common to all human beings. All of this was worked out long ago in ancient Realist philosophy.

> The most fundamental of the self-evident first principles is the *principle of identity*, which says that what is, is, or that each thing is what it is. The principle of identity is the philosophical formulation of the spontaneous knowledge that there are certain fundamental consistencies of being which are ultimate, and which common sense expresses in such statements as, "Eggs are eggs," or "A tree is a tree." (See St. Thomas, ST, I–II, 94.2.)

> The *principle of non-contradiction* is the negative statement of the principle of identity, and states that a thing cannot be and not be at the same time and in the same respect. Common sense says that "A tree is not an egg" . . . the *principle of sufficient reason*, which states that each thing must have a sufficient reason for its being, and the *principle of causality* . . . declares that every being which comes into existence must have part of its reason of being outside itself.[9]

These are not hunches, but fundamental things that are perceived as true without any need of a systematic apparatus of demonstration. Daniel J. Sullivan, quoted above, presents simply the obvious error contained in Descartes' method:

> Descartes, in an effort to make proof doubly sure, demanded
> that we prove the existence of things outside the mind . . .
> when he demanded proof for the existence of the outside
> world, [he] started a false problem. . . . The fact of the exis-
> tence of the outside world is not an abstract truth. . . . That it
> exists at all is something that we discover, not prove. . . . For
> the philosopher to ask proof of the actual existence of contin-
> gent things, including his own existence, is to betray the evi-
> dence of the fundamental intuition of his senses and intellect. It
> is to ask proof for what does not need proof, for what indeed
> cannot be proved, since it is prior to proof and is implied in all
> demonstration.[10]

In other words, if one is to doubt self-evident truths, even for
the sake of a deliberate scheme to finally reconstruct them as true,
there is the simple but quite serious problem that presents itself, that
without a starting point of some certitude, the mind cannot con-
fidently proceed through the acts of reasoning at all. As Sullivan
succinctly observes, "before the intellect even has the chance to for-
mulate the doubt of being, the intellect rests in the certainty of existence."[11] Furthermore, once this fundamental knowledge is doubted
then the thread of contradiction runs throughout all the processes of
reasoning to follow. Descartes did attempt to deal with this problem
by positing his famous first principle, *cogito ergo sum*, which I deal with
briefly later. But first, recall that Sullivan's distinction that to "discover" being, existence, reality, is, in the general context of this
study, a poetic thing—to prove is scientific. In fact, Descartes rejects
all the functions of knowledge that have been described as possessing
a poetic aspect to them.

To repeat, then: a large problem with the *Discourse* is that not
everything is known clearly and distinctly as the *Method* exclusively
calls for. As a matter of fact, there are different kinds of certainty;
one, for example, in ethics, another in mathematics. Even with the
most rigorous application of deductive reasoning, certain subjects of
human inquiry do not admit to the same degree of certitude. To
know that $2 + 2 = 4$, indubitably, is not the same kind of knowledge
as in knowing that a definition of justice is giving to each his due;
nor, is either one of these like the certainty I have that someone loves
me. To demand that each field of inquiry, that all knowledge, yield a
high degree of demonstrative certainty is, finally, *un*reasonable. The
subject (object) of study, of course, is the determinate factor, and
only mathematics, as Descartes holds, is capable of demonstrative

certainty; whereas, common experience allows for much that is the result of probable reasoning. The modern philosopher, Etienne Gilson, asks in this regard:

> Are we sure that everything that *is* is susceptible of a mathematically evident interpretation? The answer, of course, is arbitrary. You have a full right to bet on the affirmative, but it is gambling, and if by any chance you happen to be wrong, you will be playing a losing game from beginning to end. Everything will be mathematically proved in your philosophy, save only this, that everything can, and must be, mathematically proved.[12]

Gilson examines the much-discussed *cogito, ergo sum* in this light as the inevitable first principle of any philosophy that insists on mathematical evidence, but certainly not the first principle of philosophy as has hitherto been known. In other words, there are other valid places to begin philosophy besides the certainty of "I think." As Gilson says, "If we need a philosophy whose certitude is equal to that of mathematics, our first principle will have to be *I think*; but do we need such a philosophy?"[13]

Therefore, with methodic doubt as the beginning of philosophy, one will be led to doubt all things except the ontological reality of that act itself. Only one certainty remains with its two parts: the self and its proof; that is, that it thinks, which is to say in this crucial beginning of knowledge, that it doubts as the method of progress to the truth. But, if it is true that there can be no metaphysics without epistemology, no hierarchy of knowledge from the necessity of the senses to the ultimate power of the intellect, then a theory of knowledge that denies this harmony proposes a notion of disharmony between the mind and the body. Indeed, under a Cartesian philosophy, the mind will be virtually isolated from the body as well as defining the mind's first function as a critical faculty. Given this, the Cartesian view is one of the great disintegrating philosophies of all time, with its tendency to set the mind against the sensory and intuitive powers of the body-soul harmony so thoughtfully discovered and carefully described from Socrates to Aquinas. John Young has reflected on this particular problem presented by Descartes:

> The fact that he started from his own consciousness instead of from the physical world outside him distinguishes Descartes' method from that of most previous philosophies. And this also

led him to make a sharp division between the soul, which he described as a thinking thing without any extension, and the body, which is unthinking and extended. As we noted earlier, critics have said that Descartes regarded man as a "ghost in a machine." We don't know things directly, he claimed; we directly know only our thoughts. This is an extremely important departure from the traditional position, which maintains that reality is known first, and we afterwards reflect on the ideas and images we find within ourselves.[14]

This quote reflects the general theory of knowledge from Aristotle to Aquinas that holds that because we know first through the senses the mind cannot *directly* know an essence, that is, something, as Aquinas said, in potency—we know first in act, actually. For example, in sensible things we do not know the potency of the color blue, but some object that is actually blue. And even in reflective intellectual knowledge, we arrive at knowledge of an essence only insofar as it is act. To say this in the context of what comes first in the order of knowledge, we simply do not, cannot, know our thoughts of things before we know the things as they are first.

The question presents itself in regard to Descartes: how is poetic knowledge or metaphysics possible without certainty beyond the thinking self? How can the mind pose metaphysical questions or make the intuitive connections of poetic knowledge without first being able to rest upon, as certain, the corporeal world? If Descartes is wrong about his new first principle—*cogito, ergo sum*—then all that follows is flawed in spite of all his good intentions toward reaching positive knowledge. Carmin Mascia, a historian of philosophy, explains the overall problem:

> The Aristotelio-Scholastic method is also deductive, but it is very different from that of Descartes. Scholastic deduction is connected with objective reality because ideas are abstractions of the form of the objects which experience presents. Thus both the concreteness of the ideas and the concreteness of the deductions based on these ideas are justified. In Descartes ideas do not come from experience, but the intellect finds them within itself. Descartes declares that only these ideas are valid in the field of reality. Thus the concreteness (or the objective reality) of an idea is dependent upon its own clearness and distinction.[15]

In addition to Mascia's criticism, Jacques Maritain, who has a great deal to say on the problems of Descartes' philosophy, remarks that what Descartes is attempting in all the rigor of his *method* is to finally see all truth in one continuous glance. "To reason," for Descartes, "is no longer *to be led* by the principle to see the consequence, it is to *see* the principle and its connection with the consequence together."[16] Maritain continues to say that this method "destroys the unity belonging to reasoning and the continuity of logical movement."[17] Unlike the definition of intentional knowledge used by the classical philosophers to describe a specific but obscure way of knowing, based on sensible perception of reality and sensible images in the memory—as St. Thomas names this, *connatural* knowledge—Descartes' intuition resembles *angelic* intuition, that is, *angelism*, as Maritain explains:

> The angel neither reasons, nor proceeds by reasoning; he has but one intellectual act, which is at once perceiving and judging: he sees consequences not successively from the principle, but immediately in the principle.[18]

Maritain sees this angelism as the greatest error of Descartes' philosophy; that is, he begins with the proposition that man is essentially a *thinking* substance, a definition hitherto reserved for angels whose intellect is "always in act with regard to its intelligible objects [and] does not derive its ideas from things, as does ours, but has them direct from God."[19]

So, in addition to the first problem noted here with Descartes' method—that of beginning the search for truth by rejecting as certain the intuitive first principles of knowledge, and replacing this with the thinking mind as the only certainty—the second problem emerges—that of his impatience with the discursive mode of the intellect. This causes a disintegration of the natural unity of the knower to know—insisting that *all* knowledge, after an exercise in the rigor of mathematical method, be angelically intuitive, only certain when seen clearly at a glance. Maritain continues:

> In Descartes the result is the most radical leveling of the things of the spirit: one same single type of certitude, rigid as Law, is imposed on thought; everything which cannot be brought under it must be rejected; absolute exclusion of everything that

is not mathematically evident, or deemed so. It is inhuman cognition, because it would be superhuman![20]

Finally, on this point, and of great significance for the drastic
change from ancient and medieval ideas of education to what is
characteristically modern, is the result that after Descartes all knowledge is now restricted exclusively to the *ideas* of objects in the intellect, and to achieve such clear and distinct ideas, "it is always by
method, or by methods, and no longer by the spiritual quality en-
nobling the intellect, that the austerity of knowledge will be measured."[21]

It is one of those grand ironies in the history of philosophy that
René Descartes, a man of faith, wished to correct a trend of skepticism in current philosophy, only to give to the Western world a system whose starting point is to produce a method of inquiry based
on doubt; in fact, a whole new category of epistemology based on
uncertainty. It was his method more than any other that ruptured
the ancient philosophical tradition and gave rise to the beginning
of the critical age of philosophy, an age whose spirit no longer rests
on the discoveries of the past, but reexamines all beliefs in the harsh
light of scientific method, which is based on a beginning position of
disbelief. In a way, it makes no difference if Descartes was convinced
that his method would lead to truth. What the world of thought is
left with instead is a preoccupation with doubt, the radical distribution of the scientific method, a critical spirit, with the mind as the
beginning point of inquiry, as opposed to the more familiar and
long-established tradition of wonder and confidence in a real existence outside the knower. And to keep the contrast in focus, Thomas
Gilby reminds us again of this departure:

> There is a solidarity of mind and nature in St. Thomas' theory
> of knowledge, though it is missed by those of his followers who
> read Descartes into it and make of the mind a sort of reflector,
> and knowledge an inspection of the reflections. They exagger-
> ate the distinction between *esse naturale* and *esse intelligible* [nat-
> ural essence and intelligible essence], and constitute two
> worlds, of real things and of produced representations. But, in
> truth, a representation is wholly derivative from and relative to
> the real.[22]

Then there is the legacy. After Descartes, other philosophers
emerged carrying some mark of the Cartesian influence. David

Hume (1711–1776) shared Descartes' radical separation of body and mind, and, that we *infer* reality from the images in our mind. However, in contrast to Descartes—although following from his radical dualism—Hume was an empiricist, allowing that no deeper knowledge than what senses and emotions can offer is possible. According to Hume and his followers down to the present day, "We cannot ever be sure the world exists, although a strong instinct causes us to think it does."[23]

It is beyond the scope of my present study to examine in detail the precise implications of Cartesianism on modern philosophy; to describe the poetic mode of knowledge remains my primary focus. However, in general, the overall influence of Descartes—intended or not—informs all of modern philosophy in its tendency to displace from reality, if not remove altogether, the order of knowing that includes the valid role of the sensory-emotional response, integrated with the will and intellect. Therefore, only a brief chronological survey of the legacy of Descartes to the twentieth century is presented insofar as these philosophies have directly touched the realm of poetic knowledge.

Without the confidence of the role of sensory-emotional powers integrated with the mind, Immanuel Kant posits that we only know *impressions* of reality, not reality itself. Also, there is a new and radical Idealism with and after Kant, that, so much like Descartes, says we can only know our thoughts, where what we call reality is merely a projection of thought with no certainty of a real and independent existence "out there."

With the initial rupture by Descartes in the integrated and harmonious view of man as knower of his world, some of the disintegrated pieces become isolated and driven to radical, even absurd, conclusions. A new empiricism, after Locke and Hume, asserts that *all* knowledge is derived from sense experience (with a limited notion of the senses, at that); therefore, it is claimed we have no knowledge, no ability to transcend this narrow order of perception, a position that jettisons traditional metaphysics, and, as a result, destroys the possibility of recognizing and understanding the poetic mode.

Most influential philosophically, and, in fact, for American philosophy of education in particular, is John Dewey. Descartes' influence on the work of Dewey is not necessarily a direct one, and Descartes' Catholicism and his certainty that there were absolutes and divine ones at that, would have parted the two greatly. Rather, it was Descartes' love of method, process, and the tools of science that are bequeathed to philosophers such as Dewey. Like Descartes, he constructs a theory of knowledge that claims what we know is instigated exclusively by a rational process, a method, actually a simple reworking of the scientific method of inquiry where knowledge is the result of controlled experiments. Where Descartes believed from the beginning that his method would lead to a more clear and distinct knowledge of truth, Dewey has separated the scientific approach from any metaphysical tradition, and advanced it solely into the realm of problem solving for whatever is the immediate need. This philosophy of Dewey, often called pragmatism, does not exactly reject the modes of knowledge spoken of here, but assigns them no real relevance in the face of scientific advances; and, at least in the case of Dewey, the entire metaphysical tradition followed in this study, is, with a kind of due respect, retired to a bygone era of particular social circumstances no longer relevant for the modern world. Dewey was no innovator in his pragmatism on this point; such rejection was based upon the influence of empiricists like Locke who stated that metaphysical speculation about the knower was not verifiable in terms of human experience. Also, in Dewey's pragmatism, like Descartes' method, there is a position of doubt that begins inquiry, where it follows that all will have to be *proved* in some kind of way, disregarding all that has been said and demonstrated here concerning the presence of intuitive knowledge. With the influences of Kant, as well as with Descartes, all learning now becomes a kind of effort and work which Dewey models after a dynamic idea of democracy of social change, where learning has as its end the fulfillment of a progressive society *always* changing toward some perfected goal. Everything is measured by the changing needs of a social end, rather than knowing and learning beginning as a natural and effortless good in itself and leading to the fulfillment of the innate desire to know and to love. Instead, Dewey states in his creed: "I believe that the only true education comes through the stimulation of the child's powers by the demands of the social situations in which he finds himself."[24]

All learning is experimental (in the scientific sense) and subject to the environment, according to Dewey. This is a position that is, of course, partly true but neglects the innate powers of the knower to know prior to experiment, and regardless of the particular environment. This radical application of the scientific method to education reduces the knower to a mere problem solver, doubting all, testing everything, until the problem is solved, which, for Dewey, constitutes the complete act of thought. But the most noticeable departure from the history of poetic knowledge is that all learning for Dewey is *dynamic* and active, as opposed to the essential passive or receptive nature of the knower as explained in the tradition from Socrates to Aquinas. The learner, with Dewey, is more of an organism, a Darwinian species, to be adapted to the needs of the community. Since Dewey reassigns first principles and absolutes regarding human nature to no more than discovered instruments of mental activity to be used to understand and control the environment, there is no set definition of what the needs of the community are, beyond the utilitarian ends of an experimental democracy, whatever that might be. Aesthetics, and all poetic impulses, are reduced to expressions of the particular society and its relative needs. In short, the entire spiritual nature of the knower, who was in the past considered unique, able to become the thing known in the order of intention and to enter into connatural sympathy with an unchanging reality, Dewey reduces to a communal learner who will master "skills" and apply "tools of learning" to form a better democracy. John Senior states the result of such a philosophy on modern education:

> John Dewey taught that schools are instruments of social change rather than of education, and that is one reason why Johnny neither reads nor writes nor dreams or thinks; but real schools are places of un-change, of the permanent things.[25]

Hard words, that of Senior's, but absolutely consistent with the tradition of knowledge and its implications for education that embrace Dewey's philosophy as the continuation of a radical departure from the contemplative aspect of education. Now, it could be that a school could influence social change in some way—that's not the issue; rather, a school as was understood since the time of Plato, conversed about those things that do not change because permanence had been discovered as standing underneath all appearances of change, and thus was a greater reality than change. Dewey, on the other hand, is fascinated with the philosophical idea of *becoming*, and thus his intolerance for the contemplative and poetic mode of education as an end in itself that asks for nothing to change or to be manipulated or improved.

Senior does not mean that Johnny cannot read the words on the page, but that is *only* what he can read. And, in addition to the fact that today's students are being asked to read more and more "information," even when presented with the classic books of adolescence and youth, they do not know how to read these in their imaginative mode, cut off as they are more and more from the real world, and certainly alien to the agrarian and craft culture that informed the world of the works of Homer, Chaucer, Shakespeare, and the Romantics. Notice that it is not just reading and writing that suffer under a pragmatist influence on how we think and teach, but such students are less likely to "dream." To dream, that is, to discover the imaginative life based upon wonder of direct experience with things as they are. But if you make the assumption that knowledge is no more than the steps from hypothesis, deduction, to conclusion for practical ends, and, further, that schools are to apply this method for adjusting to the changes that inevitably occur as part of a dynamic materialistic democracy, then dreaming is out. To dream in the sense Senior means, is just the opposite of what either the modern skeptic or practical educator thinks is a mere waste of time spent in airy nothingness, but instead requires some object whose ultimate reality is perceived because of its permanence upon which the imagination begins to muse. In such states of mind, youth rehearse and experiment vicariously with all kinds of real-life situations.

When Dewey writes about moral, religious, aesthetic, or educational topics, these subjects all fall under the same practical and dynamic treatment. With the rejection of the speculative and metaphysical tradition of philosophy because it is not meaningful for current political and social conditions, and the ultimate rejection of the necessary first principles and self-evident truths, it only follows that Dewey would conclude "the task of future philosophy is to clarify men's ideas as to the social and moral strifes of their own day. Its aim is to become so far as is humanly possible an organ for dealing with these conflicts."[26] To express simply what Descartes and Dewey have brought into the world of thought and education, in contrast with the former presence of the poetic mode, is to say that poetic experience is useless, it doesn't do or make anything happen, least of all solve conflicts, as a pragmatist would understand. Remember, with the poetic way, we are in the realm of the will that loves, the intuitive mind, the alert senses that possess an estimative judgement of things, and the habit of being connatural with nature, all of which

Dewey would finally reject because, one, it did not follow a scientific process of thought to arrive at its conclusions, and, two, it claimed no particular end in the social realm.

While I believe that Dewey would be displeased with some of the methods of Cartesian French education—he would favor a more active and experimental atmosphere—I think he would approve of the idea of presenting, for example, a classical curriculum of litera-ture and science subsumed and applied to current conditions of commerce and political life. Since, like Descartes, he isolated one mode of knowledge and elevated it to rule all others—the practical, in the case of Dewey, the mathematical, in the case of Descartes— we see schools that still advertise a liberal arts curriculum with a reading list from the Harvard Classics or Great Books, but find that these subjects are mostly taught in the mode of science and practi-cality where graduates of such schools tend to pursue careers in law, medicine, engineering, and politics.

What links Descartes and Dewey is their trust in scientific methods of thought, shortcuts really, and that they both, in different ways, either call into question where thought begins (for Descartes, in the mind alone), or that the objects of thought are constructed by the mind only as a result of inquiry, as with Dewey. But as I said ear-lier, it is ironic that Descartes did not intend to foster skepticism, nor did he intend to bring forth a John Dewey. Descartes believed in eternal, unchanging truths as just that; whereas, Dewey recognizes these, but under a much different theory of knowledge:

> Timeless truths have to be represented by him [Dewey] as being simply instruments for application in knowing the one world of becoming, instruments which constantly show their value in use. In other words, their significance is functional rather than ontological.[27]

There is no "function" or "use" of wonder in the poetic mode of knowledge, or really in the dialogues of Plato, and this is one of the great reasons there is such an impatience, a disdain, even a hostility toward poetic education in our day. Even the settings for the conver-sations of Socrates are far from the modern idea of a classroom, many of them out of doors, and *The Republic* takes place almost en-tirely in the living room of Cephalus. Even as much as intelligent ed-ucators will admit the reasonableness of subjects that are simply good in themselves without utilitarian ends, admitting also that young students should not experience the distraction of grading systems and the whole mathematical apparatus of evaluation, no one has yet ever started an elementary school in this country in the poetic and gymnastic mode. In a moment, we may see why.

It's not that Dewey rejects all general notions. It would be impossible to construct a philosophy such as Dewey did without holding general ideas. And Dewey has admiration for the ancient tradition, the work of Aristotle, for example, especially his logic, as an expression of Greek culture *at that time*. But, for Dewey, "the attempt to preserve the Aristotelian logic when the advance of science has undermined the ontological background of essences and species on which it rested is 'the main source of existing confusion in logical theory.' "[28]

The passive nature of poetic knowledge is held to be either irrelevant or simply false under the rise of Dewey's experimentalism and rigors of inquiry. The universals embedded in particulars, grasped first intuitively, are no longer held to be valid knowledge. Even "the basic logical principles are not eternal truths, transcending the changing empirical world and to be apprehended instinctively; they are generated," according to Dewey, "in the actual process of man's active relation with his environment."[29]

Dewey's *process* of thought is a legacy from Descartes' *method*. It is not denied here that we can certainly think by means of a process and a method, but it is the fallacy of saying it is the only valid way to think—that is the point that advances the demise of poetic knowledge. Furthermore, Dewey contributes to and extends the idea that all thought and knowledge is labor, the work of the *ratio* over the passive reception of the *intellectus*.

Dewey's so-called pragmatism, as it filtered down to the masses who largely never read a word he wrote, fit neatly into the American view of education for the good life. It was perfect, in its popular versions, for the American oligarchic man, that is, the practical businessman seeking to not only retain, but to increase his property and profits. Ideas were important to these descendants of the European industrial revolutions and the new notions of the wealth of nations, insofar as they worked toward increasing the common wealth of the country and the personal wealth of those practical and clever enough to succeed. The typical American businessman had no time for philosophy—he was smart enough to know it required real leisure—but he loved what he understood of pragmatism. Quite often the oligarchic man was honest, hardworking, and fair; he even might quote a poem or two he had memorized and enjoy reciting a verse on special occasions. But how could he ever see the use in pursuing a life of contemplation and leisure, since there was no "use" in these things anyway? And when the needs of oligarchic America begin to be felt in the schools and colleges, when schools themselves became more and more places where the "product" and "commodity" of education was "produced," then what there was of the poetic mode was assigned to the token English or humanities teacher, so that the students would have a *practical* sense of literature, history, and philosophy. Then, when schooling was finally over, the student could plunge into the "real world."

Interestingly, Dewey's scientific and practical philosophy with its emphasis on dealing with the conflicts of social change was also attractive to some Marxists, although this fact is not surprising, for both systems of economics, industrial capitalism and communism, inevitably in the first case and absolutely in the second, are materialistic and have little or nothing to do with eternal truths, or beauty, or goodness in any transcendent way. Furthermore, both societies are steeped in their separate ideas of progress, a materialistic progress advanced by a scientific philosophy such as dialectical materialism, or of the optimistic future brought about by the marriage of science and capitalism—in both worlds pragmatism can be at home because of its regulating all knowledge to the service of any progressive society that has jettisoned the past and is in search of the means to control the future defined in materialistic terms. The problem for poetic knowledge in such a milieu is that it is neither progressive nor collective, for it is a subjective initiation into the eternal now of things and dwells upon the permanent things that neither progress nor regress, but are. Sooner or later, the education for a student under either way of progressive, materialist life will be informed by the dominance of the practical ends of the state.

Finally, in all fairness to Dewey, I must say that some of his insights particularly put forth in *Experience and Education, The Child and the Curriculum,* and, *The School and Society,* are perfectly expressed against the stale and routine organization that had become the education in his times, that is, the inheritance from Descartes and later the Empiricists. He also understands very well the need for the gymnastic and literary experiences of children—these books are shot through with expressions of a real philosophical knowledge of the classical tradition of education. There is much to be admired, for example, in the popular Dewey idea of learning by doing. But, sooner or later, Dewey brings all to bear on the question of whether any of the traditions or methods of education, new or old, will benefit the immediate state of social life or not, and whatever the ends of that particular society, they will be determined by scientific experience of what seems to be good for the state at the time.

From this point on, philosophy of knowledge tends toward nihilism. Ludwig Wittgenstein and A. J. Ayer ultimately reject traditional philosophy altogether—a kind of despair of knowing anything beyond sense experience. Ayer stated:

> We shall maintain that no statement which refers to a "reality" transcending the limits of all possible sense experience can possibly have any literal significance; from which it must follow that the labors of those who have striven to describe such a reality have all been devoted to the production of nonsense.[30]

Phenomenology, fathered by Kant, though certainly more complex than the new empiricism, still begins in a consciousness that is vague and distorted so that any claim to reality requires effort and more exertion of the will to clarify what the senses may or may not be receiving. For a thing to be known a whole context has to be sought and a great labor of analysis must brood upon the significance of every event. Implicit in phenomenology is a deep distrust of the judgment of sense and all the integrated intuitive powers of knowledge that have been associated with not only poetic knowledge, but all knowledge.

Finally, existentialism, now so widely invoked by theologians and atheists alike, begins with a radical subjectivism that, under the terms of the former is always in danger of "creating" a God so personal as to become private and indistinguishable from man; and, with the latter, rejecting all first principles and meaning, so that suicide can become a positive act against a meaningless and therefore absurd world.

What is the common link that these prevalent modern philosophies have with Descartes? Three can be named: one, they all begin with the consciousness, the mind, as the starting point of reality, as opposed to an independent existence outside the knower; two, doubt, as in the modern scientific mode, is the method of procedure to establish, if possible, certitude, or some experimental social agenda; and, three, following from number two, all these philosophies distrust, if they do not reject, the traditional view that the senses, inner and outer, are intimately integrated in the act of knowing with the will and the intellect, and have, as it were, a cognitive power in themselves, a light whose source is the illuminative energy of the mind that knows reality immediately and certainly.

To summarize, then, in the spirit of Maritain: these modern philosophies stemming from Descartes all violate a primordial disposition of man, doing violence to his very nature as a specific being, who is capable of knowing his world as a *whole* being, integrated and entire, body and soul, recognizing unselfconsciously and spontaneously, that all is real and good. It is only when an exaggerated and isolated status of the mind is assumed, and removed from its proper integration within the knowing powers, that Descartes and his legacy gain prominence.

The implications for education, especially for learning in the poetic mode, as a result of the Cartesian revolution should not be difficult to trace since modern education is dominated, in one way or another, by its influence. Any school of philosophy that claims that one particular science (mathematics and scientific method in the case of Descartes and his followers) must be applied to all other subjects of knowledge, will impose a formal rigor upon the entire curriculum, eliminating even the contemplative nature of mathematics and science. Sooner or later, it is all reduced to "facts." This approach bypasses the contemplative nature of knowledge, leaving the student disconnected from his nature and the nature out there. Alone, though armed with Facts, such a student is likely to become arrogant with a sense of dominance over nature when the universe is seen more and more as an obstacle and problem to be conquered instead of a companion reality to be learned from. In one of the most serious and significant books to emerge from the 1960s and 1970s, *Small Is Beautiful*, its author, E. F. Schumacher, saw where this disintegration of man with nature had led:

> Modern man does not experience himself as a part of nature
> but as an outside force destined to dominate and conquer it.

He even talks of a battle with nature. . . . If Western civilization
is in a state of permanent crisis, it is not far-fetched to suggest
there may be something wrong with its education . . . [and] if
so much reliance is today being placed in the power of education to enable ordinary people to cope with problems thrown
up by scientific and technological progress, then there must be
something more to education. . . . Science and engineering
produce "know how"; but "know-how" is nothing by itself; it is
a means without an end, a mere potentiality. . . . the task of education would be, first and foremost, the transmission of ideas
of value, of what to do with our lives.[31]

Since the older tradition of the West says that we are a part of nature, not isolated from it, it will be only in its contemplation that we
will discover the nature of things intuitively, so that we will know
"what to do with our lives."

In spite of the fact that modern philosophy has either neglected
or rejected traditional metaphysical considerations concerning the
nature of the human being, even questioning if there is such a thing
as human nature, each century nonetheless has heard the voice of
warning not to neglect the spiritual dimension of existence. Prior to
Descartes, the upheavals in Europe leading to the Reformation,
then beginning with the counter-Reformation, the Roman Catholic
Church continued to insist on man's spiritual and therefore superior
nature by retaining in its schools and seminaries the Aristotelian-
Thomist tradition of philosophy. This was true in the church's pro-
fane and sacred studies too, making a conscious effort to emphasize
the contemplative nature of all subjects in the curriculum. For nearly
thirteen hundred years, the church had handed on the doctrine of
faith and morals to its people largely in what this study would call
the poetic mode: the sensory-emotional appeal to the mind experienced in the silence of defused light and shadow of Romanesque
chapels; the use of gold, silver, and jewels for the vessels used at
Mass; later, the stories of the faith told in stained-glass windows; in-
cense, bells, chant, decorated vestments; the measured and dignified
movements that made up the ceremonies, especially of Mass; and,
the ever-present cross often decorated with precious gem stones to
reveal the paradox of victory in suffering and death in the mystery of
the life of Christ. This certainty of the ability of beautiful things to
"teach" the observer religious truths through the sensory powers
illuminated by the intellect is nowhere better expressed than by

Abbot Suger of the twelfth century, writing of the abbey church of St. Denis and the cross there of St. Eloy:

> Thus, when—out of my delight in the beauty of the house of God—the loveliness of the many-colored gems has called me away from external cares, and worthy meditation has induced me to reflect, transforming that which is material to that which is immaterial, on the diversity of the sacred virtues: then it seems to me that I see myself dwelling, as it were, in some strange region of the universe which neither exists entirely in the slime of earth nor entirely in the purity of Heaven; and, that, by the grace of God, I can be transported from the inferior to that higher world in an analogical manner.[32]

In one way or another, all these expressions emerged from the central and official prayer of the church, called the liturgy, as handed down in its longest tradition in the West, in Latin. The liturgy, as a whole, is made up of the prayers, chants, and Scripture readings contained in the Roman Missal for the celebration of Mass and in the Breviary, which contains the psalms, hymns, prayers, and Scripture commentaries that every priest, monk, and religious aspirant is obliged to read several times each day. Because the knowledge of God is not directly proportioned to the reason, St. Thomas Aquinas says the mode of poetry, though defective when compared to metaphysics, is necessary to express supernatural truths and in this way is superior to metaphysics. That is, "poetica scientia" in the "modus symbolicus" is appropriate, not to the *study* of religion, but to the acts of religion, namely, the worship and adoration of God. (I Sent prol., q. 1, a. 5, ad 3.) It is the poetic mode of the liturgy, not its rubrics nor any rational discourse on its interpretation, that calls the mind upward to things of God.

But now, in the Renaissance, and after, while the beauty of the Catholic churches was certainly retained, as well as the liturgy, the emphasis in teaching in the schools was on the appeal primarily to the rational mind with added discursive counterpunching for dealing with the new Protestant theology. Also, after the Reformation and the Council of Trent, there was a growing tendency to *instruct* the Catholic people in the articles of the faith; to admonish and warn them, to preach sermons rather than offer the more meditative homilies—all of this being an understandable reaction given the more defensive position now taken by the church. In other words, priests tended to avoid simply illuminating and digressing poetically on some point from Scripture; they also had to account for the attacks raised by the reformers. The doctrine was preserved intact, but the *style* of teaching through preaching changed, departing from the more personal "from the heart" discourses typical of the Middle Ages, where the priest often drew upon the common experiences of an agrarian and craft culture, where the elements of nature—stars, sun, moon, fields, animals, seasons, and daily family life—served as signs and metaphors of the mysteries of the Christian life.

But after the Council of Trent, when a more systematic approach to explaining the faith is adopted to accommodate and call back the populations of fallen-away Catholics, there is more reliance now on *method*, and the appeal is now more to reason and the rigors of apologetics. There is, as a matter of fact, a movement toward the scientific idea of knowledge in all this that slowly begins to eclipse the confidence in the integrated "judgment of sense" of the human being; where feelings and emotive powers become more and more distrusted by Catholic philosophers and theologians, as the Protestants begin to enshrine the subjective response to religion. Within two hundred years of this great split in religion in Europe, the Cartesian influence is present in the Catholic approach to education and handing on the faith, a faith now presented more as a problem to be explained, a demonstration that requires proof; whereas, the poetically rich expressions of that faith, as given voice by Abbot Suger, St. Francis of Assisi, St. Benedict, St. Bernard of Clairvoux, and St. Bonaventure, are increasingly considered lovely but "accidental" accouterments in the expression of the faith. John Calvin's new "system" of theology and radical interpretation of predestination virtually denied the freedom of the will and assigned to the universe the presence of only one will, God's. This contributed to the overall demoting of the spontaneous and integrated powers of the human being to know the truth, becoming especially suspicious of the transcendentals of beauty and goodness. The narrow and harsh aspects of Calvinism finally worked their way into the Catholic seminaries producing a Catholic version, known as Jansenism, soon to be labeled and condemned as a heresy precisely because of its denial of the human being's powers to naturally, freely know and love God.

Then, there was the reaction to the Cartesian and Empiricist influence that took place in the eighteenth and nineteenth centuries, namely, that time called the Romantic Age. Given the hindsight of the twentieth century, the spirit of the poetic impulse can be found attempting to assert itself in, for example, the work of Jean Jacques Rousseau, William Wordsworth, and Ralph Waldo Emerson, as somewhat representative from the countries of France, England, and America. Again, my treatment here is only cursory but sufficient to demonstrate the presence, and persistence, of poetic knowledge, although shorn of its original integration.

A clear distinction of the new disintegrated view of the knower is easy to see in Rousseau, although it is equally clear Rousseau is searching for the once-familiar presence of, say, the role and power of the senses, as he says in *Emile*.

> He [the child] wants to touch and handle everything: do not check these movements which teach him invaluable lessons. Thus he learns to perceive heat, cold, hardness, softness, weight, or lightness of bodies, to judge their size and shape and all their physical properties, by looking, feeling, listening, and above all, by comparing sight and touch, by judging with the eye what sensation they would arouse when touched.[33]

Furthermore, Rousseau understands perfectly well the traditional psychology of these sensory powers: "His sensations are the raw material of his mind; they should be presented to him in fitting order, so that memory may at future time present them in the same order to his understanding."[34] Rousseau, directly opposed to Descartes' preference for the mind as the starting point of certain knowledge and his ensuing angelism and method of scientific discovery, would instead immerse the child in the sensory world of nature as the first and best teacher and would delay advancing toward any isolated intellectual conclusion:

> May I venture at this point to state the greatest, the most important, the most useful role of education? It is: do not save time, lose it. . . . Let us transform our sensations into ideas, but let us not jump from the sensory to the intellectual.[35]

In his most moving appeal for recognition of the importance of learning proportionate to the senses, as well as for the fulfillment of childhood in general as a distinct age of development, he says:

> Love childhood, indulge its games, its pleasures, its delightful instincts. . . . Why pave the way for future regret for yourselves by robbing them of the short span which nature has allotted

them. As soon as they are aware of the joy of life, let them re-
joice in it, so that whenever God calls them they may not die
without having tasted the joy of life.[36]

And yet, as Rousseau's *Emile* proceeds, one sees that, as perceptive and even traditional as he is concerning the life and role of
the senses, he does not really advance beyond the senses. He fails to
see the real purpose of them as they are integrated with the emotions, will, and intellect—the emotions (via the senses) moved by
wonder; the will, naturally attracted to the good; and, the mind inclined intuitively to the truth.

Also, Rousseau's radical optimism about the nature of the
human being alone in nature denies the self-evident contingencies of
human experience and the pervasive evidence of the human being
to act contrary to happiness. As deftly as he dispenses with the role
of reason, he begins his great work on education by attacking society
and *all* social institutions for introducing evil into the world. "Everything is good as it leaves the hands of the Author of things; everything degenerates in the hands of man. . . . Everything is only folly
and contradiction in human institutions,"[37] he says, and only a return to our primitive (sensory) origins can save us. It is well known
that Rousseau was reacting, understandably, to the influence of
Calvinism and the doctrine of human depravity, as well as to its
Catholic counterpart, Jansenism. But in so reacting he also dismissed what all of philosophical reflection and common observation
had concluded: that man, alone in nature, or in the community of
civilization, consistently acts against his better judgment and therefore is in much need of integrating his sensory-emotional life with
the life of reason, which, in turn, must submit, for true happiness, to
the habits of virtue that frequently call for the reasonable restraint of
sensory-emotional responses that would defeat happiness.

The result of Rousseau's Naturalism produces a radical individualism that not only is torn from the obvious necessity to follow
a teacher of some kind beyond nature, but is also *unnatural* in that it
rejects the natural human faculties of the will and intellect. This naturalism produces an anti-intellectualism and disproportionate glori-
fication of the senses where the will and intellect are directed
downward to an inverted intelligence. For example, Rousseau
boldly exclaims: "Let the child do nothing on anybody's word.
Nothing is good for him unless he feels it to be so."[38]

Because the integration of all the knowing powers is no longer informed by the reality of an objective good, Rousseau's passionate desire for self-sufficiency in the learner leads to alienation, asserting (as it so clearly does) that we learn alone and exclusively in the subjective mode, except for the experience of a very ill-defined nature. Ironically, Rousseau denies the very nature of the Nature that he would have Emile return to, for everywhere in that nature can be seen the lesson of dependency, integration, harmony, and order, which all logically presupposes a larger ordering principle that we, as learners, depend on. One of the natural results of Nature, growth, is that men form societies, no matter how crude and primitive, and pass on knowledge one to another as teachers and students within families, societies, and schools. Only a blindly stubborn vision of a prefallen nature and/or a denial of common experience of man's contradictory nature prevents Rousseau from seeing that social institutions—families, societies, schools—*are* good insofar as they reflect the whole nature of man.

William Wordsworth, though less controversial than Rousseau, and really the most rational of the Romantics, still, in the broad sense, is a child of Rousseau's Naturalism. For the eighteenth and nineteenth centuries, Wordsworth articulates the case for poetic knowledge most profoundly, though more often as a dirge at its passing:

EXPOSTULATION AND REPLY

"Why William, on that old grey stone,
Thus for the length of half a day,
Why, William, sit you thus alone,
And dream your time away?
"Where are your books?—that light bequeathed
To Beings else forlorn and blind!
Up! up! and drink the spirit breathed
From dead men to their kind.
"You look round on your Mother Earth,
As if she for no purpose bore you;
As if you were her first-born birth,
And none had lived before you!"
One morning this, by Esthwaite lake,
When life was sweet, I knew not why,

To me my good friend Matthew spake,
And thus I made reply:
"The eye—it cannot choose but see;
We cannot bid the ear be still;
Our bodies feel, where'er they be,
Against or with our will.
"Nor less I deem that there are Powers
Which of themselves our minds impress:
That we can feed this mind of ours
In a wise passiveness.
"Think you, 'mid all this mighty sum
Of things for ever speaking,
That nothing of itself will come,
But we must still be seeking?'
"—Then ask not wherefore, here, alone,
Conversing as I may,
I sit upon this old grey stone,
And dream my time away."

From one point of view, the whole poem is an argument, mildly hostile, a dialogue of deep dispute, about the entire question of man's purpose, what we should know, and how we should learn. It is a gentle and characteristic touch of Wordsworth that his opponent is a "good friend." But that does not alter the real division of ideas that separates the speakers. Matthew is concerned that William is wasting time, a response, in this context, that is ignorant of real leisure and at the same time underlines the ascendancy of the materialistic view of man where our existence is defined first by *doing* rather than *being*. Matthew argues for books, that is, the intellectual approach to nature without which, he believes, we are "forlorn and blind." Without the protection of books, he fears William will be merely dreaming. Here, Descartes' insistence on clear and distinct ideas comes to mind, and the "work" implied in Kant's emphasis on *ratio*, rather than the *simplex intuitus* of the knowing powers. Wordsworth calmly answers so as to instruct Matthew on how we know in the poetic mode, how it all begins in leisure:

The eye—it cannot choose but see;
We cannot bid the ear be still;

Our bodies feel, where'er they be,
Against or with our will.

This is the complete trust in the integration of the senses, emotions, and the mind, to know what is beautiful, good, and true, "In wise passiveness," where our "Powers," that is, all the faculties of body and soul, "of themselves our minds impress." Wordsworth says that to know and be certain of reality, and its goodness, one does not need to be "ever speaking," as in discourse, or "still be seeking," as in doubt. Matthew is worried that William will be "alone," that he will be cut off and will miss reality without the aide of books and activity; whereas, Wordsworth, along with the ancients and the tradition prior to Descartes, is very much engaged with reality— sympathetically, connaturally—and quite content in being still and, in this sense, to "dream."

There is a remarkable story surrounding the works of Wordsworth and a contemporary of his not unlike the character of Matthew from the poem just quoted. It is a story that is dramatically illustrative of the necessity of poetic knowledge.

The boy genius and articulator of Utilitarianism, John Stuart Mill, reveals in his *Autobiography* that as a result of his father's efforts to actually educate him to become a genius in the Rationalist tradition, bypassing if not indeed rejecting altogether the poetic mode as anything serious, eventually led to his depression and thoughts of suicide. When Mill, fortunately, begins to realize the cause of his emptiness, perhaps not a better example exists in English of the consequences of elevating all knowledge to the critical and analytical. Mill recalls:

> I saw . . . that the habit of analysis has a tendency to wear away the feelings: as indeed it has, when no other mental habit is cultivated, and the analyzing spirit remains without its natural complements and correctives.[39]

This was no mere mood or fit of melancholy:

> I was thus . . . left stranded at the commencement of my voyage, with a well-equipped ship and a rudder, but no sail; without any real desire for the ends which I had been so carefully fitted out to work for: no delight in virtue, or the general good,

but also just as little in anything else. . . . There seemed no power in nature sufficient to begin the formation of my character anew, and create in a mind now irretrievable analytic, fresh associations of pleasure with any of the objects of human desire.[40]

Then, as if by accident, as Mill says, he finds himself reading a book of Marmontel's—*Memories*—that recounts the death of the author's father when he was still a young boy. Suddenly, the scene fills Mill with compassion and he is moved to tears. At this moment, Mill says, all darkness was lifted. Vicariously, he had experienced the emotions he had so long neglected. By the act of sympathetic (and spontaneous) knowledge he had *become* Marmontel and, in so doing, had experienced the powers of his whole nature: "I had now learnt by experience that the passive susceptibilities need to be cultivated as well as the active capacities, and required to be nourished and enriched as well as guided."[41] But this was just the beginning, and it is here that the knowledge of poetry cultivates the poetic in Mill:

> This state of my thoughts and feelings made the fact of my reading Wordsworth for the first time (in the autumn of 1828), an important event in my life. . . . These poems addressed themselves powerfully to one of the strongest of my pleasurable suspectibilities, the love of rural objects and natural scenery. . . . What made Wordsworth's poems a medicine for my state of mind, was that they expressed, not mere outward beauty, but states of feeling, and of thought colored by feeling, under the excitement of beauty. They seemed to be the very culture of the feelings, which I was in quest of. . . . I needed to be made to feel that there was real, permanent happiness in tranquil contemplation. Wordsworth taught me this, not only without turning away from, but with a greatly increased interest in the common feelings and common destiny of human beings. . . . The result was that I gradually, but completely, emerged from my habitual depression, and was never again subject to it.[42]

There are two very important points to note here. First, Mill is introduced to the "permanent happiness of tranquil contemplation," which occurs as a result of noticing nature in the poetic, and not the scientific, mode. Pantheism and appeals to mystical experience are avoided in this way, since the objects of nature will obviously pass away but not the contemplation of their beauty, which, as one of the transcendentals of being, is therefore a spiritual immutable quality. Poetry, especially of the lyric kind, and poetic knowledge, do not give mystical experience in the religious sense, but do touch on these permanent things Mill desires, that is to say, poetic knowledge reaches to the eternal and thereby gives rest to the soul. Second, Mill, as a result of the cultivation of his emotions "under the excitement of beauty," is drawn closer to, not apart from, his fellow human beings. The notion of becoming self-indulgent, eccentric, and isolated as the result of being under the influence of poetry is an image from the radical romanticism of a Baudelaire or Poe. With Mill, it is the normal integrating and balancing influence of discovering the poetic in life that is clearly seen. It is poetry and the poetic sense of things that give *form* and meaning to his feelings and draws him closer into the human family.

As a final generalization from his experience, and consistent with the insights of poetical education beginning with Socrates, Mill concludes that "unpoetical natures are precisely those which require poetic cultivations."[43]

Wordsworth's ability to awaken and cultivate the poetic sensibilities did not end, by any means, with Mill. John Ruskin, living at about the same time as both men and having had, like Mill, the dubious honor of being a child prodigy, "was ruined before his thirteenth birthday. He was ruined, one qualifies, in terms of his fully human potential."[44] In this case, it was the paintings of J. M. W. Turner first, then the poetry of Wordsworth, and to a lesser extent, Shelley, that matured Ruskin's insights into poetic knowledge. In Ruskin can be heard again the awareness of the degrees and distinctions of knowledge, especially the difference between science and art, "the difference between the mere botanist's knowledge of plants, and the great poet's or painter's knowledge of them. . . . The one notes their distinctions for the sake of swelling his herbarium, the other, that he may render them vehicles of expression and emotion."[45] It also appears that Ruskin has arrived at, by whatever means, the exact difference between metaphysical knowledge that describes causes and poetic knowledge that takes us, by way of sympathetic, connatural knowledge, into the experience of the thing itself: "The metaphysician's definition fails yet more utterly, when we look at the imagination neither as regarding, nor combining, but as penetrating."[46] Likewise, it is clear that Ruskin is fully aware of the traditional understanding of the interior sense, imagination, and how it possesses a near-metaphysical impulse due to its integrated involvement with the intellect:

> The imagination will banish all that is extraneous; it will seize out of the many threads of different feeling which nature has suffered to become entangled, one only . . . so that all its work looks as pure and true as nature itself. . . . Imagination . . . the faculty itself, called by what name we will, I insist upon as the highest intellectual power of man. There is no reasoning in it; it works not by algebra, nor by integral calculus; it is a piercing pholas-like mind's tongue, that works and tastes into the very rock heart; no matter what the subject submitted to it, substance or spirit.[47]

In addition to Ruskin's contribution to the tradition of poetic knowledge in terms of connatuality, he also understands that while such knowledge lacks the precision of science, yet it discovers something more significant than particular exactitude, especially, for example, in the words of poets:

> There is in every word set down by the imaginative mind an awful under-current of meaning, an evidence and shadow upon it of the deep places out of which it has come. It is often obscure, often half-told . . . but, if we choose to dwell upon it and trace it, it will lead us always securely back to that metropolis of the soul's dominion.[48]

And, in contrast, in the absence of imagination:

> I believe it will be found that the entirely unimaginative mind *sees* nothing of the object it has to dwell upon or describe, and is therefore utterly unable, as it is blind itself, to set anything before the eyes of the reader.[49]

Whereas, Ruskin concludes, "The imagination sees the heart and inner nature, and makes them felt, but is often obscure, mysterious, and interrupted, in its giving of outer detail."[50]

As eloquent and accurate a statement as all this is for the life of the poetic mode in its sensory powers, the Romantics, in their reaction to Rationalism, tended to isolate the passions and the imagination and then to distribute them as the supreme powers of knowledge. Ruskin claims, above, for example, that the imagination is the highest intellectual faculty. Perhaps Wordsworth less than the others, but the Romantic movement in its more radical expressions, forgot that poetic knowledge is cognitive, that is, that the emotions, being cognitive powers, are not mere feelings but intimately integrated with the intelligence.

By the nineteenth century these European reactions in philosophy and literature are given expression in America by, among others, Ralph Waldo Emerson. In Emerson can be heard something of Plato, Aristotle, Buddha, Rousseau, usually in bits and pieces. Nonetheless, the cause for poetic knowledge over the scientific clearly emerges: "The imagination must be addressed. Why always coast on the surface and never open the interior of Nature, not by science, which is surface still, but by poetry?"[51]

Emerson, as a member of the Brookfarm experience, understands very well how contact between the whole person, the body-soul composite of the human being, is a prerequisite for higher learning, grounded in things, not ideas: "A man should have a farm or mechanical craft for his welfare. We must have a basis for our higher accomplishment, our delicate entertainments of poetry and philosophy, in the work of our hands."[52]

All true, as far as it goes, but the integration of former times is missing in Emerson's work, that is, the harmony of the senses, emotions, will, and intellect, as well as the integrated society of a preindustrial culture. Now the emphasis remains on the individual, alone in a materialistic world, more and more entangled in a political context, struggling to fulfill a transcendent nature in an increasingly mundane industrial democracy. One senses in Emerson that the reason only part of the poetic mode is understood and emphasized is because American society is already splintered and disintegrated from the principles of an harmonious society, torn then as now between the two dehumanizing economic systems of socialism and liberal capitalism. Emerson considers education as a logical place to begin a reform for reawakening the poetic mode in man but, with a kind of despair, concludes: "I confess myself utterly at a loss in suggesting particular reforms in our ways of teaching."[53] At best, teaching for what he understands of the poetic life of the soul becomes subversive:

> I advise teachers to cherish mother-wit. I assume that you will
> keep the grammar, reading, writing, and arithmetic in order;

'tis easy and of course you will. But smuggle in a little contraband wit, fancy, imagination, thought.[54]

These last are appeals to the lively mind, for "wit" is a spontaneous
way of seeing, as in a *witness*, one who sees and has the evidence of
experience in his memory; and "fancy," not to be confused with its
contemporary opposite, *fantasy*, is a traditional term for poetry that
offers itself to the intellect in pictures of real things in the imagination. In Emerson's estimation, this process, this "contraband," is indeed cognitive—it leads, he says, to "thought."

Admittedly, these voices from France, England, and America
have been presented in a most general way. However, they are representative of the reaction to the wound received to the integrated
view of man, as well as carrying within themselves an incomplete
view of pre-Cartesian integrated psychology. Evidence of the depth
of this wound is seen in that even though they champion what resembles intuitive knowledge, they themselves are disintegrated from
the whole vision of man held by the classical and medieval tradition
of psychology and epistemology. This is understandable: they speak
from a world now dominated by science, mechanized war, and the
materialistic view of nearly everything. It is a world intoxicated—or
depressed, or both—by the biological determinism of Darwin's theory of evolution, the material determinism of Marx, and Freud's theory of the unconscious and dark drives that account for man's
behavior. The rise of capitalism with its radical individualism, resulting in larger populations harshly separated by greater differences in
real goods and wealth; a deepening subjectivity in philosophy and
religion; all continue to contribute to an overall *Zeitgeist* of loneliness,
alienation, and increasingly desperate behavior. Two Industrial
Revolutions pass, displacing not just rural workers but the village
craftsmen and shopkeepers, so that an entire way of life is swept
away, a life not only closer to the poetic foundation of civilization in
its work, games, music, and art but also closer to the ancient ideals of
justice, which had been the *raison d'être* of Plato's great contribution
to Western culture, *The Republic*.

Without a real and spiritual vision of life, that is, without the
habit of living out the poetic mode and all its material and immaterial satisfactions, *money* comes to represent the tangible prize of materialism for the West, its accumulation into the hands of a relative few
becomes the new trophy for having conquered a new adversarial re-

ality: nature. England felt this revolution more keenly than all of Europe, and the English poets and writers wrote painfully of the death involved. Oliver Goldsmith has "celebrated" this end of a way of life for England, but really for all the Western world as well:

> Ill fares the land, to hastening ills a prey,
> Where wealth accumulates, and men decay:
> Princes and lords may flourish, or may fade;
> A breath can make them, as a breath had made;
> But a bold peasantry, their country's pride,
> When once destroyed, can never be supplied.
> A time there was ere England's griefs began,
> When every rood of ground maintained its man;
> For him light Labour spread her wholesome store,
> Just gave what life required, but gave no more:
> His best companions, innocence and health;
> And his best riches, ignorance of wealth.

I would insist that to point out this demise in Western civilization stemming from the rejection of man's integrated nature, and the rejection of his poetic nature in particular, is no mere "nostalgia trip" or intransigent refusal to live with the realities of the twentieth century. The voices, similar to Goldsmith's, were widespread in his day, and they continue down to the present time in one way or another. For example, as I mentioned in chapter 2, Cornelis Verhoeven's study of the separation of wonder from philosophy reveals the devastating effects on education. According to Verhoeven, what passes for general education today is actually a barrier to knowledge in the absence of the poetic element of wonder.

> General education is . . . a substitute for knowledge among people for whom that knowledge is too dangerous and too demanding. . . . It creates and preserves mediocrity. It does not demand that contact with things, the piercing of man's self-righteous subjectivity which is precisely the beginning of knowledge. . . . At best it displays mountain peaks, but saves one the trouble of climbing them.[55]

Verhoeven continues to describe, exactly and passionately, the result of distributing the scientific mode of knowledge throughout the education experience:

The great temptation of education is to insist that one should memorize the results of science instead of flinging open its sources. This is why it costs us so much trouble in later life to delve deeper into what we have learned in a bookish and thus apodictic, authoritarian, and quasi-definitive manner. All too often at school the curiosity that might lead to closer acquaintance is nipped in the bud, and we are left with a collection of slogans and quotations that we call general education. This then is our portion of the fuss and bother they call science and, having lived through it, we can go on to other things. We have "had" it at school, but we have not got it, it has not got us, and we will never get it. Unless some intellectual crisis intervenes we are, after such a schooling, condemned to lifelong mediocrity.[56]

However, the poetic mode in education did survive, barely, and it is time to locate its understanding and implementation in the nineteenth and twentieth centuries.

5

Voices for Poetic Knowledge
after Descartes

We must teach beauty not from horror of ugliness but rather
attraction to beauty. Beauty should ignore ugliness as the
God of Aristotle ignored an imperfect world.
Charles Péguy

My original plan for this study of poetic knowledge included
an extensive section on an experimental school in Maslacq,
France, founded in 1940 and lasting approximately ten years. André
Charlier, the school's founder and headmaster, based this school on
the traditional principles of what we have described here as the poetic mode and its application to education. All of the background on
this school is written in French, and it soon became clear that to
translate all that was necessary for a full description of the school at
Maslacq was a task beyond the present work. However, I have ren-
dered a few freely translated documents of André Charlier, and
from one of his former students, that give an insight into the general
mood and style of the school.

André Charlier had possessed a career as a musician but had
also been drawn to the military life, and had become a French offi-
cer during World War II and a resistor to the German occupation.
After the war, he became a professor at a university in Normandy
and by all accounts remained a solitary man until the opening of the
experimental school at Maslacq.

The setting of Maslacq is an example of the thoughtful consideration to beauty so that the location of the school can be said to
teach in the poetic mode just as strongly as the approach to the curriculum. André Charlier said:

There was to Maslacq a charm that all who came in contact with it felt. The thing about something that charms is that one doesn't really know what it is. I often wondered about this myself, when in the hottest days of summer I was more or less alone in the castle where the silence and the freshness had an extraordinary quality. I always had difficulty deciding to take the train to ever go elsewhere. . . . When one walked the countryside, either on the heights of Castetner or in the desolate and small valley of Sauvelade with its monastic church, one could believe himself to be far from this world. . . . Carts are still pulled by cows, more than by oxen, which goes without saying is not too favorable to the production of milk. These carts have short axles and cannot carry heavy loads. The paths, between two hedge rows, are just large enough to allow these carts to pass. Therefore, one doesn't pass such a road quickly, and furthermore, one doesn't find a reason to go more quickly.[1]

And a student arriving at Maslacq in November of 1940, Gérard Calvet (now Dom Gerard, Benedictine Abbot of Monastère Ste. Madeleine, at Le Barroux, France), remembers well these same carts:

We arrived at night fall, going from Orthez to Maslacq, in a cart pulled by a mule that advanced slowly under a fine rain. How my heart beat while entering the big dark castle! Fortunately, my big brother was there with me. The same evening, Mr. Garrone wished us all welcome, and recalled that France was not in mourning at this return, though each of us must have resembled such a a state.[2]

André Charlier continues with his description of the "playground" of his students:

The village is laid out in rows, where, among the small hills, there are houses of the peasants who live peacefully rising with the sun each day and surrounded by a grand solitude. . . . In this village outside the castle, there are two manorial houses, modest but with an air of distinction. The hand of the grand French peasantry has touched the nobility of the rooftops, the shape of the barn doors and the chimneys. . . . I often leave the farm of the castle just to contemplate this work of art that no carpenter or architect of today could conceive. It is all proportionate to the soul . . . all of this spoke to the mind a more intelligible language than that of good books.[3]

Of course, good books were necessary, and Dom Gerard gives an insight to Charlier's way of teaching:

> From an infantry captain, he became again a teacher, an excellent teacher, who taught his pupils to *speak* in Latin. . . . I [also] remember exactly a text of Péguy that André Charlier came to read to us, as he often did in the large study of the castle.[4]

We learn from these brief recollections and elsewhere that André Charlier taught his students to speak Latin by simply speaking Latin to them; that he read aloud to them first so that the music and the gymnastic of the language could be absorbed; that, as a musician, he taught them to sing by singing the songs of their traditions and simple Gregorian chants; and, as important as all the rest of their formal education, he gave them a cold and drafty castle but with warm fires in the old fireplaces of the great halls; he gave them the outdoors of Maslacq, the village, the peasants and their farms and crafts, the narrow roads, the hills and the shepherds.

More than ten years later, after the closing of the school, André Charlier spoke directly, as well as he could, about what had taken place at Maslacq: "It is a thing of which I would be incapable to explain, because I don't know what I made there. . . . We were a handful of friends—students and professors—who were open to one another and to the taste of the truth."[5] There is profound importance in these simple, brief sentences as to the understanding of a school in the poetic mode. It is clear from the first comment that Charlier was a spontaneous and unpretentious man himself, willing to allow himself to be lead by the principles he believed in rather than imposing the reigning Cartesian curriculum of his day. And when he mentions that the school in essence was "a handful of friends," of teachers and students, who had tasted the truth together, then we have arrived at the beginning and the end of all education as understood in the context of this book. I will return to this theme in the conclusion of chapter 7.

But note well that the poetic education that took place at Maslacq was accompanied by a kind of rigorous regard for order. This is especially necessary in dealing with adolescents, and even more true for the boarding school for young boys that André Charlier founded. All his military background and poetic common sense comes to bear on this issue when he addresses the older students, his

"Captains," or dormitory leaders, who will be caring for the younger students. The difference here though is that the order is to be seen as natural and good and not foreign and imposed for the sake of discipline without a reason. In other words, the order that Charlier asks his Captains to help maintain is not a good in itself—as if to enshrine a mechaninistic showpiece of merely "well-behaved boys." The order is called for so that, as he says, souls can bloom. And discipline, for Charlier, is something that cannot be imposed by words and commands—first, the Captains must be a living example of what they ask of others, then only a few words are necessasry for correction. The end of these aspects of education such as order and discipline are never isolated as ends in themselves but are viewed as the giving of a higher good to all and the means to cultivate friendship. The following is taken from Charlier's first letter to his Captains, written September 27, 1942, after the first two years of the school's existence. The writing of these letters was a practice he continued over the years as well as his practice of reading to them and his teaching of Latin and music.

> Now that the return to school approaches, remember that it won't be any less difficult than last year, because you will have a lot of new friends. Our present building unites us all, only too numerous, in one house; whereas, we are large enough now to have two houses. However, it is necessary that we have a good beginning, otherwise the whole year will be compromised. I want to give you my instructions in writing so that there is not a possibility of uncertainty. I will first put you on guard against dangers of your function. There is, first of all, small dangers in the privileges that one concedes you, and that you interpret gladly as an excuse for greater freedoms to which you believe you have the right. But nothing is more false. Your function, rather, is service. You must be more demanding on yourselves than you are on others. You will never succeed in creating real discipline if you permit yourselves what is refused to others. Today's children are not accustomed to ever forcing themselves; above all they unconsciously look for what is pleasing to them. So, at Les Roches [the actual school by the village of Maslacq], if we do not succeed in correcting this tendency, we will have missed our mission and we are lost. I want Captains that are the most exact, the most hard-working, the most disciplined, and the most anxious for order from all points of view. I warn you that it will often fall to me to refuse you what you will

ask. But you will accept this if you remember that I must always have in view the general interest of the community, something that often escapes you. As a result, I don't want recrimination from you, but your joyful obedience.

The other danger, and one that is fundamental, is that you often pretend to think you can form your younger friends. You see what this supposes: you believe that your own character is perfectly shaped and that you are capable of directing yourselves. Be modest. Be humble. . . . What I ask above all from you, is to be rigorously strict about everything that pertains to the material order of the house. . . . It is necessary to create conditions of life so the soul can bloom. Order is one of these primordial conditions that should be working within you. Then, you will always be ready to help your friends in their difficulties and in their pains, small or big. . . . Goodness must be one of your qualities of predeliction. . . . But don't try to act as if you are chaplains — if you are living examples, two words will be sufficient to straighten out any problem. Especially don't try to be shrewd, that is, to appear what you are not: you will immediately be discredited. I insist therefore on this point as the most important of your role: you must be essentially creatures of a certain order. This order is necessary for every living soul in the house. Everything that you will do, even in the smallest of details, will do as much as anything to win the creation of this order. Don't believe this is unworthy of you, it is all important: the cleanliness of the house, the strict accurateness of boys in all acts of their life, their belongings, their language. It belongs to you to make sure that all is clean in gestures and in words. Perceive slackness, vulgarity, and cheating, as if these were a curse. I want boys that are upright, that look you in the eye, and who speak firmly. I tell you again: be humble. I repeat: don't count too much on yourselves. Look for strength where it is: only the spiritual view can give it to you. And it will give to you the radiance that illuminates your souls and the desire to pass it to others.[6]

Notice there is not one word in this opening letter for the new school year about studies or homework or grades. Nor are the recurring themes of order and humility in Charlier's letter a departure from the poetic mode, though it may sound at first like the old saws of moralist education. Rather, these habits of virtue are all mentioned as means to the end of the cultivation of an inner goodness that will illuminate their souls. In this way the Captains are not to become clones and rational robots of a rule-enforcing headmaster, but instead, because their own obedience is to be joyful, they are to be living examples of order and goodness and humility so that only a few words should be required when problems arise among the younger pupils. The goal here is always to help friends (he does not refer to them as students), in their difficulties as a result of a soul ordered to self-discipline through a poetic sympathy with the harmony of order and friendship.

A good portion of a book by André's artist brother and philosophical ally—Henri Charlier's *Culture, École, Métier*—was translated into English exclusively for this chapter.

Henri Charlier begins where one must for a genuine renewal in education along traditional lines—not with buildings, texts, or even students, but the teachers themselves and their formation. It must be remembered, reading Charlier, that by the nineteenth century the schools and seminaries in France were informed by the spirit of the Cartesian method with scientific principles being applied to all subjects of the curriculum. The system appropriate to mathematics had been imposed on all branches of knowledge and was the style in which teachers for these schools were trained. Edmund J. King has observed, with many others, that

> The Frenchman wants a short-cut to the "principles"—or at least to the theoretical part of the curriculum which can be mastered intellectually and stored in the mind for passing competitive examinations which lead to good jobs. An approach to learning by way of experiment and experience does not much appeal to French educators. . . . In fact, Frenchmen are proud to boast that their educational system is "Cartesian." Descartes stressed that the intellect is paramount; for him it was the rational process, not the near-animal propensities of the body, that gave man his essence. Instead of encouraging educators to think of personality as a harmony of complementary activities, the French view emphasizes the ascetic cultivation of "the mind." "We are priests of the intellect," says the representative teacher.[7]

Writing within the context of a Cartesian formation of teachers in France, Henri Charlier points out that the tradition of the crafts and trades have more in common with integrated learning than the present system for training teachers:

> It never occurs to the teachers themselves that the methods through which they form their minds are not universal at all, as they believe—but very peculiar to schools. This peculiar art is very favorable to didactic demonstration and very handy when forming other teachers—it is the art of logic interpreted through language. But all the trades (crafts) have another logic which is not taught except in the trades themselves, and this absence is one of the aspects of what is called the crisis in teaching.[8]

Charlier is invoking the sensory-intellectual connection contained within traditional crafts where the "logic" of one step naturally following another is experienced more by the whole person, engaging more of the powers of the learner, than by the abstract appeal to the intellect alone. Remember that the context here is twentieth-century French schools where, for example, an entire course in physics can be taught from a book without one actual demonstration of an inclined plane, or the action of a lever or pulley, where all such laws from nature are reduced to mathematical problem solving using numbers and symbols to stand for gravity, leverage, and so on.

In spite of some superficial affinities in terms of learning by doing, no doubt Dewey and Charlier would disagree in the ranking of final ends and metaphysical assumptions; that is, what education is and what it is for. For example, Dewey focuses on perfecting some skill to be set later in a larger social context of a smooth-running democracy; whereas, Charlier sees in the craft of, say, carpentry a self-perfecting of the student whereby the student will see poetically (that is, with sensory and estimative sense) the invisible principle of some logical necessity. He explains:

> A child learns logic just as well by adjusting a tenon and mortise as by doing a math problem; the necessity is the same, but the logical aspect of it is *interdependence* and not deduction. . . . In fact, there is in the craft a logical view, a visible necessity which is the logical archetype in almost any trade. The, "I think, therefore, I am," of Descartes is the archetype of all the absur-

dities verbal logic ends up with. This "therefore" corresponds to nothing real whatsoever. It would mean that one knows of his existence only because one knows one thinks! Actually, what one has is, "I am thinking." It is a statement impossible to deny. But to make existence depend on the fact that one thinks is to be a dupe of the necessities of language, and the mathematical language to which Descartes was accustomed, is worse. The more the system of verbal (and mathematical) logic is reinforced, the harder the academic requirements become; the more they are pushed in the same direction, the denser the exams become. Also, the more anxiety will be felt because this system is not suited for most minds for observation and reasoning.[9]

Therefore, Charlier says that for teachers "it is indispensable that teaching break loose from a sort of academism of letters or of thought which tends to judge of everything by means of general ideas. . . . Teaching must fill up with intellectual *experience* and not with ready-made formulas."[10] So out of touch with reality and *la nature des choses* (the nature of things), so preoccupied with the cultivation of the intellect cut off from the life of the senses, Charlier says, that the closer teachers come, "to the trade workshop the better they will be, because the crisis in teaching is nothing else but the crisis in the intellectual apprenticeship."[11] This is not unlike the understanding Socrates had for the necessity of what he called "gymnastic" for his beginners, to learn the interdependence of the sensory faculties in contact with nature and crafts. This is learning in the poetic mode, and, for Charlier, to learn by language alone is simply the opposite of gymnastic and the logic of crafts. Language means the realm of formulas and general ideas bereft of their actual antecedents. Under such teaching, there will be no images offered to the memory of the real things placed there by actual experience of the way things are. Concerning the necessity of images formed from sensory contact with the real world and kept in the memory, indispensable for learning, recall Charlier's comment on Descartes and the emphasis given to the language of logic, and it is clear that one cannot simply *think*; one has to think about some *thing*. This requires that there be an image in the memory upon which the intellect can gaze. Education that is forced to teach in the realm of abstract ideas formed from mere language is virtually impossible—one cannot imagine ideas without the interdependence of concrete things. As Charlier says, through the crafts, as his example of sensory knowledge, we remotely (poetically) approach metaphysical reality: "Logic learned by the carpenter's apprentice conforms more to Being than logic learned through language."[12] In this way, the scientific method of education has even debased the real study of science. However, there was at least one French scientist in the nineteenth century, the renowned entomologist, Henri Fabre, who would have agreed completely with Charlier. Against the trend of his times to simply perpetuate the lifeless museum idea of the study of insects, Fabre was the scientist of tireless, naked-eye observation of living things out in the weeds and sedges and hills of Provence. He dramatically recorded what he saw in his "Laboratory of the Open Fields," and in thousands of pages of careful and affectionate observations. Charles Darwin called Fabre the "incomparable observer."[13] How deeply Henri Fabre intuitively understood the poetic mode as applied to real science is everywhere in his reflections:

> Others again have reproached me with my style, which has not the solemnity, nay, better, the dryness of the schools. They fear lest a page that is read without fatigue should not always be the expression of the truth. Were I to take their word for it, we are profound only on condition of being obscure. Come here, one and all of you — you, the sting-bearers, and you, the wing-cased armour-clads—take up my defense and bear witness in my favor—tell of the intimate terms on which I live with you, of the patience with which I observe you, of the care with which I record your actions. . . . And then, my dear insects, if you cannot convince these good people, because you do not carry the weight of tedium, I, in my turn, will say to them: "you rip up the animal and I study it alive; you turn it into an object of horror and pity, whereas I cause it to be loved; you labor in a torture-chamber and dissecting-room, I make observations under the blue sky to the song of Cicadas . . . you pry into death, I pry into life." And why should I not complete my thought: the boars have muddied the clear stream; natural history, youth's glorious study, has, by dint of cellular improvements, become a hateful and repulsive thing.[14]

At the turn of the century in America there was a lone voice that also understood the need for and the wisdom of *la nature des choses* and the need to fill up first on experience from the real world, as Charlier called for. Dr. Thomas Shields, professor of education at

Catholic University, recalled in his autobiography, *The Making and Unmaking of a Dullard,* that his inability as a school boy to grasp the simplest lessons of arithmetic was eventually lifted and illuminated by the natural surroundings of his life on a Minnesota farm with the day-to-day chores of that life. "The constant variety of scene and of occupation that came with the changing seasons provided me with the best possible sensory motor training. This training formed the basis of all my subsequent mental development."[15]

Here are many clear examples of the major principles that form the foundation of prescientific, pre-Cartesian learning.

> The physical development which I have referred to rather than described, was of course not directed in accordance with any theory or with any deliberate view of education. . . . It must be remembered that the work was not that of a factory; it kept a boy out-of-doors and in close contact with nature, and it was not confined to any one occupation . . . all the senses were appealed to in turn. The smell of the fresh up-turned soil, the perfume of the wild rose, and the odor of the new-mown hay are still with me, as are the calls of the cat-bird, the whistle of the bobilink, the humming of the bees.[16]

Over two thousand years earlier Socrates had called for such experiences as the foundation for dialectic, when he prescribed in *The Republic* that

> our youth dwell in a land of health, and fair sights and sounds, and receive the good in everything; and beauty, the effluence of fair works, shall flow into the eye and ear, like a health-giving breeze from a purer region, and insensibly draw the soul from earliest years into likeness and sympathy with the beauty of reason.[17]

All around Shields is the poetic world from which he stores up image after image in the memory upon which all later reflections on the nature of things will brood:

> With these sights and sounds of nature are inseparably entwined in the tangled skein of memory the outward signs of a human activity that blended with nature's processes. I can still feel on my feet the soft, wet moss of the meadow bottoms, and see the rhythm of the twenty mowers, and hear the swish of the

scythes through the soft grass, and the music of the whetstones on the steel blades.[18]

As poetic as these impressions are, they are not poetry. Shields was not a poet in the sense that Frost was; rather, he was a man who knew the thrill and value of poetic experience and has recalled how such experience of the senses leads directly to knowledge; in his case, to measurement and number, the arithmetic concepts in school he had been at a loss to comprehend:

> We used to raise several thousand bushels of grain on our farm. When I was a boy of nine or ten, it was my task to "hold sacks"; that is, I held the bag while my father emptied into it three half-bushels of grain. Each time the measure was emptied, I lifted the bag so as to pack down the grain; in this way I learned through the sense of sight and through muscle sense the size and weight of a half bushel, a bushel, and a bushel and half of grain. This experience was repeated over and over again thousands of times each year. I was also in the habit of counting the sacks as we stood them up against each other, until I became able to recognize with a fair degree of accuracy when there were in the pile twenty sacks, the number that made a load.[19]

Now, notice the gradual progression from the necessity of material objects and the sensory experience of them to the reliance upon the image in the memory, to concept:

> In the years that followed I tied and weighed a great many thousand bushels of wheat, but never, I think, without mentally calculating the bushels and pounds . . . although I soon learned to dispense with the use of my fingers in counting and dealt wholly with sense images; but they were sense images of real bushels of wheat and not artificial symbols of which children's minds are sometimes fed.[20]

This is precisely the order of learning called for by Charlier and helps to explain his use of examples from the trades and crafts as the "teachers" of interdependence and Being.

Shields goes on to recount the numerous examples of how his eyes and ears were trained and how, through "muscle sense" in using a hand saw, he was able to judge the thickness of wood and to judge with accuracy the length of boards in putting up and replacing fence. In this way all manner of spatial relationships were mastered, concepts he was unable to understand from books used at school. It was always the power of images and memory that led him from the wonder of reality to understanding, as opposed to the Cartesian influence that followed an abstracted method of learning: "These memory pictures played a much larger role in my case than they do in the systematic training that is usually given in the schools where the children deal with actual blocks of all sizes and shapes."[21]

Thomas Shields, remarkably, went on to become a Roman Catholic priest as well as a professor of education at Catholic University—this farm boy who had been labeled a "dullard." This particular history of his makes his following reflections on physics and education even more poignant for the role of the poetic mode:

> A large part of mechanics naturally grows out of a knowledge of the lever. And, during the haying season each year, the constant use of the haypole and pitchfork gave me a thorough knowledge of the lever. . . . When we begin to teach mechanics with deducting from abstract principles, we are simply reverting the natural order of the mind's growth . . . [and] when our enthusiasm for the inductive method leads us to overwhelm our pupils with a multitude of details before they have obtained a general view of the subject, the usual result is an uncoordinated mass of facts, from which the pupils are unable to extract the great fundamental truths; and without these truths there can be little real progress toward the mastery of any science. . . . [Therefore] to begin the teaching of mechanics with the definition of a machine as a transformer of energy is a very different thing from beginning to study the same subject in its concrete, germinal form, the lever.[22]

Over and over again, Shields demonstrates with examples, the ancient discoveries that the bodily senses possess a kind of cognitive power, and, therefore, there can be no knowledge unless it first pass through these senses. In the next passage, there is a comparison by Shields that is the same made by Charlier when the latter spoke of the ability of the student to grasp the principles of logic through carpentry. Shields says:

> Young children, in playing with a see-saw, come to understand the meaning of the lever of equal and unequal arms long before

their minds are sufficiently developed to grasp the meaning of
abstract definitions and mathematical formulae.[23]

And, like the Charlier brothers, Shields notices the deep interdependence of things that is grasped by children in this play:

> They understand that a downward pressure on one arm of the
> lever is changed into an upward on the other arm, and it does
> not take them long to discover that a child sitting out on one
> end of the see-saw will balance two or more children seated
> near the fulcrum on the other end. They understand, too, that
> the longer the arm, the larger the movement. In this way there
> is laid up in the minds of the children a secure foundation for
> the future study of the science of physics.[24]

Again, this is exactly the filling up of experience that Charlier speaks
of so necessary for an integrated knowledge of reality. Shields then
recalls his own discovery of the principle of mechanics, the lever, in
his experience with the pitchfork:

> The concept of the lever is developed much more fully by the
> use of the pitchfork ... [the weight] is at one end and the
> power and fulcrum are one in each hand of the hay maker. If
> the right hand be held in the middle of the fork handle and the
> left hand at the extreme end, twice the weight of the hay is sus-
> tained by the right hand while a downward pressure equal to
> the weight of the hay is exerted by the left hand. Now, the rela-
> tive positions of the hands on the fork handle are constantly
> shifting, and so the haymaker learns through his muscle sense
> the meaning of the relative positions of the lever as it moves
> round the axis rotation.[25]

It was just such farm-life experiences that awakened Shields's
intellectual life. And it was this "dullard" who one day noticed in
sheer delight that the principle of the wheel is actually based on the
principle of the lever. Once he saw that all the subjects he was failing
in school—especially mathematics and science, because they were
presented in abstract formulae—could now be seen and understood
in his everyday world, his intellectual life became a joy. The statement of the ancients that learning begins in wonder through the
senses—that is, the poetic mode of knowledge—was proved again.

The lesson of the proper progression of knowledge became deeply impressed in him:

> The sensory-motor reaction lies at the basis of mental life and until this is developed and made the standard of interpretation, the knowledge contained in books and language remains sealed. But once we have secured a vigorous development along these lines, it will be found comparatively easy to divert the flow of mental energy into other channels.[26]

Nor did Shields forget the importance of the first movements of seeing and sensing, the emotion of joy as the "other channels" of knowledge are encountered: "There is no real progress in intellectual life," Shields concludes, "until the *delight* in the discovery of truth becomes the controlling motive."[27] In other words, this poetic mode spoken of so often here and given example by Shields is no mere gimmick simply to catch the attention of the learner to entice him on to more serious studies. Delight is, according to Shields and to the entire tradition which he reflects, "the controlling motive" of *all* intellectual life.

Returning to Henri Charlier, the same counsel is heard to move away from merely passing on abstract formulae with their fixed systems of learning. "The inventors of the wheel," Charlier writes, "the inventors of the yoke, were not mathematicians, but rather observing minds endowed with imagination."[28] The "observing mind endowed with imagination" describes exactly one with the poetic view of reality, a view without which science loses its integration in the order of knowledge and, when applied to market technology, loses its regard for the humane with consequences now recognized by ecologists and environmentalists as global dilemmas.

Not only does Charlier inveigh against a learning that is largely abstract and prematurely analytical, but he also says the means of transferring this kind of education—by mere language—has become imprecise: "Words no longer offer any precise meaning, they can no longer define things for the three quarters of the people who still use them."[29] This lack of precision imposed on language is partly the result, Charlier says, of a teaching that has been "to have children retain as much as possible in the memory. . . . That the memory may be filled with innumerable bits of knowledge amassed by generations of men is completely useless as the mind does not know how to relate these facts into ideas."[30] We need only remember the example of Professor Gradgrind insisting on "Facts" about a horse (about everything), rather than the idea formed from the real experience and knowledge of a horse, to illustrate Charlier's meaning. Charlier observes that this system of education even falls short of teaching the practical side of knowledge:

> They are teaching not a true practical science, or an art that is truly practical, but a kind of abstract theory of the practical, or even a scientific manipulation of quantity they seem to think is practical, but which distances the students as much from life and trades/crafts as pure intellectual science; whereas, the true practice of crafts with every blow of the hammer comes up against a nature of things which admirably forms the intelligence not only as far as the practical side is concerned, but also forms reflection on nature and the spirit of things.[31]

Charlier's insistence on traditional crafts is no mere metaphor for learning in the poetic mode. It is neither "artsy craftsy," nor mere vocationalism. For Charlier, the crafts offer a real knowledge in themselves and, because they possess real knowledge, can be used as metaphor. It is learning that begins in the *actual* without isolating the mind as the object of knowledge and instead places the learner in an integrated experience that calls into play a sensory-intellectual insight:

> The mind of man escapes quantity, for it cannot be quantified, nor can his emotional life or his sensations. Science can very well try to reduce our sensations to quantity, and assume from this a very powerful upper hand on nature, and even a kind of symbolic thought . . . nonetheless, man is still most amenable to the *l'esprit de finesse*, to intuition, which distinguishes qualities . . . the true spirit of teaching is not to know many things but to understand how to distinguish ideas.[32]

This ability to distinguish qualities and ideas by means of *l'esprit de finesse* is based on the experience and observation of *la nature des choses* as they are discovered in, for example, the traditional trades and crafts. "A narrow-minded (scientific) spirit is the disastrous result of this [education]," says Charlier, "because it gives young people an encyclopedic knowledge before showing them first how to use this knowledge."[33]

Modern education, for Charlier, now stripped of its sensory-emotional foundations, is informed by the result of teachers trained in mathematical, philosophical systems—quantitative and abstract systems of learning. Here he offers a more complete reflection of his use of the trades in education. In reading this it is important to remember Charlier has in mind the traditional crafts that endured up to preindustrial, pretechnological times. Also, this traditional view distinguishes *homo sapiens* from *home faber*, man as maker, two aspects that complete our nature. For the purposes here, Charlier's crafts are to be understood as a paradigm of the experience of poetic knowledge:

> Most men have to think in their trade. The great thinkers all had their trade, their crafts, whether they were psychologists or scientists, like Pascal and Descartes, or apostles and leaders of souls like St. Paul and St. Augustine, or sculptors like Michelangelo, or poets like Aeschylus. Contemporary education, weighed down as it is with so much diversified knowledge, and said to be made to prepare people for life, has a rather profound defect, that it is separated from the trades. It separates young people from their natural craft and even from all crafts and trades.[34]

Thus, under modern education,

> the child . . . is introduced to a kind of intellectual work which, all things considered, is rather easy: reading books and compiling facts. At the end of his studies he is not capable of doing any other work than reading books and compiling facts. So, he becomes a bureaucrat, an employee, a professor, or tax collector. He doesn't even realize that he can do anything else . . . he himself thinks only of leading others on toward the same routine.[35]

In passing I should point out that among the many contemporary observers who recognize modern education as "intellectual work," described by Charlier and mentioned earlier by Josef Pieper, there is the recent work of David Elkind, a student of Piaget, who

has documented in several books the harm in such education. His titles alone reveal the concern: *The Hurried Child*; *All Grown Up and No
Where to Go*; and, dealing with the same psychological fallout of hurried education on the preschool level, *Miseducation*.

Charlier anticipates how Quixotic, at best, his ideas will appear
to many of his modern readers:

> Philosophers and teachers who think themselves to be special-
> ists of the universal, will probably be the last to accept the idea
> that learning, to learn a craft seriously, is to fashion and form
> someone's mind to distinguish ideas, to abstract and generalize.
> These village craftsmen of the seventeenth and eighteenth cen-
> turies who left us so many admirable pieces of furniture that we
> still find in the places where they were made, did not always
> know how to write. And yet, what wonderfully civilized quality
> we find in their work! To buy a tree trunk with the idea of
> forming from it a wardrobe, to bring the work to fruition, this is
> really what we mean when we say to truly know one's trade; it
> is, a philosopher would say, in the order of "making." But there
> is a plan, an organization in a wardrobe, there is a *logic* of the
> operations, a generalized order which must be seized by the
> mind in the abstract. Out of hypotheoretical pieces of wood
> that the carpenter sees only in his imagination and that he
> compares to a plan which is the very *idea* of the wardrobe, his
> mind then learns to abstract and to generalize as seriously as
> upon the venerable examples: "Peter is a man," or, "a rare
> horse is expensive."[36]

This describes exactly what Thomas Shields saw in the completion of his daily chores, this "logic of operations" experienced
with his "muscle sense" when he described his discovery of the principle of mechanics in the lever when using a pitchfork. With the
advancement of the modern machine and the presence of mass-
produced products made of exotic synthetic materials, with the resulting transfer from man the maker as craftsman to man the mere
operator of these machines, it is no wonder modern readers may
find it difficult if not impossible to see the very real and serious dimension of knowledge in these experiences and crafts. Furthermore,
it is only from these crafts described by Charlier, often produced by
illiterate men, that have that "wonderfully civilized quality," where
one admires such work with a reciprocal poetic response as being

"something very much like perfection," according to the highest principle of intuitive aesthetic judgment. A test of this truth would be to contrast the idea of someone walking round and round a microwave or a child's plastic toy, commenting with admiration on the beauty and loving workmanship of such items.

But Charlier is precise as to what he means about this sensory, poetic approach to learning that ultimately involves all the faculties of perception, as when he spoke earlier of the "interdependence" of things learned when, for example, adjusting a mortise and tenon:

> A cabinet maker learns to think while doing his apprenticeship, and to think very profoundly if he is a great cabinet maker, after having thought of the theory of the assemblages, the parts that go together, he can also think of a theory—in so doing, he touches the very source of knowledge.[37]

As mentioned earlier, it is clear that Charlier's examples presuppose trades and crafts, and apprenticeship, prior to mass-produced products made with power tools and machines. In the factory's setting, instead of the traditional workshop, the machine that exactly cuts and perfectly joins the parts together comes between the learner and the materials, robbing him of the real experience and opportunity to know with his senses the "logic of operations" and the "interdependence of things." Machines, then, tend to destroy the cultivation of poetic knowledge, leaving the average worker, in the factory, in the office, and even in the typical appliance-equipped modern kitchen, ignorant of a whole realm of reality, as well as bereft of much needed sensory and emotional satisfaction. The problem of this lack of knowledge in the presence of the modern machine was passionately observed by the twentieth-century artist and sculptor, Eric Gill. It is not difficult to think of modern education alà Gradgrind as Gill attacks the factory and machine:

> It is difficult to think of any introduction of machinery into already existing workshops which had any other object than that of lowering the costs of production and increasing the quantity of things made, and therefore the profits. No machine has ever been invented for *improving the quality*. . . . The majority of things made today are not made by men at all. The majority of men today do not make things. They only do what they are told.

They are not responsible for the thing which results from their obedience. They are not responsible workmen. They are not artists. They are puppets. They have been reduced (as the theologians put it) to a subhuman condition of intellectual irresponsibility. They are more interested in the process than in the product. . . . Machinery makes the workman less necessary and, eventually, unnecessary altogether.[38]

No less concerned is Walter John Marx, in his book, *Mechanization and Culture*:

So long as we turn efficiency of operation into an end in itself, we not only raise up insoluble social problems but defeat the very purpose of human work. Efficiency is allied to speed-up or the stretch-out and is often simply the mechanizing of man so that he may better keep up with the machine.[39]

The terms *quantity* and *efficiency* that so much dominate the vocabulary of modern life and work are tell-tale concepts indicating the rise and dominance of science and its technological applications over the poetic sense of life. They point to a mode of knowledge, the scientific, that has come to be considered superior to the extent that nearly all positions to the contrary that seek to reintroduce the life of leisure, beauty, and a "civilized quality" to human work are dismissed as hopelessly unrealistic and irrelevant to the progress achieved by modern man.

In spite of the virtual disappearance of the small workshop and the dominance of the vast marketplace of mass-produced goods, Charlier's example of the crafts still illuminates his educational principles. These men—Charlier, Fabre, Shields, Gill—were not odd and eccentric cranks but philosophical companions in a tradition that reaches from Socrates to Aquinas and beyond. Among his contemporary philosophers, Charlier, like Maritain, found support from Henri Bergson:

Thus Bergson said, and very justly so . . . "We are too much tempted to see in manual labor nothing more than a kind of relaxation. We forget that intelligence is essentially the capacity to manipulate material, that it began, at least, this way, that such was the intention of nature. How then could intelligence not profit from an education of the hands?" a knowledge which comes completely from books compresses and suppresses activities which only ask to take flight in order to come to life. Let the child have a chance of doing manual labor, but do not hand over the task of teaching to a kind of unskilled laborer. Rather, let us address ourselves to a real teacher who can perfect the sense of touch, to the point that it becomes a refined sense of touch: intelligence will then climb right from the hands to the head. In all areas of studies our teaching has been too verbal.[40]

Charlier then begins to complete his picture of learning in the poetic mode by examining a trade and craft with which he was familiar and which, at least in France, has changed very little over the centuries. Along with the example of the cabinetmaker, this portrait of man the maker should dispel the misunderstanding that the poetic mode has nothing to do with the practical:

We have taken the example of a wood worker; that of a peasant would perhaps be even more convincing, because there is no craft where the intuitive spirit and the sense of observation is more used. Wine growers also have seen their vines die from phylloxia, who have re-established them two and three times without success, and who have started again, who have made a whole new vineyard adapted to the modifications of the seasons, to new parasites, to the soil chemistry, and finally to the terrain of one slope or another—and I have seen them at work—these were truly wonderful men. The whole world has nothing more to do than imitate their work and methods. . . . They can be compared only to the most famous physiologists and doctors. In the varieties of seasons, of soils, discerning the causes of the condition of the plant, and generalizing correctly from this, requires not only observation, but a most delicate induction and deduction, which, still as a young man, I could only admire this intellectual power.[41]

In concluding this example Charlier never loses sight of the educational principles contained in the craft, and neither does he make the mistake of Rousseau's Romantic individualism by trying to isolate from society, and from a tradition of culture, this noble peasant:

I realize fully that an average knowledge of chemistry, geology and history, can add to this experience [of the wood worker and wine grower] . . . but these crafts are superior in a way that can never be taken away from them, that is, they teach there is a nature of things. A professor can have fallen into great error, can be mistaken, and he can stay there his whole life destroying thousands, ten thousand intelligences, but nonetheless will continue to have a good job and will have a very comfortable retirement afterward. But if a peasant fails to plant his fields two times in a row, he's ruined. This is the origin of what is called the good common sense of the peasant: he knows there is a nature of things and that we cannot change them. The mind of a great vine grower is a *formed* mind—a mind which has been formed to observe, to induct, to abstract, to deduce, to generalize. Without a doubt, this man is not what you would call a cultured man, he's lacking in the general experience that comes from the knowledge of history and past civilizations. But it doesn't take much at all to really cultivate deeply and profoundly the intelligent man who truly possesses a craft, a trade. He needs some experience in reading provided by a cultured man . . . [but] everything is profitable for this man, everything is extra, and he often wins out as far as intellectual prudence is concerned because his method has been formed as a result of contact with facts, because he thinks according to nature, and because he is used to seeing nature put to the test, to test his conclusions about things.[42]

Later, in Charlier's *Culture, École, Métier*, he says how aspects of this same kind of craft knowledge can be introduced into the school under the subjects of a traditional curriculum: "We rely on a complement of education to change a superficial literary spirit which is opposed to poetry, philosophy, and to profound thought . . . [therefore] it is essential to introduce into the studies physical education and music."[43] However, Charlier is quite aware, and opposed, to the modern idea of "sports":

It is not that we must enshrine sports. Sports-men are not as strong as they appear to be. They are often afraid of hurting themselves. When I see them go to sophisticated ski resorts, I can't help but think the real winter sport is the cutting of wood in the forest.[44]

In the tradition of the ancients, Charlier has in mind the Socratic idea of gymnastic, all those things that cause one to be aware of their body, waking it up, as it were, and making the senses alert to reality: "The essential of gymnastics is the training to race, including different types of jumps and climbs. But physical labor must be added, which gives resistance, brings one back to the hard realities of life."[45] In this same tradition, Charlier considers music:

> In the ancient times and in all the middle ages, music was a part of the studies. Why? And why this pre-eminence given to music rather than to any of the other arts? Music is the most violent of all the arts, and the one which most powerfully affects the senses. Music is very useful in forming sensitivity. . . . The slightest beat of the drum, even if you are thinking about something else, will produce a physical effect far more powerful than any painting.[46]

And further:

> For the Greeks, the word "music" meant poetry, music, and dance, all at the same time. They never separated them. That proves they had common sense. The screams and wild movements of the young today would have shocked them. They would have asked, "Where were they educated?" The answer would have been, ". . . at the closest high school." Dance is the best way for youngsters to calm their senses and control this violence of a young vitality which they usually use in a wrong way. We are not speaking of the dancing of the dance halls, but of outdoor dancing: the ancient folk dances. . . . Strength, grace, fervor of life, and a sort of majesty coming from the complete gift of one's self are the fruits of dance.[47]

All these topics of Charlier—crafts, cutting wood, running, jumping, singing, dancing—are considered in the gymnastic and poetic modes and become the stuff of poetic education. It is not only prior to scientific knowledge, it is, as Charlier says, "superior in a way," because they teach first and deepest *la nature des choses*, the nature of work, song, dance, and so on, and not simply a knowledge about these things.

What Charlier has described here is a less formal explanation of the more detailed discussion of Aristotle and Aquinas concerning connatural knowledge, that sympathetic, intuitive way of knowing that takes us inside the thing by way of the senses. In this way, we come closer to the *experience* of the thing's existence where its principles are yielded up to the whole body and mind without the aid of abstract intellectual discourse. This is exactly the way of knowing discovered and called for by Thomas Shields.

As Charlier returns to his original thesis in the beginning of his book, that any reform in education must begin with the reform of teachers under a pre-Cartesian formation, with an initial focus on sensory and emotive experience, he has no illusions how difficult this would be: "In our time, alas, intellectual life is directed by men who have no direct contact with the nature of things, men who live in cities where the art is to mask the nature of things."[48]

However, he could not have known that there were at least three men in America who, nearly thirty years after Charlier's book first appeared and with no knowledge of his work or his brother's school at Maslacq, France, founded a two-year humanities program at the University of Kansas that Charlier would have recognized immediately as having grasped the key principles he had called for in the formation of a faculty and the reform of education. It is that program that is examined in the next chapter.

6

Poetic Knowledge and the Integrated Humanities Program

Tell all the Truth but tell it slant—
Success in Circuit lies
Too bright for our infirm Delight
The Truth's superb surprise.

—Emily Dickinson

"To awaken wonder was the major work of the muses and of the Integrated Humanities Program," writes Robert Carlson, professor of English at Casper College in Wyoming. Carlson pursues the role of poetic knowledge in education in the same way that has been surveyed throughout this study:

> Western tradition has divided the long itinerary of liberal education into three stages, each contributing something of its own to the three purposes of liberal education—to humanize, to acculturate, to make happy. These are the stages of poetry, liberal arts, and sciences. According to Plato, the first step in the long itinerary of liberal education is the elementary or poetic stage. . . . These descriptions of the poetic stage of development mention the powers within the young student—senses, memory, imagination. Poetic education begins to humanize by developing these powers.[1]

Carlson's book, *Truth On Trial: Liberal Education Be Hanged*, also includes a chapter that documents in detail how poetic education in the IHP begins to humanize by developing these powers in one particular student. And, it is at this point that I now turn directly to the IHP, for it is one thing to have traced the philosophical history of poetic knowledge and presented a case for its rightful place in learning and education—theoretically. It is quite another matter to have discovered where these ideas were actually applied, as in the case of Maslacq, France, and more recently in America, where in the last years of the IHP I had the opportunity to know and experience the poetic mode in practice. That this program existed at all is extraordinary, given the almost complete demise of traditional humanities programs in the United States; that it lasted for nearly fifteen years in the midst of some of the most intoxicated times for educational "change" and that it was so clearly successful seems to be in the order of the miraculous.

In 1971, three professors at the University of Kansas, Dennis B. Quinn, Franklyn C. Nelick, and John Senior,[2] began a four-semester program for freshmen and sophomores called The Pearson Integrated Humanities Program. The IHP, as it came to be called, was taught, as we shall see, according to the principles of the poetic mode of knowledge, carefully adapted for a young college-age audience.

This was a time of great upheaval on many American campuses. The tendency, even now, might be to recall these times of campus unrest as largely related to the protest against the war in Vietnam and student activism in regard to civil rights. However, the original catalog printed for the IHP reveals another aspect of student dissatisfaction in the early seventies, at least, at the University of Kansas:

> In recent years college freshmen and sophomores have complained with increasing bitterness that they are treated as second-class citizens at the big universities. Many underclass courses are taught by graduate students rather than by full-time faculty, beginning classes are routine and dull; the underclassman is a mere number, never knowing or being known by any faculty member; the freshman-sophomore curriculum, consisting principally of unpopular "required" courses, is fragmented, incoherent, and directionless; typical college courses have nothing to do with the fundamental questions of life.[3]

The IHP was a curious approach, by modern standards, in meeting these fundamental criticisms. It used the traditional great and good books, yet it was not a Great Books Program—far from it. It revived the traditional receptive attitude of the students attending lectures, but they were not allowed to take notes; they had to *listen*. In fact, these twice-a-week, hour-and-twenty-minute meetings were not lectures at all but, rather, conversation between the three professors, one from classics and two from English, who had come to know one another through their shared ideas of education and had become friends. The conversations were, by design, unrehearsed and spontaneous, begun by simply taking up some moment from the *Odyssey*, or from Herodotus, or *The Republic* that interested one of the teachers, then exploring it with anecdotes, stories, connections with other readings, following wherever the theme took them. Now and then, they would acknowledge directly the presence of the nearly two hundred students in the hall, but for the most part the experience was one of listening and watching a real conversation take place among three men who were themselves sincerely caught up in their own topic and friendship. As a result, students were caught up with them, for the mode of conversation, as opposed to canned lectures or the tedium of analyzing a text, is a poetic thing, and it was the intention of the professors not to talk about teaching in the poetic mode but to actually do it. Precisely because of the serious attention needed to conduct such spontaneous talks, it was a rare conversation that was not complemented by an intense silence as the students discovered that they could, after all, really listen when the distraction of note taking was laid aside; and it was an equally rare class period that did not erupt at some point in real laughter. Laughter of this kind is also poetic in that it comes to us as a surprise of suddenly seeing the connection between two dissimilar things. One of the recurring themes of the IHP was that while life was not "fun," it certainly was often funny.

During the week, between Tuesday and Thursday lectures, smaller groups of students met to memorize poetry, truly by memory, since no text was used, but conducted by another student who had himself the poems of the program in his memory. In this way, the professors spoke of *doing* poetry, rather than studying or analyzing it. It was in the order of music and gymnastic at the same time, since in the first place most of the poems memorized were lyrical and, in the second place, by withdrawing all books or handouts of poetry, nothing came between the student and the poem, not even his eyes.

The brochure for the IHP, and often topics of conversation, spoke of professions and careers more as vocations, as "callings" to a life's work, rather than the usual tired prospects for the top-dollar jobs of the day. These were invitations to consider being sailors, soldiers, cowboys, mothers and fathers of families, poets, and stressing the cultivation of crafts and farming. No wonder that the picture of Don Quixote was soon adopted, by the students, as the emblem for the program.

The professors of the IHP clearly recognized the steady falling off of students' abilities to read, speak, and write on a college level taken for granted only a generation ago. But the goal was never to improve test scores. They would say that the tests themselves and the entire system built up around such Cartesian measurement instruments were an indication of the problem in modern education.

In other words, everything in the IHP was, in one way or another, the result of the awareness of the poetic mode of knowledge. This was the awareness of wonder, in the books and in the teaching, and the awareness that these texts and much of the teaching needed to point the senses and emotions toward the objects of delight and wonder. This is why the IHP did not teach philosophy—Plato and Cicero, for example, were always read and commented on in the literary mode, never in terms of argument or debate. The atmosphere was intended to be meditative, not disputatious. Thus, the conversations replaced the modern sense of lecture and were closer to the medieval idea of *lectio* where the teachers spontaneously delivered a commentary on some text. This was, in turn, derived from the practice of the ancient *rhetors*, Cicero, for example, where the professors were aware and at ease working within this tradition. The students, as mentioned earlier, freed from the distraction of taking notes and trying to listen to the teacher with a book in hand at the same time, could now participate in this conversation among the teachers by being physically passive so that they could be emotionally and intellectually receptive as listeners. As the professors pointed out, to receive is not to do nothing: a baseball catcher does a great deal, but he is still the receiver of the activity of the pitcher. Furthermore, they explained to the students that every conversation requires an attentive listener, alert and sympathetic; otherwise, the occasion deteriorates into mere discussion, a kind of noise, really, losing the meditative silence within which what is being said can be pondered. Listening then, it was explained, in this way is a poetic thing. *Conversation*, a word whose etymology was revealed by the professors to show how it meant to turn together around some subject, was a sign of friendship and an activity that involves the alertness of the whole person, not just the mind but the eyes and ears, noticing gestures and tone of voice that indicate meaning and nuance within the give and take of such dialogue. On the other hand, lecture appeals mainly to the intellect and even more so, to the extent lecture is prepared and planned, relies less and less on the intuitive connections within the memory of the speaker. In the end, lecture of this kind eliminates the surprise and delight in learning. The analogy of a traditional jazz band, improvising on a familiar theme, was used by the professors to describe their spontaneous conversations.

The example of these professors, teaching by way of their personal conversation, speaking as naturally as if around a table where a leisurely lunch was taking place, making quick connections with the similar and contrary ideas contained in the other books of the program, from daily life, or meandering, wandering around and around the topic, digressing to personal experiences relevant to the subject—all taught the students, indirectly at least, the joy of the memory and a healthy independence from books and notes and all the gimmicks so often used to keep this generation's attention. Also, it was the presence of the three professors in friendly, lively conversation that personalized the impersonal education decried by many students then and referred to in the IHP brochure. Usually, by the end of the semester, the professors knew most of the students' names, largely as the result of the continuing conversations that took place after class between the students and the teachers that often continued throughout the week in the teachers' offices with smaller groups.

Given the fact that their physical childhood had passed and the students were in various stages of middle and late adolescence, direct early experience of reality in games, sports, and crafts was not possible. (It is instructive to mention that all the professors of the IHP believed or soon came to believe that what they were doing on the college level, in spite of the obvious success, was needed much sooner, beginning at the elementary level making the necessary adjustments in texts, etc.). More significantly, an entire preindustrial culture was missing from these students' experience, and in its place was our familiar modern life, artificial and insulated more and more from direct experience with nature and reality. Still, the IHP eventually added activities that led students closer to poetic experience. In addition to memorizing poetry, students also learned calligraphy, the art of beautiful writing. Night-time outings were organized for naked-eye star gazing where students learned to recognize several of the constellations and their main stars and the Greek stories that accompanied them. Each semester the students learned by heart several traditional songs, usually sung by the older students before lecture, so that by midsemester one could hear an entire auditorium filled with the song lyrics of "Drink to Me Only with Thine Eyes" or a Stephen Foster favorite. This quickly produced a sense of delight in the students, not only in the simple refrains but in the fact that now these poems and songs were placed within them and were part of who they were. This is what the professors meant by *doing* poetry, or song, as opposed to studying them. The senses and emotions were being called on to experience the transcendentals of beauty, goodness, and truth, rather than offering mere definitions to be learned for an examination. Letting the stars, the poems, the songs come in directly through their senses, learning to control a flowing ink pen with just a little careful attention so that their usual scrawls became beautiful written characters, was already accomplishing the end of poetic education.

Each spring, preparations began for the IHP waltz, an event that the students suggested and organized. Fellow students gave dance lessons, others saw to hiring an orchestra to play the music of Strauss, and the University ballroom was rented for the evening. Many of the female students made their own evening gowns, while the young men arrived in rented tuxedos. Many parents of the IHP students attended the annual spring waltz as well as professors from other departments of the university to gaze on this amazing transformation—a roomful of young people normally decked out in flowery tops and bell-bottom pants, now moving in time, like twirling blossoms on a clear pond of water, to the music of civilized nineteenth-century Europe.

Literally and figuratively, in this way the IHP was a musical education, observing in poetry, dance, song, star gazing, and calligraphy, an understanding of what Socrates, Aristotle, Aquinas, Shields, and Charlier all called for as preliminary and prerequisite music and gymnastic for humanizing the student prior to any advanced studies. The IHP neither encouraged nor discouraged higher studies beyond its program in any general way. What they offered was minimal for all. To become a scholar, to study philosophy or literature or law, was a decision for individual students in concrete cases.

Furthermore, the professors taught the books from the classics of literature, history, and philosophy in the poetic mode, rather than in any analytical way. Not only because many of the great books lend themselves to appreciation at the literary level, but also because of the deprivation of traditional culture in modern life, the professors presented these texts imaginatively to the students. They made use of concrete examples from everyday life, from traditional life, from childhood, all to give a vicarious experience of philosophy, history, and so on. Presenting *The Republic* and *The Persian Wars* in this way, in the manner of story and personal experience, allowed for the students' participation within the arguments about justice between Socrates and Thrasymachus. As a matter of fact, before teaching *The Republic*, the professors wanted the students to know Socrates. They did this by reading *The Apology* first, where the ideal of a just man dying for the love of wisdom deeply impressed the students who were still idealistic enough to be moved by such good-natured heroism. And, since Herodotus wrote his history largely in the form of stories, digressions, and anecdotes, it was a natural approach to view all of history as an unfolding story that also commemorated "the deeds of great men," instead of presenting history as the scientific analysis of social, economic, and geographic contingencies.

Consistent with this approach in the IHP, the works of Aristotle and Thomas Aquinas were omitted in the two-year program due to the obvious difficulty and the nonpoetic form of presentation. Furthermore, the choice to exclude these works from a freshman-sophomore program was in keeping with the whole idea of the place of poetic knowledge in the hierarchy of education. The *Metaphysics* of Aristotle, for example, and the *Summa Theologica* of St. Thomas presuppose years and years of experience, first in direct contact with nature, with music and gymnastic, followed by a slow and patient journey through what came to be known as the *trivium* and *quadrivium* of classical and medieval education. The professors' decision in this regard proved to be a sound one, for many of the IHP students went on to formally study and obtain degrees in philosophy, law, and theology. On this issue of delaying these higher studies, there was a more or less friendly quarrel between the IHP and the traditional liberal arts program at Thomas Aquinas College in California, a very rigorous and intellectual Great Books program that attracted many brilliant students. The TAC faculty and students tended to regard the IHP as "romantic," undisciplined, and not really serious. But the professors of the IHP were unmoved by this criticism, other than to, with mirth and goodwill, agree with them! To plunge freshmen into formal philosophy and to lead such studies in a tutor-directed roundtable discussion would sooner or later force a method of learning to which they were so opposed: that of bypassing the sensory-emotional cultivation and instead feeding the mind more exclusively with general abstract formulas. The IHP professors were fond of paraphrasing a statement of Cardinal Newman's that while it is possible to train youth in the rigors of formal philosophy, what one often gets as a result, without the prior humanizing of the poetic mode, are disputatious young students, not unlike Bitzer, the prize pupil of Gradgrind, who knew on command all the facts about a horse but did not know what a horse *is*.

In addition to the weekly lectures, the IHP also offered Latin, taught in the beginning entirely by the oral method, that is, without the use of a textbook or formal grammar. This course was, as everything was in the IHP, presented in the poetic mode. The students, by listening carefully and repeating what they heard, learned to *speak* very simple Latin from their memories much like children begin to learn their native language without any study of grammar, without any books. This was gymnastic in that it allowed for direct wrestling with the Latin; it was musical in that it brought forth much delight and laughter in the challenge and mistakes of trying to conduct an entire lesson without using any English, pointing, gesturing, acting out, the words and meaning instead. Books and grammar were not excluded altogether if the student decided to continue with Latin, but they were simply delayed so that the mind would not be filled with paradigms and rules and all the systems of a disintegrated language. Rather, the student would have in the memory the sounds of Latin words and phrases used in real conversation. Once again, the emphasis was *to do* Latin, not to study it.

The IHP also conducted a course in rhetoric, but again without a formal study of classical styles or painstaking research assignments. The students followed a simple literary approach—from Aesop's fables and Grimm's tales—to introduce them to reasoning by noticing the perfect arrangement of beginning, middle, and end, a logic of thought, and cause and effect. In so doing, the program exposed itself to more criticism from outsiders, some of whom considered such an approach childish and silly. But the professors had

left nothing unconsidered, and in presenting rhetoric in this way
from the ground up they followed exactly the literary formation ex-
pected by Plato and Aristotle in their schools, as the number of refer-
ences to Aesop and Homer in their works demonstrate. The IHP
faculty knew that the students were also remotely reliving parts of
their childhood in these delightful, timeless stories. This rediscovery
of their childhood, which for many of them had been unfulfilled, was
of great importance in the two-year program. The professors knew
that a materialist society, with all its utilitarian goals that suffocate
the poetic nature of the human being, had rushed many of the students through childhood, that time of leisure in which the wonders
of reality are encountered simply as wonders. As this entire study has
demonstrated, there can be no real advancement in knowledge unless it first begin in leisure and wonder, where the controlling motive
throughout remains to be delight and love. Without the reconnec-
tion with their childhood and the appropriate emotions, the students
would not be reachable. The approach proved sound, as a large portion of the IHP students became teachers in elementary and high
schools, in colleges and universities.

It was never the plan of the IHP to simply teach the books of
Western culture, but rather to discover the roots of that culture and
give, to the extent possible, the actual experience of that civilization.
Therefore, in the first years of the program, the IHP traveled to Europe for a complete semester, once in 1976 to Ireland and in following years for between-semester tours to Greece, Spain, and Italy,
where the professors and their one hundred or more students continued to read and talk about the books of the West. Now, they
could walk together on the roads and bridges built by Caesar, sail on
the waters that brought Odysseus back from Troy, see medieval castles and monasteries, sit in humble Irish taverns and listen to the stories of sheep herders, sailors, and a town drunk or two.

With the direct experience of a still-visible traditional Western
culture, so clearly connected with the details in the classic literature
being read, the teachers of the IHP achieved one of the main goals
of the program, to *integrate* experience for the students and to allow
them to see that experience, remote or direct, had meaning, and
that there was a thing called "the Western experience" that was really a part of a larger experience of the world to which they right-
fully belonged. There, near the monasteries and cathedrals, the
villages and colorful vibrant cities, the castles, the cottages, the

winding roads, the vineyards, the large pastoral landscapes of rural life, was evidence that there had been and still was to an extent, a civilization that had kept and valued as its foundation the poetic sense of life.

None of the three professors has written at any length a systematic philosophy of education to explain what they did in the IHP. Like poets themselves, once their muse was upon them, they tended to act in accordance with the principles that moved them, not always conscious of or intending any particular outcome for themselves or the students: they simply treated with love and affection, and with a great deal of wit and mirth, whatever was the subject at hand, allowing that subject to lead them wherever it would. Quite often, one of them would say, speaking for the others, that the reason they were present at all was because they enjoyed what they were talking about and enjoyed the company of one another. They would talk this way whether the students were present or not.

However, they all have contributed some brief essays and recorded some informal audio tapes that reveal their reflections on aspects of the poetic mode of knowledge. (Professors Quinn and Senior have completed books of their own, Quinn on wonder mentioned earlier, and Senior on *The Restoration of Innocence*). In a booklet published about the IHP, John Senior, professor of classics and one of the founders of the program, offered a definition of the course's name. There is much to be learned about the thoughtful background for the IHP in these little meditations:

> *Integrated* means "united by a reason within the nature of the thing," like an organism, rather than externally, like a collection, say of books in a library arranged for our convenience. A modern university is a collection of subjects loosely united by the demands of business and the professions for trained personnel and arranged for the convenience of its administrators. However, the great tradition in philosophy has held that knowledge is analogous, that is, one integral structure having many parts but moving together and arranged from within by its intrinsic nature.[4]

Senior then proceeds to define with commentary the next two terms:

> *Humanities* means those aspects of integral knowledge directly bearing on the human species insofar as it is human—that is,

insofar as man has intelligence, memory and will and the properties that follow from these such as freedom, laughter, the enjoyment of poetry and the other arts, the appreciation of formal
excellence in nature, workmanship or sports. The humanities
are prescientific based on ordinary experience.[5]

This last sentence in Senior's definition of humanities is an important one in separating what the IHP did from other humanities
courses that simply surveyed the general ideas and themes of Western culture following a systematic plan. In fact, the appeal to "ordinary experience" as the key to the humanities places this knowledge
in the grasp of everyone and apart from the exclusively intellectual
approach of the specialist. It reminds us that a central aspect of the
poetic mode of knowledge is that it is common, natural, to all. Senior develops this point next:

> Some critics have accused humanities teachers of making
> fraudulent claims to encyclopedic knowledge—how can one
> professor be an expert in so many fields? they ask—and by the
> very question have tacitly and mistakenly assumed that all real
> knowledge must be specialized and that knowledge is the only
> end of education. Whereas in reality science simply makes
> common sense explicit, clear and detailed. . . . Science without
> the more general knowledge is pathetic, lost, like a surveyor
> who doesn't know the lay of the land or a blind optician. Mod-
> ern education has become increasingly suicidal in the en-
> croachment of science on schools and liberal arts colleges
> where students traditionally have learned, through gymnas-
> tic and the imaginative arts—poetry, music, history, nature
> study—the love of these things, not their dissection and analy-
> sis. The purpose of the humanities is not knowledge but to hu-
> manize—it is the indispensable prerequisite to science because
> the love of the subject is the motive and purpose of science.[6]

To place the motive of education, and the humanities in particular, in the realm of love, is to recall the essential energy of poetic
knowledge as it calls to the senses and the emotions. We are re-
minded of St. Augustine's statement that to *know* a thing we must
some way come to love it. Senior's comments on the "encroachment
of science on schools" echoes Newman, Shields, Charlier, and even
the great scientist of nature, Henri Fabre. Because of the influence of

the Romantics' reaction against rationalism and their overemphasis on the emotions as sentiments and feelings, we must remember that love as it is used here means a real grasp of reality integrated with the emotions, will, and intellect. Love is knowledge.

Then, Senior treats the last term:

> *Program* . . . is equivalent to "agenda." The word is properly used at theaters and prize fights, improperly by government agencies and universities to mean a "collection," an artificial unification of activities. Some think education is "programming" in the improper sense; and when they don't approve of the results, they initiate "deprogramming." . . . the Integrated Humanities Program is not a course, not the running through of a prescribed sequence in the humanistic sciences such as literary and historical analysis—it is not an attempt to advance knowledge at all, but rather, as the word "program" implies, to read what the greatest minds of all generations have thought about what must be done if each man's life is to be lived with intelligence and refinement.[7]

Statements that stunned newcomers to the program, such as that the IHP "is not an attempt to advance knowledge at all," are absolutely consistent with the fundamental position of poetic knowledge. Knowledge at the poetic level considers neither ends nor means, so that in this sense there is nothing to advance, only to experience. For example, in the case of furniture there are chairs and tables placed together in such a way that we may sit and have a meal. But sometimes we consider these things in themselves apart from any purpose as in the case of their beauty: a Shaker-style chair, for example, set on a polished wood-plank floor, against a white-washed wall with the sunlight from a bare window falling in beams and shadows across the room. It is a serene view, and for that moment completely without purpose, yet the viewer is certainly filled with a profound and mysterious sense of the real and of the beauty of this reality, a deep and penetrating intuitive knowledge of existence. This absence of the hurry-up energy to advance knowledge is restated elsewhere by Senior:

> We don't study history to use the past, to profit from past mistakes or to broaden our horizons; we rather celebrate the great events of Marathon, Roncevaux or Valley Forge and Gettys-

burg so that what men died for there, as Lincoln said, "Shall not perish from the earth." And so it is with all the subjects of liberal education; their purpose does not lie "concentered all in self."[8]

Senior is not denying that there is such a thing and a place for real scholarship in historical and literary matters; but at the level of beginners liberal studies must remain "prescientific," that is, in the realm of the cognitive powers of the senses and emotions with our intuitive responses to the transcendentals:

> The student who opens his heart to Homer, Plato, St. Augustine, the author of the *Song of Roland*, Dante, Chaucer and Shakespeare, doesn't get, he gives; he learns to love these authors whose Beauty, Truth and Good shine through the dark divine and human matter of their works like swarms of stars in the honey-combed night of time; he gazes on them with the thrilled fear we call "awe" or "wonder," the way a lover gazes upon his beloved, who would be shocked and ashamed at anyone who asked what he was *going to get out of her!*[9]

In the student handbook for the IHP, an article under the title "What is the Philosophy of the Humanities Program?" we find, first, an answer to the charge that the IHP teachers are imposing their own ideas on the course; second, a restatement of the end of liberal education; and, third, the acknowledgment of the student's ability to respond to a body of knowledge naturally, intuitively, without drill or analysis:

> The subject of the course is emphatically not the convictions of the teachers, for, as St. Augustine says, "Who would be so stupidly curious as to send his son to school in order that he may learn what the teacher thinks?" What Plato says is far more important than what we say of him, but it is not the point of education to learn even the convictions of Plato. The greatest of Plato's students, Aristotle, declared that as much as he loved his teacher, he loved truth still more. Mark Van Doren . . . puts it this way, "The teacher, of course, must have authority over the student before he can be respected in the way the student wants to respect him. But authority comes naturally with knowledge that is lucid as the liberal arts make knowledge lucid. The teacher who is not a liberal artist may indoctrinate

or charm, but he will not teach. Indoctrination makes the teacher's thought prevail, but teaching is less a matter of what either the teacher or the student thinks than of what the mind itself, the third person, decides and says."[10]

This natural reflex of the mind, "the third person," is Van Doren's acknowledgment of education that takes place in what the IHP calls the "prescientific mode," that is, knowledge at the poetic level.

Dennis B. Quinn, professor of English and cofounder of the IHP, has written an essay responding to some critics of the program. There were those who said the teachers were conducting a class without pedagogical foundation. These critics were, actually, confused by the absence of lesson plans, textbooks, syllabi, notes, and particularly by the spontaneous three-way conversation that served as lecture. Quinn titled his essay "Education by the Muses." "Of the many reasons why IHP remains mysterious," he began, "I shall treat but one; namely, that it is taught in the poetical mode."[11] But before explaining the poetical mode, Quinn deals with the radical change in the perception of humanities courses in the twentieth century, especially in light of the rise of career education and professionalism:

> Everyone recognizes that in higher education the liberal arts in general and the humanities in particular are suffering a serious decline. Vocationalism is driving more and more students toward professional schools or training programs where a marketable skill can be learned quickly. . . . The humanities have lost their allure because they have thrown away that which constitutes their distinctive appeal. I mean the love of knowledge for its own sake. . . . The humanities have been professionalized and scientized to the point where the ordinary undergraduate with a budding love for poetry or history or art or philosophy finds his affection returned in the form of footnotes, research projects, bibliographies, and scholarly jargon— all the poisonous paraphernalia that murders to dissect.[12]

This particular complaint about the plight of modern humanities education helps to explain the IHP's response of poetical education, since it is the encroachment of a Cartesian education that makes such a bleak contrast to the traditional approach to the humanities. Now Quinn contrasts the IHP with the trend of devaluing humanities and liberal arts and describes what is meant by "Education by the Muses":

> In *The Laws*, Plato's spokesman says, "Shall we begin then, with the acknowledgment that education is first given through Apollo and the Muses?" The Muses are the deities of poetry, music, dance, history, and astronomy. They introduce the young to reality through delight. It is a total education including the heart—the memory and passions and imagination—as well as the body and intelligence.[13]

Then, moving from the principles of education by the muses, Quinn gives an illustration from common experience:

> The nursery rhyme and fairy tale first present the phenomena of nature to the child. "Twinkle, twinkle, little star," is a Musical . . . introduction to astronomy that includes some primary observation of the heavenly phenomena and stirs the appropriate emotion—wonder. Now it is precisely this emotion that provides the motivating energy of education.[14]

In other words, Quinn is merely applying to this experience of childhood the statement of Aristotle that learning begins in wonder. But because of the ever-present reaction of the Romantics to the rise of materialism, a reaction which tended to idealize the emotions over the intellect, Quinn cautions: "Mistake me not: wonder is no sugary sentimentality, but, rather, a mighty passion, a species of fear, an awful confrontation of the mystery of things."[15]

Leading us to confront the "mystery of things" is essentially the art of the poet who directs our attention to the ordinary experience of life and reminds us how extraordinary it really is. In this sense, acting as poets, the professors taught in the mode of wonder to first engage the sense-imagination of their students whether the subject was history, philosophy, or literature. Quinn elaborates on this:

> Through the Muses the fearful abyss of reality first calls out to that other abyss that is the human heart; and the wonder of its response is, as the philosophers have said, the beginning of philosophy—not merely the first step; but the *arché*, the principle, as one is the principle of arithmetic and the fear of God the be-

ginning of Wisdom. Thus wonder both starts education and sustains it.[16]

Establishing that the IHP was taught in the poetical mode, at the level of wonder, keeping within the prescientific area of knowledge, Quinn echoes what was said earlier concerning connatural knowledge under the psychology and epistemology of Aristotle and St. Thomas Aquinas. Here, he chooses the term *participatory* to explain connaturality:

> Education by the Muses is participatory. To sing a love song is not identical with being in love, but it is to participate somehow in that experience. When a child sees the twinkle of the stars he knows it directly; when he chants the rhyme he knows the twinkling indirectly by participating in it. Poetry and music and even astronomy at this level are not to be studied but to be done. Later, perhaps, one may learn the physical causes of this phenomenon of stars: this kind of knowledge is not participatory, however; it is a higher, more intellectual, and more abstract kind of knowledge, but it does not eclipse that original participated experience, and, indeed, it sees something that eludes the highest science.[17]

As I explained in chapters 2 and 3, poetic knowledge is that which gets us inside the experience; it is, in this sense, vicarious and remotely real experience of the thing itself, rather than descriptive or analytical knowledge. As Quinn remarked in a personal conversation:

> Poetry and poetic education operate though the estimative sense, which has a kind of judgment of sense. It is the highest of the interior senses and, like poetry, is cognitive. When St. Thomas Aquinas says that poetic knowledge is defective, he means as compared to metaphysical knowledge, that is, one could say that faith is defective when compared to science. But the poetic way is real knowledge, just as faith is real knowledge.[18]

This is why Senior says that not even the acquisition of advanced knowledge is the end of humanities; in the poetic mode one experiences things rather than examining them in any critical spirit. Quinn says that when the muse of poetry, history, or philosophy begins to sing to the receptive student, "the stories they tell do not explain; they imitate or re-present their subject; they render it present."[19]

Briefly, then, scientific education explains; critical education dissects; poetic education, by way of the integrated senses, experiences. Therefore, the position of the teachers of the IHP was that in the order of knowledge, experience comes first, but experience of two kinds, direct and imaginatively participatory. Because Dewey and the more empirically minded educators denied or ignored the metaphysical and transcendental dimension of the senses and emotions, only actual experience of things for them brought knowledge, and even this had to be a direct experience that involved manipulating the environment in some way to wrench knowledge from it. But both direct and vicarious experience are poetic under the philosophy of the IHP, insofar as they remain uncritical and content to begin to learn in "wise passiveness."

Frank C. Nelick, professor of English and the third member of the IHP faculty, observed that with the coming of the Renaissance, the innovations of literary self-consciousness emerged—a science (after Descartes) of literature, made easier by the invention of movable type where texts could be analyzed and "knowledge could be reduced to words and put in print."[20] In other words, the poetic mode even for the study of literature was being lost to student and teacher. It was the end of an oral and conversational tradition and the end of the reliance on memory, which, as the Greeks believed, was the mother of the muses. Nelick says that poetry—and he uses the term comprehensively—"is an art and, as such, has an end proper to it."[21] This is to say on the other hand, that modern science has no end in the philosophical sense because it seeks to simply analyze things, to take them apart and identify these parts, and there cannot be an end to an activity that disintegrates, that is not directed throughout to the wholeness of the thing. Whereas, poetry, as a craft and representative of the mode of knowledge under discussion here, is an art and is therefore ruled as other arts that have as their end completion, some point of finality and rest, as the art of woodworking has the chair or table as its end, as sewing has the making of clothes as its end, arts that are opposite of the ongoing aggressive spirit of science that endlessly inquires and probes as if that were its end.

Contrasted with the rise of scientific inquiry and method, Nelick said:

> The older notion of knowledge existing in the great dialogue of minds in articulation was greatly lost in their [the scholars of the Renaissance] restless and acquisitive enthusiasm; "teaching" was replaced by "scholarship"; and libraries first came to be regarded, as they are now, the repositories of wisdom. In all ways, this discovery encouraged concentration on relationships between words rather than between things.[22]

This last sentence of Nelick's is from the same spirit and perception of Henri Charlier, made over thirty years earlier, that without concrete experience of things or as Nelick says, "between things," learning becomes the dupe of the necessities of mere words, abstract ideas, formulas, and empty logic. An education that no longer takes seriously the poetic mode of experience falsely elevates the mode of science. When science is applied to all the subjects of the curriculum, classrooms resemble laboratories, no matter how colorfully decorated, and the subjects of the humanities suffer most. For example, Nelick notes that "from the Renaissance until the present time most literary study has been concerned with the properties of style and the nice handling of narrative than with an identification of the realities which great poetry exposes."[23]

Although there has been care taken to distinguish between poetic knowledge and the art of poetry, it should be obvious that poetry itself is a natural means of teaching in the poetic mode. This was very much the case for the IHP where literature was the great vehicle of vicarious experience. Not only was there the memorization of poetry each semester, but the students read the great epics of Homer and Virgil, Chaucer's *Canterbury Tales*, a selection of Shakespeare's plays, and Cervantes' *Don Quixote*. In addition, Quinn, Nelick, and Senior, and a few other University of Kansas faculty taught classes in poetry outside the regular IHP schedule that were well attended by their students. Nelick's class in poetry was a steady favorite and it is clear from his following statement that of all subjects, poetry must be taught in the poetic mode:

Traditionally, the final cause of literature has been considered instruction of the person by delight. Poetry aims to delight by the recognition on the part of the reader or auditor of the similarities between things. . . . Virtually every critic who has concerned himself with the purpose of poetry has concluded that the sense "delights in things duly proportioned, as in things similar to itself." And to the extent that poetry represents, or pictures, or imitates nature, it deals with reality and in so doing instructs.[24]

Thus, these three professors were established philosophically in the mode of learning discovered as essential by the Idealist-Realist tradition. It was passed on by them under the name of the poetic mode, or as Quinn calls it, education by the muses. It is all the same, really, because when Nelick says that "Poetry is not an advanced thing; it is exactly as Latin is, a first thing. It is a child's thing,"[25] it is what is meant when Quinn remarks:

The Muses present life fresh, as if seen and experienced for the first time. In philosophy Socrates is the great beginner, the great freshman, who never lost his amateur status, who insisted that philosophy is nothing more than what the word means literally, the love of wisdom.[26]

So, this was the essential *way*, not method, of education for the IHP, a program that existed for nearly fifteen years as a college within a university; although as a funded and official program, the IHP lasted only ten years, with Quinn and Senior teaching the sequence of courses for five more years. The IHP achieved national recognition from time to time and eventually became "controversial" to the point that all of its funding was withdrawn and all its official support canceled by the administrators of the University of Kansas. Then two of the professors, Frank Nelick and John Senior, retired due to poor health, leaving Dennis Quinn to teach a steadily decreasing enrollment as the trend toward technical training and professionalism increased rapidly in the 1980s, and now that the IHP courses fulfilled no "requirements" for students.

However, the three professors, Quinn and Senior in particular, continued to meet informally with many of their former students, and the two teachers began to make audio tapes of their conversations about the books and the education of the IHP. In one of these taped conversations made in 1990, their thoughts can be followed on poetic knowledge and, typically, related topics ranging from horses to religion, illustrative digressions reminiscent of the former IHP "lectures":

Senior: What is poetic knowledge? It is not simply expression—
            we are talking about an experience, and you have to ex-
            perience the experience. The philosophers call this
            connatural knowledge—it is not abstract knowledge.
            Here, somebody knows something, but the only way to
            know what he knows is to know it yourself in the same
            way that he knows it. For example, you touch a hot stove,
            and you say, ouch. Then you say to somebody: you think
            stoves are hot? How do you know that? And, you say,
            touch it for yourself. You can repeat this kind of experi-
            ence, but it is very dangerous. So, we have another way,
            and that is by doing the experience in *sympathy*. We don't
            actually do it, but we can do it in our imaginations. This
            is what is meant by connatural knowledge. Children do
            this in play, imitating animals, for example. And there is
            a way of understanding, say, horses, through connatural-
            ity, and that's what poetry does.

Quinn: And it is not some form of inferior knowledge that you
            eventually outgrow, that you surpass as you get wiser.
            You may get wiser, and you may study horses in a very
            thoughtful way, I don't mean in a purely scientific way,
            but you may be around them and come to know about
            their anatomy and all that sort of thing—and, you will
            have more, but it will never replace that connatural
            knowledge, and it won't measure up to it either. It won't
            be as exhaustive or as great.

Senior: This is [also] a profound point in theology, and a lot of
            theologians apparently forget it. St. Thomas Aquinas
            says that abstract knowledge—and this is a very ironic
            fact—that the higher and higher you go in abstraction,
            the clearer and clearer your *understanding* gets, that is,
            your *intellectus*; but the less your *knowledge* gets. For exam-
            ple, if you study the *Summa Theologica*, those first ques-
            tions, you will arrive at an *understanding* of God. . . . But

St. Thomas says, remember, that nothing of what you learn is ever as rich or as perfect as your devotion to Jesus Christ. And you must always, he says, *advert*, that's the word he uses, you must always in abstract knowledge advert to the singular, about which there is no science. There is no science of the singular. . . . Theologians, for hundreds of years, I think, have forgotten that. If you go through books on moral or dogmatic theology, they never advert to the singular. They go on and on with propositions . . . [but] a concept is not a thing. St. Thomas makes a distinction between concept, what the human mind grasps in abstraction, and he calls it an *ens quo* . . . *ens* means an existent being, anything that exists; but *quo* means, by which, or by means of which. . . . So that an *ens quo* really means, *an existent by means of which*. But, in itself, it isn't anything. For example, the concept of God is not God. It's a way, a sign, an instrument *by which* the mind can come to know God—but God Himself is not the concept. We have a concept *of* God, but concepts are not the thing. What philosophy rests on that distinction!

Quinn: Mr. Senior is using the example of God, but it is true of a horse, a fly, or a flea, which is another example that St. Thomas uses. That is, we must always advert to the singular in any realm of thought.

Senior: So, you started out by saying that poetry is not a theory—it's not clear, it's the least intellectual. But we must never confuse cognition with intellectual—*cognitio* with *intellectus*; that is, there is *sense* knowledge. There is even *emotional* knowledge. St. Thomas says that emotions are also a form of knowledge. That is, if you are afraid, for example, there is something to be afraid of. Fear is a kind of knowledge. And love. We're human beings, we're not angels, and our cognition is sensuous, that is, the five exterior senses, but also our internal senses, which are our emotions. These are all ways of knowing. The will is a way of knowing, when you will something very strongly there is a kind of knowledge in it. You must never make the mistake in thinking that the only kind of knowledge is intellectual knowledge.

Quinn: That is a terrible confusion. We are human beings, and
              because we are human beings, the whole apparatus,
              the senses, the emotions, the will, every other aspect, the
              imagination, the memory—they're all hooked up to the
              intelligence. To say, oh, that is just an emotional argu-
              ment, for example, is to act as if we are only animals. An-
              imals do not have intellect. But I would say that in
              animals there is some mode of knowledge, it's not intel-
              lectual, but it is a mode of knowledge—even in their fear,
              they *know* what they fear.

Senior: The mouse knows perfectly well things about cats. It's
              not rational, it's not intellectual, but it's knowledge.[27]

7

The Future of the Poetic Mode of Knowledge in Education

I listened, motionless and still;
And, as I mounted up the hill
The music in my heart I bore,
Long after it was heard no more.
William Wordsworth

inally, to summarize to the extent that it is possible, I offer some concluding distinctions between the poetic and scientific modes of knowledge, remarks on education, and what a school in the poetic mode might look like today. These closing reflections are drawn to a large extent from my own experience of the IHP when, alas, it was in its final days, but also from years of conversations with Quinn and Senior that have continued to the present about this topic of knowledge, as well as from my experiences as a teacher at the elementary, secondary, and college levels.

The recognition of poetic knowledge is absent in teaching under the modern scientific approach, because science, by its nature, is bound to measure external reality, and there is nothing penetrating, sublime, or lovable about, for example, a diagramed sentence, a chart of historical dates, or a dissected frog. In fact, I will use these three examples to illustrate the point.

When a sentence is broken into its parts for the purpose of learning how to read and write, a child may become a whiz at identifying nouns, verbs, and adjectives, but the integrity of the language as that living thing capable of communicating living ideas is violated. Scientific grammar is studied, if at all, at the end of years of exposure to the literature of one's tradition. The same principle drawn from the poetic way of education can be said of learning a foreign language. Latin, for example, begun in the elementary grades, should be spoken by the teacher in easy phrases and sentences that identify familiar objects, with equally easy questions asked about these of the students who must answer in Latin by repeating what the teacher has said. Gently, and with lots of room for merriment, the teacher corrects the inevitable mistakes, orally, always in Latin. In fact, for the duration of the lesson, no other language except Latin is spoken by the teacher or the students. After about five or six years of this approach, increasing the vocabulary and actually teaching grammar indirectly by continually pointing out—in context, in Latin—the different endings for different occasions of usage, then formal grammar could be taken up. Even at this point, the parts of speech should be given a meditative treatment—nouns, for example, are terms that give names to things: how else would we know things without a name? The words of the declensions are rich sources for etymologies, such as *genitive*, a word that indicates in its many forms the origin of things, nations, people, tribes, kindred, so that the little word *of* that we use in English represents a whole concept of belonging to something essential. In this appeal to the imagination, the declensions come back to life rather than being presented as mere categorical bins into which certain words are dumped. And verbs are those words that recreate the movement of life, which easily calls for the observation that in some way all things have movement, a statement that will immediately elicit arguments from young minds about the stability of rocks and mountains.

But prior to teaching scientific grammar, I have found in my limited experience, it takes a class of second graders about ten minutes or less to discover the correct form of the verb in the following exercise repeated several times by the teacher:

> "Roma in Italia *est.*"
> "Italia et Hispania in Europa *sunt.*"

Of course, the teacher can employ the use of holding up fingers, drawing on the chalk board, and body language. The students do not know exactly why "est" changes to "sunt," but they do know that it does when there is more than one thing mentioned in the preceding statements, and more importantly, they know to make these adjustments in an integrated way, that is, with their whole persons—their voices, while learning to listen closely as their whole being and not just their minds come alive in such an exercise—as opposed to the dry sands of a grammar drill at the end of a printed text that relies more on the rational process. By withholding the use of English, students are froced to *do* Latin, with all the inevitable mistakes, they begin in this way to participate in the language.

Historically important dates and names are not only necessary to know when learning history, but for students these can also be enjoyable, if those precise things are left embedded in the *stories* of history. With older students, reading the histories written by the makers of history—Caesar's *Conquest of Gaul*, for example—gives an immediacy to the subject and deepens the vicarious experience of the events. In either case, textbooks of history should be avoided, for these are far too abstract for young minds, books about books, usually, that merely summarize events. Even for older students, in high school for example, the best foundation for Ancient Greek history is still Homer—the *Odyssey* and the *Illiad*.

When a flower is taken apart and examined as pistil, stamen, stem, and petals, each part is seen exactly and a certain curiosity is indeed satisfied; however, curiosity is not wonder, the former being the itch to take apart, the latter to gaze on things as they are. Curiosity belongs to the scientific impulse and would strive to dominate nature; whereas, wonder is poetic and is content to view things in their wholeness and full context, to pretty much leave them alone. Stated as simply as possible, science sees knowledge as power; poetic knowledge is *admiratio*, love. In other words, take the students outside, regularly, and turn even a backyard into a laboratory of the open fields. Once again, textbooks at this level are a burden, they get between the student and the things of admiration. Let them make their own notes and pictures, poems and stories, about what they have seen. Biology is the observation of living things, not dead things. And this includes all the elements of nature. I remember never being comfortable with the famous story of the cannon ball and bag of feathers being dropped from the tower of Pisa, that they would arrive at earth at the same time, until it was pointed out to me that this experiment could only conclude this way if it took place in a vacuum! The absence of wind, a breeze, even the presence of air itself, are realities of nature and scientific factors of friction and resistance that would cause, as our common sense tells us, the cannon ball to fall to the ground first.

So, with dissection or isolation there is no longer an experience of the flower—only parts—and the thing called a rose is gone. Recalling a similar observation on the narrow scrutiny of science, Dennis Quinn mentions that D. H. Lawrence said, "to the scandal of physicists, 'Whatever the sun is, it is not a ball of flaming gas.' "[1] In this sense, too, neither is a glass of wine simply an ounce or two of alcohol, or a pipe of blended tobaccos mere nicotine. Water is only H_2O in a laboratory demonstration that isolates its parts, and will never be thought of as such by the thirsty man. Our lives are lived out more in the poetic mode, in spite of the apparent dominance of science, for, after all, we do not in our daily experiences, say things like, "That was a beautiful ball of flaming gas last evening," or, "I would like an ounce or two of alcohol with my dinner tonight." And no one seriously asks for a glass of H_2O, but only ironically, in making fun—of science.

When one has cultivated the habit of seeing in the poetic mode, science loses its privileged and usurped position in the nature and order of knowledge. For example, if you lived in or near the mountains and it was the month of April, and during a morning rain you were with a child who looked up and noticed that the peak in front of you was covered with a dusting of new snow, and then asked why, the conversation could go something like this:

Child: Why is it raining here but there's snow on the mountain?

Adult: Because it's colder higher up and the moisture is snow up
            there and rain down here where it's warmer.

Child: That doesn't make sense. When you go up higher you get
            closer to the sun. It should be hotter.

Adult: Well, the air is thinner higher up and so things don't get
            as warm.

Scientifically, it would seem, the adult responses are generally true, but the little dialogue, from the point of view of poetic knowledge, is a failure. The authority of the child's senses have been confused and called into doubt by the incompleteness of the adult's answers. As a matter of fact, the child is more correct in its intuitive inductions in the ultimate sense of truth, poetically and scientifically, for, once passing beyond our thin atmosphere, deeper toward the center of our solar system, one indeed will experience more heat, dangerously so, as Icarus and the Greeks knew. Poetically, with no contradiction to the facts, the adult could have added:

> Yes, if you go close enough to the sun, you'll burn up! In fact, when Icarus flew toward the sun his wings of wax melted and he fell back into the sea. Also, when we climb mountains, we might need more air to breathe if we climb high enough, but it is also easier at the height to get sunburned.

However, it is also to be remembered that the human mind is limited—one of the great lessons of poetic knowledge—and even under the power of connatural knowledge, or formal metaphysics, it cannot fully account for the presence of flowers, rain, the sun, or anything. Scientific knowledge accounts for the material world even less because of its necessary attachment of observing externals. This is why scientific knowledge can give the impression of dominance over nature, because only material reality can be disassembled, manipulated, and destroyed, giving the appearance of complete dominance to the finite mind. An education that rejects the poetic mode actually rejects the essential stage of discovery of reality. Advancing to the conclusions of science without the gymnastic and poetic foundations casts an aura of unreality on all knowledge that follows. Recall Descartes's *Method*—a shortcut to the truth, as if that were possible—in this regard.

The fact is, we are not moved by thought alone but by the integration of an idea and desire, the desire for union with reality, and all our composite being perceives reality as good. If education does not cultivate the natural desire for union with reality with the understanding that the poetic and gymnastic modes are real knowledge, then it delivers something profoundly inferior to the reality and powers of the human being. For desire of the real to rise up, there must be something real to arouse it, and gadgets, computers, and gimmicks used to hold attention, all taking place in classroom environments technologically insulated from reality, are simply parts of the generally unlovable atmosphere of modern education—unlovable because they are all efficiency, utility, and no longer beautiful.

But, in this conclusion it would be a mistake not to briefly return to the four modes of knowledge spoken of by John Senior at the beginning of this study. While he presented them in their traditional

understanding and order, it must be said that for all the defense of
the poetic mode here, the other three degrees of knowledge have
equally been debased in modern times and are in great need of
being returned to their original status. For example, metaphysical
knowledge, *scientia*, that is, absolute certitude, is for the most part rejected by the modern world. How often do we hear the unconscious
contradiction: You can't be certain of anything, everything is relative, there is no truth, and so on. Next, in the descending order, is dialectic, which has been taken over by modern science and has
elevated the value of a laboratory demonstration to the place of
metaphysical reality. Then comes rhetoric, which now has the con-
notation it deserves, given that its practice is almost entirely in the
hands of politicians and other vested interests. It is a mode of proba-
bility far adrift from at least the Socratic tradition that insisted its
purpose was the persuasion toward the *truth*. The modern student of
rhetoric who would deny this is not so modern after all: the Sophists
of Socrates' day taught ever so eloquently that whatever was "true"
was defined by whoever was in some position of power and influence. It was, finally, the anger of the Sophists at Socrates' refusal to
admit to such a corruption of logic, among other things, that
brought about his execution.

At the level of poetic knowledge, to know something we have
to experience it in some way, and knowledge by connaturality, the
poetic mode, gives experience of this kind because it is sympathetic
knowledge. Again, it is love, desire, that inspires real knowledge, and
far from being confined to feelings, this must include the love from
the will. When it is seen how poetic knowledge operates, Thomas
Gilby explains this integration:

> Besides this influence of the will acting on the mind as a stimu-
> lus there is, in the second place, a more penetrating influence,
> more intimate, profound, formal, when love does not only
> work upon knowledge but works into it. Not only does the de-
> sire of the will now impel the mind to know, but in its passion
> for the concrete it overflows into the mind, to produce a reac-
> tion above and beyond the logic of the situation, a mysterious
> experience which is not so much a rational judgement as a
> sympathy, a knowledge by affinity, nature, compassion.[2]

Scientific knowledge, on the other hand, does not, cannot, give an
experience of the whole thing—only external reality, the surface, the

parts, are held as real. It is a priority of the scientific mode that it be free of emotional responses to reality. When this scientific view enters into education, then only the deliberative aspect of the will is emphasized, and effort to learn anything is considered a virtue. When this has entered into religious education, it has often been taught that the love of God and neighbor always requires an act of the will, that is, effort. But under the view of poetic knowledge, such effort only makes sense after first recognizing that it is *natural* to love God and to desire the good of our neighbor. It is also natural that God, as our Creator, loves us and that we should have some integrated experience of His love. *Tribue, quaesumus; ut ipsam pro nobis intercedere sentiamus*, reads part of a prayer in the Little Office of the Blessed Virgin Mary, widely known by all classes in the Middle Ages; that is, "Grant, we pray, that we may *discern by our senses* her intercession |to God| for us." While it is true that the Latin *sentire* carries with it the act of intellectual knowing, it is also undeniable that this word means such knowledge is sensually perceived, that is, experienced by the senses as well as the mind.

On the other hand, acts of the will, or prayers, that require clinched teeth and the rush of adrenalin are normally infrequent; but if it is thought that effort is the only function of the will where mysteries are mistaken for problems to be solved and obstacles to be overcome, then the active movement of the will is radically distributed and resembles more the emotion of fear and anger. If all a person has left at the end of religious education is a joyless determination to love and obey God—"I *will* love God, I *will* obey God!"— a resigned and sad tolerance for their neighbor—"I don't *like* him, but I will love him for the sake of God"—then they have missed the natural growth of love mentioned by Senior: "Love grows in five cumulative (not disjunctive) stages, each defined by its object: parents, animals, boys, girls, God."[3] One's mother and father, pet, wife or husband, and neighbor are not abstractions or concepts, and if we are to believe the entire Western tradition of philosophy and the Christian tradition, nor is God. The Puritan and Jamsenist often attempt to skirt the more complete obligation to love neighbor by exclusively calling for this love because God has commanded it—neglecting to add that because we are all created in His image, we therefore must be in some way lovable—not just tolerated. And this is not to be merely a cool and intellectual love, but one that also includes the emotions, for God and neighbor. It is simply a fact that

some of the harshest words of Christ are reserved for those whose
hearts are hard and cold enough to scandalize children, dishonor
their parents, and neglect the care of their neighbor.

But the great question for students and teachers who would
discover the poetic mode of knowledge is not whether it can be de-
clared valid or not—it can, either by pointing to the long tradition of
its recognition in a survey such as this one or by simply reflecting on
their own experience to see that such a mode exists within themselves. Rather, because the awareness of poetic knowledge requires,
not exclusively but to a profound degree, a poetic culture found in
daily life and in ordinary experience, the question is: Is such a life
possible in a highly industrialized, technological society based on the
idolatry of materialism? If poetic experience first plays upon the
beautiful, the wonderful, the proportionate thing that is intuitively
pleasing to our senses, where are we to find this beauty in the noise,
glare, and glitz, the noxious air, the tasteless food, the vulgar democ-
ratization of manners, the desensitization of emotions and resulting
wanton violence from suburbs to cities to nations, that so inform the
life of the twentieth century? Are there even any tables, chairs, cups,
and bowls (outside of museums or a few craft centers) whose hand-
made simple beauty caused the manly Odysseus to gaze in wonder
at such ordinary objects? What ideas of substance present themselves from our daily life and work, so that at mealtime around the
table (if anyone still eats together) is there conversation of some reflection on the permanent things? How often, if ever, do we encounter some setting, some person, some song, some moment where
we can say within our hearts and minds that the experience was
"something very much like perfection?"

Frank Nelick paused at such questions as these and his response was not encouraging:

> It is possible for poetry and the poetic order of knowledge to be
> lost as, say, culture or religion; it is certainly, by all accounts,
> later than we think. To paraphrase Nietzsche: Poetry is dead
> and the uneducated specialists have killed it by making it extra-
> ordinary, uncommon and, in their own image, eccentric.[4]

The modern world, indeed, has gone a long way in destroying
the occasions for a normal sensory life in contact with natural beauty
and the occasions of poetic experience. In cities, small towns, homes,

and schools, it is largely a life insulated from reality, a world of electronic images and music, machines in the home and in the office that separate us from our work, exercise machines and professional sports and no real gymnastic sense of the world. For the poetic sense of life to make a real "comeback," to treat just one area, both atheistic communism and liberal capitalism would have to disappear as well as the huge and crushing industrial-technological nations they have produced. An economy based on working and living proportionate to the whole human being within a stable family unit, and not relative to the State and its materialist ends, would have to come into being. Frankly, it all seems impossible viewed this way, without perhaps, some enormous global catastrophe first.

Without a sympathetic culture that reflects the poetic sense of life, teachers who work in the poetic mode have very little to point to for present examples; we prove our position often in the negative, by the absence of poetry. Yet, the close of the twentieth century also forces us to look more closely, for there still is a nature, and a human nature, that can respond to reality and to the permanent things. It is simply more difficult now. Therefore, it seems that poetic education can be engaged in now but on a small scale, perhaps as small as one home and family at a time, but I would hope one classroom, one small school at a time. The recent rise in private schools and home schooling are opportunities for the application of poetic education without the constraining bureaucratic requirements from state and federal education agencies.

But what is needed is a school completely dedicated, I would say, devoted to the education that observes first of all the poetic and gymnastic modes of knowledge. And a school, based on the tradition from Socrates to the IHP described here, is also based on that great species of love: friendship. As Senior says, a school first of all is a faculty of friends. Before buildings, before books, even before students, a school is a gathering, often of just a few friends, learning together, who love the same things and love to reflect and remark about them in conversation. The presence of such friendships and their love of concrete and mysterious realities, is what attracts students to such a school.

In the absence of a school in the poetic mode of knowledge for children, then next best for our time would be a school for teachers. Here, teachers who already know even vaguely that something is missing in all they were taught about modern education, or those brave hearts who would like to be teachers but not like the ones they now see, could gather to trace the history, and experience for themselves the legacy covered in this book. For, there must be no confusion about this: that while the poetic mode of education teaches finally by the muses, as Quinn says, this does not mean there is not much to be done, deliberately and consciously, to learn to trust these ways of knowing again. As Jacques Maritain carefully observed:

> If the very act of the perception of the beautiful takes place without discourse and without any effort of abstraction, conceptual discourse can nevertheless play an immense part in the *preparation* for this act. . . . the aptitude for perceiving beauty and pronouncing a judgment on it, presupposes an innate gift, but [it] can be developed by education and instruction.[5]

I would only add what should be obvious by now, that such instruction for teachers, even though dealing more in concepts, should also be in the poetic mode.

Either school is urgently needed to carry at least a small flame of the memory of this educational heritage, which is ours by right, into the twenty-first century.

But the main problem with either school—aside from the necessities of funding—is that they are both extremely simple proposals, a fact that seems to puzzle and frustrate the modern school planners who still construct schools using complex corporate organization models, with boards, committees, administrators, and, finally, the two classes of workers, teachers and students.

Yet, it is still a school that is needed, and so little is required for it, or even wanted, to establish the poetic school of education: no expensive buildings, just tasteful; no amenities or luxuries; no funds for expensive textbooks, special equipment or audio-visual aides; no indoor swimming pools or gymnasiums or elaborate playground equipment; no expensive laboratory devices; no computers and no televisions. Not only is the poetic and gymnastic mode preserved with this deliberate "poverty," so that very little comes between the student and the teacher and the subject at hand, but thousands upon thousands of dollars are saved as well, which instead should be placed in an endowment for the modest salaries of the teachers who must work with the security of tenure so that they may give undivided attention to their students. Small is beautiful, less is more, in this case, and students of such a school will not only regain the proper use of their senses, they will at the same time discover their reason which, while being good in itself, would also answer the charge that such a school would not prepare the students for the "real" world. And what indeed is the real world of a school? To present just one example, a school where the temperature is controlled through devices mounted on a wall that invisibly lead to some underground plant of machines, or a school where each room is heated by an airtight wood stove in winter, and where tall windows are thrown all the way up to catch the breeze in late summer and spring? The second example is simultaneously gymnastic and poetic, as the harmonious notes played on the scale together, for when such a school is considered it must be understood that everything teaches. With the spacious windows of buildings arranged toward the sun for the better part of the year, there is little need for electric lights. Teach by the light of the day, and when on infrequent days it is too overcast to see the chalk board or the books, have conversation, or music, or games, or go outside. Such children will have a fond familiarity all their lives of living with the seasons and changes of weather, for the memory of light and shadow as given by the sun and clouds. When we no longer believe that these are important details of sensory and emotional growth, grounded in the real, and reverberating the beautiful, true, and good, then we construct elementary and middle schools that resemble too closely medium security prisons— few windows, one level and a flat roof, mostly concrete and brick, and actually quite expensive to maintain, since they are also constructed for the convenience of housing costly air conditioning and heating systems.

Keep in mind, then, that a school in the gymnastic and poetic mode, designed to truly recover education, is not a "romantic" idea, or an easy school, especially when compared to the cushy surroundings and "feel-good" methods of most modern education. Students in the real school, for example, would be cold before the room took in the heat of the wood stove, and they would be hot unless a breeze could be found to enter through open windows. But like the memories of light and shadow, the memory of cold and hot, the smell of the open field for playground and science, the drowsy afternoons after a simple but healthy lunch, the sometimes tedious drills for math, would all be recalled in a sympathy that had joined the passive and active powers of body and soul. And recall at this point what André Charlier said about order at Maslacq, so that souls could bloom, an order based largely on self-discipline now so foreign to the average school setting as to be disbelieved as possible without the aid of threats, bribes, and even the presence of police. And yet, order as viewed by Charlier or Senior (or Socrates, Aristotle, or Aquinas, for that matter) is also part of nature; therefore, in spite of human perversity, or call it original sin, the sense and satisfaction of order as a species of beauty still resides within the soul and can still be drawn out by the alert and sympathetic teacher.

Teachers and parents often want to know about books for such a school and how they would be taught. In the school of the poetic mode of education, there are very few books indeed, and the ones used, in a sense, choose us before we chose them; that is, these are the books of our tradition, which is the Western tradition. No amount of forced multiculturalism in the schools can change the fact that we are born at a certain time into a certain culture and tradition, and no amount of study of, for example, the culture of the East, will make us any more Eastern when reading translations of Tibetan folk stories, as will be our culturally instinctive response to the world of the stories of Grimm and Andersen. And, turning this the other way, a school in the Orient would do well to read those stories that have been handed down to them by their tradition. It is not a question of being exclusive or xenophobic; it is rather to recognize that the taking on of another's culture and traditions is unnecessary and inappropriate at this level of education. The study of Chinese literature, for example, would be a very good thing to do, gathering as much information about Chinese philosophy, politics, life, and manners, not to mention some attempt at learning to translate the language—all necessary collateral studies precisely because the story or poem was not written in our tradition and we would need to do as much 'homework" as possible to recreate the circumstances for its appreciation. But to accomplish the conditions for reading stories from China is the work of the graduate student on the way to becoming a specialist, an expert in a particular field. The school of the poetic mode remains a school of beginners.

Furthermore, to teach in the integrated way, so that students see that knowledge is not a set of discrete subjects to be mastered but rather a whole that instructs by delight, one book could suffice for an entire curriculum. For example, at the fifth-grade level, one of the books I once taught was Jack London's *Call of the Wild*, another was

Dana's *Two Years Before the Mast*. I discovered that each book at certain points introduced situations of arithmetic, geography, history, and science that raised questions about each subject that the class did not know the answer to—and in several areas, neither did I. Because the students were first of all already engrossed in the story of the book, it became quite easy to pause and make a digression into these other subjects. Poetry, drawing, and even music were also subjects that presented themselves throughout the reading. Likewise, in a religious education setting or in a school that desired to draw out any universal moral principles, it was quite clear that the natural sympathies aroused by the occasions of injustice and cruelty, as well as the events of courage and success, taught the children in the mode of vicarious *experience*, rather than by the abstracted principles of catechisms and by deliberate reduction of stories to moralism.

It was a kind of thrill for both myself and the students to realize that within one book, and one that they were coming to love, their whole life as a student was contained. But the end of such an education is not more and more books or even necessarily smarter students. Poetic and gymnastic education has as its end the cultivation of the senses, the imagination, and the will, not the elevation of the I.Q. Nor is there the presence of the twice-removed distance of the impersonal textbook or the cumbersome bookkeeping with work sheets, handouts, or the conventional means of evaluation under this way of teaching. My student examinations on what they read was determined by writing something about the experience of the book, talking about it, drawing about it. Even the "hard" subjects of math, where perhaps calculations for distances were determined, always had the full context of the story underneath them as the foundation of reference, rather than the cold black and white numbers in a lifeless story problem in a textbook.

So, to repeat, that the books of this fifth-grade class example, or any of the titles drawn from the list of great and good books, are not the end of education and certainly not intended to produce "bookish" students with overstimulated minds. It is not a school for parents to be able to say: My kid is smarter than your kid. The books, while being good in themselves, are first of all to be enjoyed. They are also occasions of something more important.

The philosophers recognize such distinctions by speaking of *causes* or ends; that is, in addition to reading the book for enjoyment, the student is able to learn about life in a vicarious way and also in some specific ways—sailing, for example, as well as learning more about the living language. Students become better readers and writers by reading and writing, not by methods of attacking the discrete topics of a language arts programs. These ends would be called *immediate* and *proximate* causes.

But there are also *remote* and *ultimate* ends. The reward teachers and students experience when they abandon all the cumbersome paraphanalia of scientific education and confront one another and the truths of the subject at hand directly and simply, is friendship. It is friendship, a species of love, spoken of by André Charlier and John Senior, that defines such a school and echos that first image in the West of the teacher Socrates, whose students playfully, affectionately detain him one day so that he will talk to them about justice, as seen at the beginning of *The Republic*. And this is why Senior says that first of all a school is a faculty of friends. More about this in a moment.

These last ends of education are more difficult to define because they point to the mysterious bond between teacher and student who have been brought together by something other than themselves, something they both love, something that begins to encompass them both. Perhaps these four causes can be better understood by using the example of a dinner party where the immediate occasion for gathering is to eat and drink, to be nourished; the proximate cause is to visit and to behave as social beings, as the term *proximus* implies, to be neighborly. But the remote end of feasting is to present the pleasant occasion for real friendship, which, in turn, may led to the ultimate and more mysterious end: to experience, poetically a participation in a transcendent feast and friendship, to be caught up in a wholeness beyond ourselves.

And so it is with teaching in the poetic mode where the conditions are present for the spark of insight to leap from one soul to another, that is, from teacher to student, sometimes from student to teacher, as Plato says in his famous Seventh Letter, "after much converse about the matter itself and a life lived together, suddenly a light, as it were, is kindled in one soul by a flame that leaps to it from another, and thereafter sustains itself."[6]

I mentioned earlier in an illustration of poetic experience that it resembles the metaphor of poetry where two dissimilar things are seen in a moment of insight to possess a similarity. Likewise, the presence of the teacher and student, and the teacher illuminating a book with the student—the object that has been placed between them—produces the third thing, like the note created by two notes played in harmony, the mutual delight in some aspect of the true, the good, and the beautiful, those transcendentals that are harmonized in the One. To have shared and loved the experience of the good, true, and beautiful, through some concrete or vicarious experience is to begin real friendship, for as Aristotle observed, true friendship is based in part on the mutual love of the good.

Several years before my experience teaching fifth graders, I had taught a class of senior high school boys. When I saw three of them about twelve years after their graduation, they were eager to tell me how much they had enjoyed my class. When I asked them why and what they remembered, they all said they only remembered that we read the *Iliad* and *The Count of Monte Cristo* together, and that they were the best books they ever read. They remembered very little of what I had said. I realized, seeing their sincerely happy faces at recalling this class, that it was fine, and good for my vanity as well, that they recalled little of what I had said but that their memory of the experience of the class was one of overall great fondness. I think this was possible because those books were read in an atmosphere of pure enjoyment—no notes were to be taken, no pop quizzes. We read a great deal aloud and would talk whole hours about one scene, recreating it in our minds, savoring some moment or event that seemed true to us.

When we compare the ends of modern education, be it in the public schools and universities or the majority of private academies and colleges, with the ends of education as conceived by the much longer and vibrant tradition recorded in this study, we see that there can be very little friendship between students and teachers and between the students themselves, at least in the sense spoken of here. First, the faculties of most schools have been brought together to instruct students in certain subjects so that they master certain skills. Students are present because by law they have to be, and by the "law" of economics, so they are told, they must use an education to get a job. Now, faculty members within this setting, as well as students, may indeed become friends, but it will not ordinarily be because of a remote or ultimate cause of education but because of the nature of human beings who tend to form friendships of some kind in social settings. Furthermore, since the pervasive influence of Dewey and his overzealous disciples have firmly implanted the idea throughout the education of teachers that there really are no transcendent truths to be seen and experienced outside their utility in solving economic, social, or political problems, then there is nothing left for teacher and student to gaze upon beyond immediate and proximate ends, nothing for them to love as good in itself. This situation is further revealed to be destructive of the poetic mode, and real friendship, because of the confusion, or ignorance of, the distinctions of the kinds of good and the friendships based on them that existed, if not always in fact at least in ideal, from the time of Socrates.

Aristotle set down in an orderly manner what had already been observed in common experience for as long as anyone could reflect on such things, that there are friendships based on utility, that is, what is perceived as the *bonum utile*, where what love there is is not based on the good of the other but upon what each can get from the other. It is for the good of ourselves that we befriend another person in this case. Then, there is the occasion of love based on pleasure, the *bonum delectabile*, similar to the *bonum utile* in that the love of the person is still based not on the good of the other but upon what pleasantness we derive for ourselves from that person. Aristotle says such friendships are incidental and are easily dissolved, because if one person ceases to be useful or pleasant then there is no reason to love them. Of course, Aristotle also points out that true friendships contain a measure of usefulness and pleasantness, for, after all, these are goods of a kind, and the truly good desire to be useful and pleasant to their friend. It is just that the useful and the pleasant between real friends must be of a higher order and not subject to change and whim. But perfect friendship, says Aristotle, can only take place between those who are good and are alike in virtue. This *bonum honestum* is reserved for those who love the good, where we desire, above all, the good of the other. So, it is not difficult to see that the immediate and proximate ends of things are closer to the utilitarian and pleasant goods; whereas, the remote and ultimate ends rise to the *bonum honestum*, that is, the honorable good, which, beginning with at least Socrates to present-day Christianity, is recognized as true friendship. When true friendship is practiced, we humbly participate in the *bonum summum*, the sum, the whole, of all good, philosophically speaking; and, from the point of view of religion, we share in the life of God Himself.

The teacher, then, who passes through, and never repudiates, their own poetic life, so that the first note of melody has been struck in the soul, can then progress on naturally and harmonize with the mode of metaphysical certitude about what is indeed true, good, and beautiful while never losing what was already known, poetically, from the beginning. (Once we see that these modes of knowledge are not only quite real but their proper order and cultivation quite serious, then it is also plain to see what scientific knowledge without the humanizing effects of the poetic mode has given the modern world, up to this very hour: the horrific destruction of mankind and his natural home, the earth.)

But returning from such a passage up and down the scale of knowledge, always with love predominating, such a teacher is best suited to lead the student waiting to begin their journey through the modes of knowledge. It is clear from all experience that youth do not really form the higher degrees of friendship—theirs is mainly at the level of what is pleasing. But given the presence of teachers who are friends and who love their students in the highest order, desiring their good, and understanding and patient of their age, students will have the model in their memory, the form of love in their minds, in a time where as a nation, as a world, we either destroy our youth in unjust wars, or by overindulgence, or by neglect and deprivation.

And now we need to take a deep breath, to have a time out, and found a school even with just a few teachers and few students, for a few years. Who knows how far the spark may leap? With all the experiments in education, with all the concern about diversity, it would seem there would be room somewhere for one small experiment in the recovery of education.

Does it all seem too much, too much like a dream? Certainly, it is a dream, but a dream in the sense of the possible—not a fantasy. To found a school as has been thought of here requires only the listening heart of perhaps just one courageous, poetic soul who has come to see—intuitively and positively in an awful delight of wonder, as well as from the heights of reason and deliberate serious thought—that our land, our homes, the heavens and the earth, and those dear and those distant from us are important not only in their nature, but, like ourselves, have meaning and purpose far beyond the reach of the current means of analysis and measurement. By re-discovering poetic knowledge, it is possible to see and teach once more that the world—seen and unseen—and the world of ourselves within, mysteriously but actually possess a life that is "something very much like perfection."

NOTES

Chapter 1. The Validity of Poetic Knowledge

1. Charles Dickens, *Hard Times* (New York: Bantam), 1981, 25.
2. Dickens, 28.
3. Dickens, 28.
4. John Senior, *The Restoration of Christian Culture* (San Francisco: Ignatius, 1983), 194–95.
5. Jacques Maritain, *A Maritain Reader*, "Creative Intuition and Poetic Knowledge" (Garden City, N.Y.: Image, 1966), 332.
6. Karl Stern, *The Flight from Woman* (New York: Farrar, Straus, and Giroux, 1965), 42.
7. Stern, 43.
8. Frank Smith, *Insult to Intelligence* (New York: Arbor House, 1986), 38.
9. Smith, 56.
10. Smith, 60.

Chapter 2. The Philosophical Foundations of Poetic Knowledge

1. Plato, *The Republic* (New York: Penguin, 1984), 130–131.
2. Julius A. Elias, *Plato's Defense of Poetry* (Albany: State University of New York Press, 1984), 3.
3. Elias, 1.
4. Elias, 213.

5. Elias, 2.

6. Henri Marrou, *A History of Education in Antiquity* (London: Sheed and Ward, 1981), 9.

7. Werner Jaeger, *Paideia: The Ideals of Greek Culture* (New York: Oxford University Press, 1945), Vol. 1, 36.

8. Jaeger, vol. 1, 36.

9. Homer, *The Odyssey* (New York: Penguin, 1983), 139.

10. Homer, 142.

11. Josef Pieper, *Leisure: The Basis of Culture*, (New York: New American Library, 1963), 73–74.

12. Pieper, 44.

13. Jean Piaget, *The Child's Conception of the World* (Savage, Md.: Littlefield Adams, n.d.), 33.

14. Plato, *The Republic* (New York: Penguin, 1984), 162–63.

15. Plato, 160–63.

16. Confucius, *The Analects* trans. D. C. Blau (New York: Penguin, 1983), 8, 93.

17. Plato, *The Republic*, 176.

18. Plato, 164–65.

19. Gerald L. Gutek, *Philosophical and Ideological Perspectives on Education* (Englewood Cliffs, N.J.: Prentice Hall, 1988), 17.

20. Plato, *The Republic*, 77.

21. Aristotle, "Metaphysics," *Great Books of the Western World*, trans. W. D. Ross (Chicago: Encyclopedia Britannica), vol. 8, 991.

22. Aristotle, "De Anima," trans. J. A. Smith, vol. 8, 664.

23. Aristotle, "Politics," trans. Benjamin Jowett, vol. 9, 542.

24. Aristotle, ibid., 542.

25. Aristotle, ibid., 543.

26. Aristotle, ibid., 543.

27. Aristotle, ibid., 543.

28. Aristotle, ibid., 545.

29. Aristotle, ibid., 545.

30. Aristotle, ibid., 546.

31. Aristotle, "Metaphysics," 499–500.

32. Jonathan Lear, *Aristotle: The Desire to Understand* (Cambridge: Cambridge University Press, 1988), 1.

33. Lear, 1.

34. Lear, 2–3.

35. David Summers, *The Judgment of Sense: Renaissance Naturalism and the Rise of Aesthetics* (Cambridge: Cambridge University Press, 1990), 61.

36. Summers, 58.

37. Aristotle, "Metaphysics," 500–501.

38. Dennis B. Quinn, *Iris in Exile: A Synoptic History of Wonder* ms., 23–24.

39. Quinn, ibid., 27.

40. Quinn, ibid., 27.

41. Cornelis Verhoeven, *The Philosophy of Wonder: An Introduction and Incitement to Philosophy*, trans. Mary Foran (New York: Macmillan, 1967), 11.

42. Verhoeven, 11.

43. Verhoeven, 11.

44. John Henry Newman, *Apologia Pro Vita Sua* (New York: Modern Library, 1948), 264.

45. George Howie, trans., intro., *St. Augustine on Education*, (South Bend, Ind.: Gateway Editions, 1969), 157.

46. Emmanuel Chapman, *Saint Augustine's Philosophy of Beauty* (New York: Sheed and Ward, 1939), 6, 8.

47. Howie, ibid., 157.

48. Chapman, 6, 8.

49. Chapman, 9.

50. Chapman, 9.

51. Howie, 88.

52. Howie, 88–89.

53. Andrew Louth, *Discerning the Mystery: An Essay on the Nature of Theology* (Oxford: Clarendon, 1989), 5.

54. Howie, ibid., 10.

55. Joseph M. Colleran, trans., intro., *St. Augustine: The Teacher*, Ancient Christian Writers Series No. 9 (Westminster, Md.: Newman, 1964), 114.

56. Colleran, 117.

57. Colleran, 117.

58. Colleran, 117.

59. St. Augustine, "The Teacher," *Ancient Christian Writers* (Westminster, Md.: Newman, 1964), 185.

60. John Henry Newman, "The Mission of St. Benedict," *Historical Sketches*, vol. 2, by John Henry Cardinal Newman (London: Longmans, Green, 1912), 258.

61. John Senior, *The Restoration of Christian Culture* (San Francisco: Ignatius, 1983), 150.

62. Newman, ibid., 214.

63. Newman, ibid., 245.

64. St. Benedict, "The Rule of St. Benedict," *The Holy Rule for Laymen*, T. F. Lindsay (London: Burns and Oats, 1947).

65. Senior, 153.

66. Newman, ibid., 252.

67. Newman, ibid., 253.

68. Newman, ibid., 264.

69. Senior, 162.

70. Newman, ibid., 267.

71. Umberto Eco, *The Aesthetics of Thomas Aquinas*, trans. Hugh Bredin (Cambridge, Mass.: Harvard University Press, 1988), 6.

72. Eco, 6.

73. Eco, 10.

74. Eco, 11.

75. Eco, 12.

76. Eco, 14.

77. Eco, 15.

78. Eco, 16.

79. Eco, 17.

80. Eco, 17.

81. Eco, 17.

82. Robert Edward Brennan, *The Image of His Maker* (Milwaukee, Wisc.: Bruce Publishing, 1956), 49.

83. St. Thomas Aquinas, *The Summa Theologica of Saint Thomas Aquinas* (Chicago: Great Books of the Western World, Encyclopedia Britannica) trans. Fathers of the English Dominican Province, vol. 1, I, Q. 76, 386.

84. Brennan, ibid., 50.

85. Brennan, ibid., 55–56.

86. Aquinas, I, Q. 77, 7, 405–406.

87. Renard, 85.

88. Brennan, ibid., 127.

89. Aquinas, I, Q. 78, art. 4, reply obj. I, 413.

90. Brennan, ibid., 128.

91. Brennan, ibid., 128–29.

92. Robert Edward Brennan, *Thomistic Psychology* (New York: Macmillan, 1941), 127.

93. Brennan, *The Image of His Maker*, 133.

94. Brennan, ibid., 134.

95. Brennan, ibid., 143.

96. Brennan, ibid., 145.

97. Aristotle, 136.

98. Summers, 206–207.

99. Summers, 207.

100. Summers, 208.

101. Summers, 161.

102. Conrad W. Baars, *Psychic Wholeness and Healing* (New York: Alba House, 1981), 3.

103. Quinn, 20.

104. Baars, ibid., 16.

105. Baars, ibid., 22.

106. Conrad Baars, *Feeling and Healing Your Emotions* (South Plainfield, N.J.: Logos, 1979), 11–12.

107. Baars, 23.

108. Aquinas, I, 5, 4, 26.

109. Baars, *Psychic Wholeness and Healing*, 1981, 23.

110. Brennan, *The Image of His Maker*, 218.

111. Brennan, 218.

112. Brennan, 218.

113. Brennan, 218.

114. Baars, *Psychic Wholeness and Healing*, 1981, 24.

115. Baars, ibid., 24.

116. Baars, ibid., 25.

117. Aquinas, I, II, Q. 22, art. 2, 722.

118. John Senior, *The Restoration of Innocence* ms., 128.

119. Baars, 29, *Psychic Wholeness and Healing* 1981 f.n. 2.

Chapter 3. Connatural, Intentional, and Intuitive Knowledge

1. Henri Renard, *The Philosophy of Man*, 69.

2. Aristotle, "Posterior Analytics," 136–137.

3. Aristotle, "De Anima," 664.

4. Aristotle, 664.

5. St Thomas Aquinas, I, 14, 1, 76.

6. Vincent Edward Smith, *Philosophical Physics* (New York: Harper, 1950), 20.

7. Smith, 20, 25.

8. Renard, 69.

9. Renard, 69.

10. Renard, 69.

11. Baars, 24. Psychic Wholeness and Healing, 1981.

12. Renard, 71.

13. Renard, 71, n 7.

14. Renard, 76–77.

15. "*Poetica scientia* est de his quae propter defectum vertitatis non possunt a ratione capi; unde oportet quod quasi quibusdam similitudinibus ratio seductur." (Poetic knowledge [compared to science] is somewhat defective of the truth, and, as a result, does not grasp things by reason; rather, the reason is "seduced," as it were, by things that resemble the truth.) I *Sentences* prol., q. 1, a. 5, ad 3. Translation by James S. Taylor.

16. St. Thomas Aquinas, II, II, 45, 2, vol. 20, 600.

17. Aquinas, 600.

18. Stern, 43.

19. Jacques Maritain, *The Range of Reason* (New York: Scribner's, 1952), 23.

20. Jacques Maritain, *Creative Intuition in Art and Poetry* (New York: Pantheon, 1953), 76.

21. Harold L Weatherby, *The Keen Delight: The Christian Poet in the Modern World* (Athens: University of Georgia Press, 1975), 126.

22. Jacques Maritain, *Creative Intuition in Art and Poetry*, 91.

23. Ralph McInerny, *Art and Prudence: Studies in the Thought of Jacques Maritain* (Notre Dame, Ind.: University of Notre Dame Press, 1988), 139.

24. McInerny, 141.

25. Aristotle, in Maritain's *Creative Intuition in Art and Poetry*, 90.

26. Maritain, 1953, 135.

27. Maritain, ibid., 135.

28. Maritain, ibid., 93.

29. Thomas Gilby, *Poetic Experience: An Introduction to Thomist Aesthetic* (New York: Sheed and Ward, 1934), 20–21.

30. Gilby, 27.

31. Maritain, 1953, 98, f.n. 37.

32. Maritain, ibid., 126.

33. Maritain, ibid., 126.

34. Maritain, ibid., 110.

35. Louth, *Discerning the Mystery*, 27.

36. Louth, 28.

37. Maritain, 1953, 119–20.

38. McInerny, 142.

39. Jacques Maritain, *The Situation of Poetry* (New York: Kraus, 1968), 66–67.

40. Maritain, ibid., 75.

41. Pieper, *Leisure: The Basis of Culture*, 73.

42. Jacques Maritain, *Art and Scholasticism and the Frontiers of Poetry*, trans Joseph W. Evans (Notre Dame, Ind: University of Notre Dame Press, 1974), 165.

43. Maritain, ibid., 165.

44. Pieper, *Leisure: The Basis of Culture*, 26.

45. Plato, Phaedrus, *Great Books of the Western World* (Chicago: Encyclopedia Britannica) trans. Benjamin Jowett, vol. 7, 116.

46. Pieper, *Leisure: The Basis of Culture*, 31.

47. St Thomas Aquinas, II, II, 27, 8, reply obj. 3, 527.

48. Pieper, *Leisure: The Basis of Culture*, 74.

49. Pieper, ibid., 31.

50. Chapter 3, n. 29.

51. Pieper, ibid., 43.

52. Pieper, ibid., 27.

53. Vincent Edward Smith, 21–22.

54. See chapter 3, n. 15.

55. John Senior, personal interview, January 1994.

56. Vincent Edward Smith, 21–22.

57. Senior interview.

58. Senior interview.

59. Willa Cather, *Shadows on the Rock* (New York: Knopf, 1931), 137.

Chapter 4. Descartes and the Cartesian Legacy

1. Theodore Brauer, *Thomistic Principles in a Catholic School* (St Louis: Herder, 1949), 101.

2. Daniel J Sullivan, *Introduction to Philosophy* (Rockford, Ill.: Tan, 1992), 79.

3. Sullivan, ibid., 80.

4. Frederick Copleston, *A History of Philosophy*, bk. 2, vol 4 (Garden City, N.Y.: Image, 1985), 67.

5. Copleston, 73.

6. Copleston, 74.

7. René Descartes, *Discourse on Method and Meditations*, trans. and intro. Laurence J. Lafleur (Indianapolis, Ind.: Bobbs-Merrill, 1984), 15.

8. Descartes, 16.

9. Sullivan, ibid., 80.

10. Sullivan, ibid., 84–85.

11. Sullivan, ibid., 83.

12. Etienne Gilson, *The Unity of Philosophical Experience* (New York: Scribner's, 1937), 132–33.

13. Gilson, ibid., 132.

14. John Young, *Reasoning Things Out* (Fort Worth, Tex.: Stella Maris, 1981), 64.

15. Carmin Mascio, *A History of Philosophy* (Patterson, N.J.: St Anthony Guild, 1957), 293–94.

16. Jacques Maritain, *Three Reformers: Luther, Descartes, Rousseau* (London: Sheed and Ward, 1944), 58.

17. Maritain, ibid., 59.

18. Maritain, ibid., 59.

19. Maritain, ibid., 56.

20. Maritain, ibid., 64.

21. Maritain, ibid., 66.

22. Gilby, 27–28.

23. Young, 65.

24. John Dewey, "My Pedagogic Creed," *Theory and Practice in the History of American Education*, ed. Hillesheim and Merrill (Lanham, Md.: University Press of America, 1980), 223.

25. John Senior, *The Restoration of Christian Culture* (San Francisco: Ignatius, 1983), 75.

26. John Dewey, *Reconstruction in Philosophy* (New York: Henry Holt and Co., 1920), 26.

27. Frederick Copleston, *A History of Philosophy*, bk. 3, vol. 8 (Garden City, N.Y.: Image, 1985), 366.

28. Copleston, 363.

29. Copleston, 365.

30. A. J. Ayer, quoted by Young, *Reasoning Things Out*, 68.

31. E. F. Schumacher, *Small Is Beautiful: Economics as if People Mattered* (New York: Harper and Row, 1975), 81–82.

32. Abbot Suger, *On the Abbey Church of St Denis and Its Art Treasures*, ed., trans. Erwin Panofsky (Princeton, N.J.: Princeton University Press, 1979), 64–65.

33. Jean Jacques Rousseau, "Emile," ed Hillesheim and Merrill, 26.

34. Rousseau, ibid., 27.

35. Rousseau, ibid., 29, 31.

36. Rousseau, ibid., 28.

37. Jean Jacques Rousseau, *Emile; or On Education*, intro, trans. Allan Bloom (New York: Basic, 1979), 37, 82.

38. Rousseau, ibid., 178.

39. John Stuart Mill, *Autobiography* (New York: Henry Holt, 1873), 137.

40. Mill, ibid., 139.

41. Mill, ibid., 146, 149.

42. Mill, ibid., 149.

43. Mill, ibid., 148, 149.

44. John Ruskin, In *The Literary Criticism of John Ruskin*, ed. Harold Bloom (New York: De Capo, 1965), x. intro.

45. Ruskin, ibid., 2.

46. Ruskin, ibid., 6.

47. Ruskin, ibid., 15, 18.

48. Ruskin, ibid., 19.

49. Ruskin, ibid., 20.

50. Ruskin, ibid., 20.

51. Ralph Waldo Emerson, "*Theory and Practice in the History of American Education*," ed Hillesheim and Merrill, 131.

52. Emerson, ibid., 189.

53. Emerson, ibid., 188.
54. Emerson, ibid., 188.
55. Verhoeven, 1972, 17.
56. Verhoeven, ibid., 18.

Chapter 5. Voices for Poetic Knowledge after Descartes

1. André Charlier, "Adieu a Maslacq," *Que Faut-il dire aux hommes* (Paris Nouvelle Editions Latines, 1972), 321–22.
2. Gerard Calvet, "Histoire de Maslacq," *André Charlier* (Paris: Itineraires, Nouvelles Editions Latines, 1972), 63, 65.
3. André Charlier, ibid., 322.
4. Gerard Calvet, 65.
5. André Charlier, ibid., 330.
6. André Charlier, *Lettres aux capitains* (Le Barroux, France: Les Editiones Ste. Madeleine, 1980), 11–14.
7. Edmund J. King, *Other Schools and Ours: Comparative Studies for Today* (London: Holt, Rinehart, and Winston, 1979), 119.
8. Henri Charlier, *Culture, École, Métier* trans. by Claude Biselx and James S. Taylor (Paris: Nouvelles Editions Latines, 1959), 13.
9. Charlier, ibid., 13.
10. Charlier, 13.
11. Charlier, 19.
12. Charlier, 19.
13. Henri Fabre, *The Insect World of Henri Fabre*, intro. Edwin Way Teale, trans. Alexander Teixeira de Mattos (Boston: Beacon, 1991), 25.
14. Fabre, 3.
15. Thomas Shields, *The Making and the Unmaking of a Dullard* (Washington, D.C.: Catholic University Press, 1940), 113.
16. Shields, 113–14.
17. Plato, "The Republic," *Great Books of the Western World* (Chicago: Encyclopedia Britannica), vol. 7, 333.
18. Shields, ibid., 114.
19. Shields, ibid., 118–19.
20. Shields, ibid., 121–22.
21. Shields, ibid., 136.
22. Shields, ibid., 143–45.
23. Shields, ibid., 150.
24. Shields, ibid., 150–51.
25. Shields, ibid., 152–53.
26. Shields, ibid., 260.
27. Shields, ibid., 179.

28. Charlier, *Culture, École, Métier,* 26.

29. Charlier, ibid., 25.

30. Charlier, ibid., 25.

31. Charlier, ibid., 27.

32. Charlier, ibid., 28.

33. Charlier, ibid., 29.

34. Charlier, ibid., 33.

35. Charlier, ibid., 34.

36. Charlier, ibid., 35.

37. Charlier, ibid., 35.

38. Eric Gill, *Beauty Looks after Herself* (London: Sheed and Ward, 1933), 129, 184–85.

39. Walter John Marx, *Mechanization and Culture* (St Louis: Herder, 1941), 130–31.

40. Charlier, ibid., 36.

41. Charlier, ibid., 37.

42. Charlier, ibid., 37.

43. Charlier, ibid., 109.

44. Charlier, ibid., 108.

45. Charlier, ibid., 108.

46. Charlier, ibid., 109.

47. Charlier, ibid., 110.

48. Charlier, ibid., 37.

Chapter 6. Poetic Knowledge and the Integrated Humanities Program

1. Robert K. Carlson, *Truth on Trial: Liberal Education Be Hanged* (South Bend, Ind.: Crisis, 1995), 36.

2. Nelick retired in 1985, Senior in 1986, both due to health reasons Nelick died in 1996. Quinn has continued his regular duties at the English department while still teaching the books of the IHP as an elective class in humanities.

3. *Pearson Integrated Humanities Program* (Lawrence: University of Kansas, English Department, 1975), 5.

4. John Senior, "Integrated Humanities Program: A Definition," *The Integration of Knowledge: Discourses on Education,* ed. Dennis B. Quinn (Lawrence, Kansas: University of Kansas, 1979), 3.

5. Senior, ibid., 3.

6. Senior, 3–4.

7. Senior, 4.

8. John Senior, *Integrated Humanities* (brochure) (Lawrence: University of Kansas, 1980).

9. Senior, brochure.

10. *Pearson Integrated Humanities Program*, 10.

11. Dennis B. Quinn, "Education by the Muses," *The Integration of Knowledge*, 8.

12. Quinn, ibid., 8–9.

13. Quinn, 9, 10.

14. Quinn, 10.

15. Quinn, 10.

16. Quinn, 10.

17. Quinn, 11.

18. Dennis B. Quinn, personal conversation, June 15, 1994.

19. Quinn, "Education by the Muses," 12.

20. Frank C. Nelick, "The Darkling Plain of Poetry," *The Integration of Knowledge*, 16.

21. Nelick, 15.

22. Nelick, 16.

23. Nelick, 16.

24. Nelick, 17.

25. Nelick, 19.

26. Quinn, 10.

27. John Senior and Dennis B. Quinn, "Job," tape 4 (Casper, Wy.: Powder River Literary Society, 1990).

Chapter 7. The Future of the Poetic Mode of Knowledge in Education

1. Quinn, "Education by the Muses," 11.

2. Gilby, 42.

3. John Senior, *The Restoration of Innocence*, ms., 132.

4. Nelick, "The Darkling Plain of Poetry," 20.

5. Jacques Maritain, *Art and Scholasticism and the Frontiers of Poetry*, trans Joseph W. Evans (New York: Scribner's, 1956), 165.

6. Plato, "The Seventh Letter," *Great Books of the Western World* (Chicago: Encyclopedia Britannica), vol. 7, 809.

SELECTED BIBLIOGRAPHY

Adler, Mortimer J. *Ten Philosophical Mistakes*. New York. Macmillan, 1985.

Aquinas, Thomas St. *Questiones de Anima*. Trans. James H. Robb. Milwaukee, Wisc.: Marquette University Press, 1984.

———. *Summa Theologica* (Selections). *Great Books of the Western World*. Ed. Robert Maynard Hutchins. 2 vols. Encyclopedia Britannica, 1952.

Aristotle. "De Anima" (On the Soul) Trans J A Smith *Great Books of the Western World*. Ed. Robert Maynard Hutchins. 2 vols. Encyclopedia Britannica, 1952. Vol. 1.

———. "Ethics." Trans. W. D. Ross. *Great Books of the Western World*. Ed. Robert Maynard Hutchins. 2 vols. Chicago: Encyclopedia Britannica, 1952. Vol. 2.

Augustine, Aurelis. "On the Teacher." Trans. George Howie. *St. Augustine on Education*. South Bend, Ind.: Gateway Editions, 1969.

Baars, Conrad W., M.D. *Feeling and Healing Your Emotions*. South Plainfield, N.J., 1979.

———. *How to Prevent the Crisis in the Priesthood*. Chicago, Ill.: Franciscan Herald Press, 1972.

Baars, Conrad W., and Anna A. Terruwe, M.D. *Psychic Wholeness and Healing*. New York: Alba House, 1981.

Bauer, Theodore. *Thomistic Principles In A Catholic School*. St Louis: B. Herder Co., 1949.

Benedict, St. *The Rule of Saint Benedict*. Trans. Justin McCann. London: Sheed and Ward, 1976.

Bloom, Allan. *The Closing of the American Mind*. New York, N.Y.: Simon and Schuster, 1987.

Bougle, Celestin. *The French Conception of "Culture Generale" and Its Influence upon Instruction.* New York: Teachers College, Columbia University, 1938.

Brennan, Robert Edward. *The Image of His Maker.* Milwaukee, Wisc.: Bruce, 1956.

———. *Thomistic Psychology.* New York: Macmillan, 1941.

Cabot, Stephen P. *Secondary Education in Germany, France, England and Denmark.* Cambridge: Harvard University Press, 1930.

Calvet, Dom Gerard. "Histoire de Maslacq." *André Charlier.* Paris: Itineraries Chroniques and Documents, 1972.

Carlson, Robert K. *Truth on Trial: Liberal Education Be Hanged.* South Bend, Ind.: Crisis, 1995.

Cather, Willa. *Shadows on the Rock.* New York: Alfred A. Knopf, 1931.

Caussade, Jean-Pierre. *Self-Abandonment to Divine Providence.* London: Burns and Oates, 1959.

Chapman, Emmanuel. *Saint Augustine's Philosophy of Beauty.* New York: Sheed and Ward, 1939.

Charlier, André. *Que Faut-il dire aux hommes.* Paris: Nouvelle Editions Latines, 1972.

———. *Lettres aux capitains.* Le Barroux, France: Les Editions Ste. Madeleine, 1980.

Charlier, Henri, *Culture, École, Métier.* Collection "Itineraries." Paris: Nouvelles Editions Latines, 1959.

Colleran, Joseph M. Trans., intro. *St. Augustine: The Teacher.* Westminster, Md.: Newman, 1964.

Confucius. *The Analects.* New York: Penguin, 1983.

Copleston, Frederick. *A History of Philosophy.* 9 vols. Garden City, N.Y.: Image, 1985.

Cunningham, William F. *The Pivotal Problems of Education.* New York: Macmillan, 1940.

Derrick, Christopher. *Escape from Skepticism: Liberal Education as if Truth Mattered.* Peru, Ill.: Sherwood Sugden, 1977.

Descartes, René. *Discourse on Method and Meditations.* Trans. and intro. Laurence J. Lafleur. Indianapolis, Ind.: Bobbs-Merrill, 1984.

Dewey, John. *Democracy and Education.* New York: Free Press, 1966.

———. *Experience and Education.* New York: Collier, 1967.

———. *Reconstruction in Philosophy.* New York: Henry Holt and Co., 1920.

———. *The Child and the Curriculum / The School and Society.* Chicago and London: University of Chicago Press, 1956.

———. *The Quest for Certainty: A Study of the Relation of Knowledge and Action.* New York: Balch, 1929.

Dickens, Charles. *Hard Times.* New York: Bantam, 1981.

Donohue, John. W. *St. Thomas Aquinas and Education.* New York: Random House, 1968.

Duska, Ronald, and Mariellen Whelan. *Moral Development: A Guide to Piaget and Kohlberg*. New York: Paulist Press, 1975.

Eco, Humberto. *The Aesthetics of Thomas Aquinas*. Trans. Hugh Bredin. Cambridge, Mass.: Harvard University Press, 1988.

Elias, Julius A. *Plato's Defense of Poetry*. Albany: State University of New York Press, 1984.

Elkind, David. *All Grown Up and No Where to Go*. Reading, Mass.: Addison-Wesley, 1984.

————. *Miseducation: Preschoolers at Risk*. New York: Knopf, 1988.

————. *The Hurried Child*. Reading, Mass.: Addison-Wesley, 1981.

Fabre, Henri. *The Insect World of Henri Fabre*. Intro. Edwin Way Teale, trans. Alexander Teixeira de Mattos. Boston: Beacon, 1991.

Fahey, Denis. *The Church and Farming*. Cork, Ireland: Forum, 1953.

Farrington, Ernest Frederic. *The Public Primary School System of France*. New York: Teachers College, Columbia University, 1906.

Gilby, Thomas. *Poetic Experience: An Introduction to Thomist Aesthetic*. New York: Sheed and Ward, 1934.

Gill, Eric. *Beauty Looks after Herself*. London: Sheed and Ward, 1933.

Gilson, Etienne. *Moral Values and the Moral Life: The System of St. Thomas Aquinas*. Trans. Leo Richard Ward. St. Louis: B. Herder, 1931.

————. *The Unity of Philosophical Experience*. New York: Scribner's, 1937.

————. *The Christian Philosophy of St. Thomas Aquinas*. New York: Random House, 1956.

————. *Thomist Realism and the Critique of Knowledge*. San Francisco: Ignatius, 1986.

Gutek, Gerald L. *Philosophical and Ideological Perspectives on Education*. Englewood Cliffs, N.J.: Prentice Hall, 1988.

Hillesheim and Merrill, ed. *Theory and Practice in the History of American Education*. Lanham Md.: 1980.

Hodgson, Geraldine. *Studies in French Education from Rabelais to Rousseau*. Cambridge: Cambridge University Press, 1908.

Howard, Thomas. *Chance or the Dance: A Critique of Modern Secularism*. San Francisco: Ignatius, 1988.

Howie, George. *Education Theory and Practice in St. Augustine*. London: Routledge and Kegan Paul, 1969.

————. *St. Augustine on Education*. South Bend, Indiana: Gateway Editions, Ltd, 1969.

————. *Humanities Program: A Special Course for Undergraduates at the University of Kansas*. (Brochure) Lawrence: University of Kansas, 1979.

Hutchins, Robert M. *Education for Freedom*. Louisiana State University Press, 1942.

————. *The Higher Learning in America*. New Haven: Yale University Press, 1936.

Jaeger, Werner. *Aristotle: Fundamentals of the History of His Development.* Trans. Richard Robinson. 2d ed. Oxford: Oxford University Press, 1948.
————. *Paideia: The Ideals of Greek Culture.* 3 vols. Trans. Gilbert Highet. New York: Oxford University Press, 1945.

Jaki, Stanley L. *Angels, Apes, and Men.* Peru, Ill.: Sherwood Sugden, 1987.

James, William. *Talks to Teachers on Psychology; and to Students on Some of Life's Ideals.* New York: Norton, 1958.

Kandel, I. L. *The Reform of Secondary Education in France.* New York: Teachers College, Columbia University, 1924.

Kelly, William A. *Introductory Child Psychology.* Milwaukee: Bruce, 1938.

King, Edmund J. *Other Schools and Ours: Comparative Studies for Today.* 5th ed. London: Holt, Rinehart, Winston, 1979.

Lear, Jonathan. *Aristotle: The Desire to Understand.* Cambridge: Cambridge University Press, 1988.

Leclercq, Dom Jean. *The Love of Learning and the Desire for God.* New York: Fordham University Press, 1960.

Lindsay, T. F. *The Holy Rule for Layman.* London: Burns and Oates, 1947.

Locke, John. *An Essay Concerning Human Understanding.* Chicago: Great Books of the Western World, Encyclopedia Britannica, 1952. Vol. 35.

Louth, Andrew. *Discerning the Mystery: An Essay on the Nature of Theology.* Oxford: Clarendon, 1989.

Madiran, Jean, ed. *Les Charliers.* Paris: Itineraries Chroniques and Documents, 1982.

Maritain, Jacques. *A Maritain Reader.* Ed. Donald Gallagher and Idella Gallagher. Garden City, N.Y.: Image, 1966.
————. *Art and Scholasticism and the Frontiers of Poetry.* Trans. Joseph W. Evans. Notre Dame, Ind.: University of Notre Dame Press, 1974.
————. *Creative Intuition in Art and Poetry.* N.Y.: Pantheon, 1953.
————. *Education at the Crossroads.* New Haven, Conn.: Yale University Press, 1943.
————. *The Dream of Descartes.* Trans. Mabelle L. Anderson. New York: Philosophical Library, 1944.
————. *The Degrees of Knowledge.* Trans. Gerald B. Phelan. New York: Scribner's, 1959.
————. *The Range of Reason.* New York: Scribner's, 1952.
————. *Three Reformers: Luther, Descartes, Rousseau.* New York: Scribner's, 1934.
————. *The Situation of Poetry.* New York: Kraus Reprint, 1968.

Marrou, Henri. *A History of Education in Antiquity.* London: Sheed and Ward, 1981.

Marx, Walter John. *Mechanization and Culture.* St. Louis: Herder, 1941.

Mascio, Carmin. *A History of Philosophy.* Patterson, N.J.: St Anthony Guild, 1957.

Maurer, Armand A. *About Beauty: A Thomist Interpretation*. Houston, Tex.: Center for Thomistic Studies, University of St. Thomas, 1983.

Mayer, Mary Helen. *The Philosophy of Teaching of St. Thomas Aquinas*. New York: Bruce, 1929.

McInerny, Ralph. *Art and Prudence: Studies in the Thought of Jacques Maritain*. Notre Dame, Ind.: University of Notre Dame Press, 1988.

Miles, Donald W. *Recent Reforms in French Secondary Education: With Implications for French and American Education*. New York: Teachers College, Columbia University, 1953.

Mill, John Stuart. *Autobiography*. New York: Henry Holt, 1873.

Nelick, Frank C. "The Darkling Plain of Poetry." *The Integration of Knowledge: Discourse on Education*. Lawrence: University of Kansas, The Integrated Humanities Program, 1979.

Newman, John Henry. *The Idea of a University*. Chicago: Loyola University Press, 1927.

———. "The Mission of St. Benedict." *The Benedictine Schools*. London: Longman's, Green, 1912.

Nuttall, A. D. *A Common Sky: Philosophy and Literary Imagination*. London: Sussex University Press, 1974.

O'Brien, Kevin J. *The Proximate End of Education*. Milwaukee: Bruce, 1958.

O'Connor, Peter. *Understanding the Mid-Life Crisis*. New York: Paulist Press, 1981.

———. *Pearson Integrated Humanities Program*. (Catalog) Lawrence: University of Kansas, 1975.

Pegis, Anton. "St. Thomas and Husserl on Intentionality." *Thomistic Papers I*. Houston, Tex.: University of St. Thomas, Center for Thomistic Studies, 1984.

Piaget, Jean. *The Child's Conception of the World*. Savage, Md.: Littlefield Adams, no date.

Pieper, Joseph. *Joseph Pieper: An Anthology*. San Francisco: Ignatius, 1989.

———. *Leisure: The Basis of Culture*. Trans. Alexander Dru. 1952. New York: New American Library, 1963.

———. *Living the Truth*. San Francisco: Ignatius, 1989.

Plato. *The Republic*. New York: Penguin, 1984.

Plato. "The Republic," "Meno," "Phaedo." Trans. Benjamin Jowett. *The Great Books of the Western World*. Ed. Robert Maynard Hutchins. Chicago: Encyclopedia Britannica, 1952. Vol. 7.

Quinn, Dennis B. "Education by the Muses." *The Integration of Knowledge: Discourse on Education*. Lawrence: University of Kansas, The Integrated Humanities Program, 1979.

———. *Iris in Exile: A Synoptic History of Wonder*. ms.

Renard, Henri. *The Philosophy of Man*. Milwaukee, Wisc.: Bruce, 1948.

Rousseau, Jean Jacques. *Emile; or On Education*. Intro. and trans. Allan Bloom. New York: Basic, 1979.

Sarton, May. *The Small Room*. New York: Norton, 1976.

Schumacher, E. F. *Small Is Beautiful: Economics as if People Mattered*. New York: Harper and Row, 1975.

Senior, John. "Integrated Humanities Program: A Definition." "The Several-Storied Tower." *The Integration of Knowledge: Discourses on Education*. Lawrence: University of Kansas, The Integrated Humanities Program, 1979.

Senior, John and Dennis B. Quinn. "Job". tape 4. Caspar, Wy: Powder River Library Society, 1990.

———. *The Death of Christian Culture*. New York, N.Y.: Arlington House, 1978.

———. *The Restoration of Christian Culture*. San Francisco: Ignatius, 1983.

———. *The Restoration of Innocence*. ms.

Shields, Thomas. *The Making and the Unmaking of a Dullard*. Washington: Catholic University Press, 1940.

Smith, Frank. *Insult to Intelligence*. New York: Arbor House, 1986.

Smith, Vincent Edward. *Philosophical Physics*. New York: Harper, 1950.

Solzhenitsyn, Alexandr I. *A World Split Apart*. New York: Harper and Row, 1978.

St. John's College. *The St. John's Program*. Annapolis, Md.: St. John's College, 1985.

St. John of the Cross. *Poems*. Trans. Roy Campbell. New York: Grosset and Dunlap, 1967.

Steiner, George. *Real Presences*. Chicago: University of Chicago Press, 1990.

Stern, Karl. *The Flight from Woman*. New York: Farrar, Straus, and Giroux, 1965.

Suger, Abbot. *On the Abbey Church of St. Denis and Its Art Treasures*. Ed., trans. Erwin Panofsky. Princeton, N.J.: Princeton University Press, 1979.

Sullivan, Daniel J. *Fundamentals of Logic*. New York: McGraw-Hill, 1963.

———. *Introduction to Philosophy*. Rockford, Ill.: Tan Books, 1992.

Summers, David. *The Judgment of Sense: Renaissance Naturalism and the Rise of Aesthetics*. Cambridge: Cambridge University Press, 1990.

Thomas Aquinas College. *Bulletin of Information, 1982–83*. Santa Paula, Calif.: Thomas Aquinas College, 1982.

Verhoeven, Cornelis. *The Philosophy of Wonder:* An Introduction and Incitement to Philosophy. Trans. Mary Foran. New York: Macmillan, 1972.

Weatherby, Harold L. *The Keen Delight: The Christian Poet in the Modern World*. Athens: The University of Georgia Press, 1975.

Young, John. *Reasoning Things Out*. Fort Worth, Tex.: Stella Maris, 1981.

INDEX